Customer Communications in Marketing
2003–2004

Customer Communications in Marketing 2003–2004

Alison Cheeseman and Gill Wood

AMSTERDAM BOSTON HEIDELBERG LONDON NEW YORK OXFORD
PARIS SAN DIEGO SAN FRANCISCO SINGAPORE SYDNEY TOKYO

Butterworth-Heinemann
An imprint of Elsevier
Linacre House, Jordan Hill, Oxford OX2 8DP
200 Wheeler Road, Burlington MA 01803

First published 2003
British Library Cataloguing in Publication Data
A catalogue record for this book is available from the British Library

ISBN 0 7506 5955 6

For information on all Butterworth-Heinemann publications
visit our website at www.bh.com

Typeset by Integra Software Services Pvt. Ltd, Pondicherry, India
www.integra-india.com
Printed and bound in Italy

Contents

welcome to the CIM coursebooks

An introduction from the academic development advisor

In the last two years we have seen some significant changes to the CIM Professional Series initiated by the Chartered Institute of Marketing. The changes have been introduced on a year-on-year basis, with Stage 1 (Certificate) changes implemented last year in 2002, and the Stage 2 (Advanced Certificate in Marketing) being implemented this year. It is anticipated that next year in 2004 the Stage 3 (Postgraduate Diploma) changes will be implemented.

As a result the authoring team, Butterworth-Heinemann and I have aimed to rigorously revise and update the coursebook series to make sure that every title is the best possible study aid and accurately reflects the latest CIM syllabus.

The revisions to the series this year included continued development in the Stage 1 and Postgraduate Diploma Series, and complete re-writes at Stage 2 to align with the radical overhaul of the CIM syllabus. There are a number of new authors and indeed Senior Examiners, in the series who have been commissioned for their CIM course teaching and examining experience, as well as their research into specific curriculum-related areas and their wide general knowledge of the latest thinking in marketing.

We are certain that you will find these coursebooks highly beneficial in terms of the content and assessment opportunities and a study tool that will prepare you for both CIM examinations and continuous/integrative assessment opportunities. They will guide you in a logical and structured way through the detail of the syllabus, providing you with the required underpinning knowledge, understanding and application of theory.

The editorial team and authors wish you every success as you embark upon your studies.

Karen Beamish
Academic Development Advisor

How to use these coursebooks

Everyone who has contributed to this series has been careful to structure the books with the exams in mind. Each unit, therefore, covers an essential part of the syllabus. You need to work through the complete coursebook systematically to ensure that you have covered everything you need to know.

This coursebook is divided into units each containing a selection of the following standard elements:

- o **Learning objectives** Tell you what you will be expected to know, having read the unit
- o **Syllabus references** Outline what part of the syllabus is covered in the module
- o **Study guides** Tell you how long the unit is and how long its activities take to do
- o **Questions** Are designed to give you practice – they will be similar to those you get in the exam
- o **Answers** (at the end of the book) give you a suggest format for answering exam questions. *Remember* there is no such thing as a model answer – you should use these examples only as guidelines
- o **Activities** Give you a chance to put what you have learned into practice
- o **Debriefings** (at the end of the book) shed light on the methodologies involved in the activities
- o **Hints and tips** Are tips from the senior examiner, examiner or author which are designed to help you avoid common mistakes made by previous candidates and give you guidance on improving your knowledge base
- o **Insights** Encourage you to contextualize your academic knowledge by reference to real-life experience
- o **Key definitions** Highlight and explain the key points relevant to that module
- o **Definitions** May be used for words you must know to pass the exam
- o **Summaries** Cover what you should have picked up from reading the unit.
- o **Further study** Provides details of recommended reading in addition to the coursebook

While you will find that each section of the syllabus has been covered within this text, you might find that the order of some of the topics has been changed. This is because it sometimes makes more sense to put certain topics together when you are studying, even though they might appear in different sections of the syllabus itself. If you are following the reading and other activities, your coverage of the syllabus will be just fine, but don't forget to follow up with trade press reading!

About MarketingOnline

With this year's coursebooks Butterworth-Heinemann is offering readers free access to MarketingOnline (www.marketingonline.co.uk), our premier online support engine for the CIM marketing courses. On this site you can benefit from:

- o Tutorials on key topics every two weeks during the term, comprehensive revision support material and access to revision days from Tactics – the highly acclaimed independent trainer for CIM courses.
- o Fully customizable electronic versions of the coursebooks – annotate, cut and paste sections of text to create your own tailored learning notes.
- o Instant access to weblinks related to the coursebooks.
- o Capacity to search the coursebook online for instant access to definitions and key concepts.

Logging on

Before you can access MarketingOnline you will first need to get a password. Please go to www.marketingonline.co.uk where you will find registration instructions for coursebook purchasers. Once you have got your password, you will need to log on using the onscreen instructions. This will give you access to the various functions outlined below.

Using MarketingOnline

MarketingOnline is broadly divided into four sections which can each be accessed from the front page after you have logged on to the system:

1. **The coursebooks** Buttons corresponding to the three levels of CIM marketing qualification are situated on the home page. Select your level and you will be presented with the four coursebook titles for each module of that level. Click on the desired coursebook to access the full online text (divided up by chapter). On each page of text you have the option to add an electronic bookmark or annotation by following the onscreen instructions. You can also freely cut and paste text into a blank word document to create your own learning notes.
2. **Revision material** Click on the 'Revision material' link and select the appropriate CIM level and coursebook to access revision material.
3. **Useful links** Click on 'Useful links' to access a list of links to other sites of interest for further reading and research.
4. **Glossary** Click on the 'Glossary' button to access our online dictionary of marketing terms.

If you have specific queries about using MarketingOnline then you should consult our fully searchable FAQ section – again, this is accessible through the appropriate link on the front page of the site. Please also note that a **full user guide** can be downloaded by clicking on the link on the opening page of the website.

unit 1
the importance of the customer

Learning objectives

In this unit you will:

o   Look at the different types of customers that you and your organization deal with

o   Examine the various ways you and your organization communicate with customers.

By the end of the unit you should be able to:

o   Understand the importance of effective customer communications in marketing

o   Identify the internal and external customers in a given situation

o   Be aware of what is meant by the terms *stakeholder* and *decision-making unit*

o   Appreciate how communication methods and messages alter depending on the context and the customer.

Study Guide

This unit provides an overview of the relationship between people and organizations and their customers. It covers indicative content area 1.1, 1.2 and 2.3 of the syllabus. Some of the unit is revisited in Units 4, 7 and 9 where there is further information about the various communication formats.

The unit links to the Marketing Fundamentals syllabus indicative content 1.1. The topics covered in this unit also link with the contents in the Marketing Fundamentals workbook in Unit 1.

The key point to be made here is that, although 'customers' are dealt with on each syllabus, from this module's perspective you are dealing with customers purely from the perspective of how you communicate with them and the impact on service delivery but not from a broad marketing perspective as with the Marketing Fundamentals syllabus.

You should take two hours to read the unit and a further two hours to complete the activities in the unit. You are advised to spend some extra time drafting an answer to the examination question you are referred to at the end of the unit.

Study tip

After reading this unit you could develop your understanding of this area by selecting two different organizations that you are familiar with. Compare and contrast the organizations in terms of size, objectives, industry sector (or whether public or private sector) and the type of customers they have to communicate with. Then consider the various ways that these organizations communicate with their internal and external customers, and consider how their communications could be improved.

Why are customers important?

As very few people live or work in isolation, communication with others is a fundamental part of most people's lives. Most jobs can be achieved only through communication, whether that involves giving/receiving instructions, sharing ideas with colleagues or giving information to external customers or suppliers. Away from work, the ability to communicate can affect the quality of personal relationships. In addition to this, communication is integral to marketing, involving as it does, communication initiatives that range from persuasive sales calls and presentations to clients, to the production of simple brochures and leaflets and the creation of sophisticated packaging, logos and advertising.

Communication is, therefore, a core skill that marketing professionals need to use daily. Consequently, the module Customer Communications in Marketing that this textbook relates to, forms the bedrock of the CIM qualification and the foundation to the other subjects you will study.

The Customer Communications in Marketing syllabus was introduced as part of Syllabus 2000 and replaced the Business Communications syllabus. Its development is in response to feedback received from employers, tutors and students. It takes account of the changes taking place in the world of marketing and seeks to test candidates' communication skills in a variety of marketing situations. Thus the focus of the Customer Communications in Marketing syllabus, and of this book, is on business communications from a marketing perspective. Much of the original Business Communications syllabus content, such as the communication process, oral communication, written communication and the interpretation and presentation of statistical information, continue to be featured.

However, the changes made to the syllabus reflect the impact of technological innovation on communications and the increasing emphasis being placed on how organizations communicate with customers. The syllabus has also been extended to consider the wide range of promotional activities used by organizations in communicating with customers.

So it is important for marketers to develop their understanding of who they communicate with, why they communicate with them and how communication can be improved. If you define a customer as 'a person one has dealings with', then clearly everyone, irrespective of job role, organization or industry sector, is affected by the issues arising from this subject.

Definition

Customer communication – In business, it is the process by which information is transferred between one individual or group and another, both within and outside the organization. The communication can take place verbally or non-verbally and may be transmitted through a variety of communication methods, such as reports, presentations, letters, advertising or in meetings.

Why do people communicate in business?

The main reasons for people to communicate in business organizations, internally and externally, are as follows:

- To *build relationships* internally and externally with individuals and groups
- To give *specific instructions* to others on a range of business matters, both procedural and strategic
- To *disseminate information* on a range of corporate matters such as the mission statement, policy issues or, in the case of the external market, on price changes or new promotional initiatives
- To *share ideas and values* on general organizational issues, possibly to maintain or subtly change the corporate culture
- To share ideas and values on work-specific issues or procedural tasks
- To *negotiate* matters of policy such as a joint venture or merger
- To *discuss* or negotiate on personal or professional matters such as remuneration and other higher- and lower-level hygiene factors
- To *motivate, interest and stimulate* employees for commitment and loyalty to the firm
- To create an awareness of the organization, its products or services and *persuade* the external market, for example, to make a purchase decision or to request further information
- To receive feedback in order to monitor whether the communication was understood and the reaction of the recipient to the message.

If you consider who you communicate with, why and how, you may be surprised at just how many people you actually communicate with, how many are inside your organization and how many are outside of it. You should also consider the people and organizations from whom you receive information.

If, for instance, you are working in the marketing department of a firm that makes and sells garden furniture, and you have responsibility for the organization's marketing communications, then in an average working day you may communicate with a large number of people in a variety of ways . . .

You may receive information by post from potential suppliers informing you about advertising opportunities. You may send a mailshot to customers on the company's database to encourage them to order products from a new brochure. You may fax a press release to a gardening magazine to raise the firm's profile. You may telephone a designer to change the layout of a brochure before it goes to print. Your line manager may e-mail you, asking you to organize a corporate event for an important business client. You may meet with a colleague to discuss how a project should be progressed. You may deliver a presentation to colleagues showing sales revenue figures in a graph. Or you may draft a report for the senior management team based on research that you have carried out.

DRIP Dyson

Dyson manufactures a revolutionary type of vacuum cleaner and has 52 per cent of the UK market. Its communications have needed to:

Differentiate it from conventional products – use of innovative technology

Remind/reassure customers that the cyclone system works better than any other and to resist the competition's attempts to gain top of mind awareness

Inform and educate the market about what is wrong with conventional appliances

Persuade potential customers to consider Dyson as the only option when next purchasing floor cleaning appliances.

Directive communications – the countryside

Marketing communications can be used to persuade target audiences in a variety of ways. For example, speaking on BBC Radio 4, Bob Waller (1996) claimed that publicity had been used effectively by the Peak District National Park. However, instead of using publicity to attract tourists, they had deliberately used their publicity opportunities to divert visitors away from particular areas in the Park, in order to repair, preserve and protect them for visitors in the future.

In 2001, with the foot and mouth crisis mounting, the government realized that its previous policy to restrict the public's access to the countryside was deterring tourism and threatening the economy. To correct this perception, it used public relations to encourage access to particular areas that were uninfected with the disease.

Source: C. Fill, *Marketing Communications, Contexts, Strategies and Applications*, 3rd Edition, 2002.

 ## Activity 1.1

Whether you are undertaking your course of study by continuous assessment or the examination route, use the skills audit form (Figure 1.1) to examine the types of communications you use and who you communicate with in your job. Spend some time to self-assess your skill level in the areas outlined in the form. If appropriate, you may want to undertake some peer assessment by consulting your colleagues and line manager about their views. If you are not working, you could consider how you communicate and with whom in your personal life. For instance, if you are seeking employment, you may use the Internet to research jobs, you may write job application letters, attend job interviews and contribute to meetings at your local sports club.

	Syllabus Ref	Current Skill level				Importance to Current Role				Likely Future Importance				YOUR COMMENTS
DEVELOPMENT AREAS:	2 CC	None			High	Low		Vital		Low		Vital		
Write business letters and memos	4.1	0	1	2	3	[ ]	[ ]	[ ]	[ ]	[ ]	[ ]	[ ]	[ ]	
Write informal business reports	4.1	0	1	2	3	[ ]	[ ]	[ ]	[ ]	[ ]	[ ]	[ ]	[ ]	
Write formal business reports	4.1	0	1	2	3	[ ]	[ ]	[ ]	[ ]	[ ]	[ ]	[ ]	[ ]	
Write direct mail letters and material	4.1	0	1	2	3	[ ]	[ ]	[ ]	[ ]	[ ]	[ ]	[ ]	[ ]	
Write press releases and articles	4.1	0	1	2	3	[ ]	[ ]	[ ]	[ ]	[ ]	[ ]	[ ]	[ ]	
Write sales proposals and quotations	4.1	0	1	2	3	[ ]	[ ]	[ ]	[ ]	[ ]	[ ]	[ ]	[ ]	
Write copy for information sheets	4.1	0	1	2	3	[ ]	[ ]	[ ]	[ ]	[ ]	[ ]	[ ]	[ ]	
Write management briefings and notes	4.1	0	1	2	3	[ ]	[ ]	[ ]	[ ]	[ ]	[ ]	[ ]	[ ]	
Conduct one to one/group interviews	3.6	0	1	2	3	[ ]	[ ]	[ ]	[ ]	[ ]	[ ]	[ ]	[ ]	
Plan and lead group discussions/meetings	3.6	0	1	2	3	[ ]	[ ]	[ ]	[ ]	[ ]	[ ]	[ ]	[ ]	
Plan and conduct sales meetings/visits	3.6/7	0	1	2	3	[ ]	[ ]	[ ]	[ ]	[ ]	[ ]	[ ]	[ ]	
Negotiate sales, price and terms	3.6/7	0	1	2	3	[ ]	[ ]	[ ]	[ ]	[ ]	[ ]	[ ]	[ ]	
Phone to gather market/sales information	3.7	0	1	2	3	[ ]	[ ]	[ ]	[ ]	[ ]	[ ]	[ ]	[ ]	
Phone to make appointments/liaise with clients	3.7	0	1	2	3	[ ]	[ ]	[ ]	[ ]	[ ]	[ ]	[ ]	[ ]	
Plan presentations/ briefings/talks	3.5	0	1	2	3	[ ]	[ ]	[ ]	[ ]	[ ]	[ ]	[ ]	[ ]	
Prepare speaking notes/scripts for others	3.5	0	1	2	3	[ ]	[ ]	[ ]	[ ]	[ ]	[ ]	[ ]	[ ]	
Prepare presentations using IT (e.g. PowerPoint)	3.5	0	1	2	3	[ ]	[ ]	[ ]	[ ]	[ ]	[ ]	[ ]	[ ]	
Make presentations to groups	3.5-7	0	1	2	3	[ ]	[ ]	[ ]	[ ]	[ ]	[ ]	[ ]	[ ]	
Visually present statistical data/information	3.5	0	1	2	3	[ ]	[ ]	[ ]	[ ]	[ ]	[ ]	[ ]	[ ]	

Figure 1.1 Skills audit form

Create visual aids/images	3.5	0	1	2	3	[ ]	[ ]	[ ]	[ ]	[ ]	[ ]	[ ]	[ ]
Specify layout for promotional material	4.1	0	1	2	3	[ ]	[ ]	[ ]	[ ]	[ ]	[ ]	[ ]	[ ]
Specify layout for printed advertising	4.1	0	1	2	3	[ ]	[ ]	[ ]	[ ]	[ ]	[ ]	[ ]	[ ]
Use IT for word processing/DTP	5.1/2	0	1	2	3	[ ]	[ ]	[ ]	[ ]	[ ]	[ ]	[ ]	[ ]
Use IT to maintain information databases	5.1/2	0	1	2	3	[ ]	[ ]	[ ]	[ ]	[ ]	[ ]	[ ]	[ ]
Use IT to maintain financial information	5.1/2	0	1	2	3	[ ]	[ ]	[ ]	[ ]	[ ]	[ ]	[ ]	[ ]
Use IT/Internet to communicate	5.3	0	1	2	3	[ ]	[ ]	[ ]	[ ]	[ ]	[ ]	[ ]	[ ]
Plan and build a simple web site	5.3	0	1	2	3	[ ]	[ ]	[ ]	[ ]	[ ]	[ ]	[ ]	[ ]
Identify role/motivation of DMU members	1.1/3	0	1	2	3	[ ]	[ ]	[ ]	[ ]	[ ]	[ ]	[ ]	[ ]
Articulate Features Advantages, Benefits statements for key targets	1.1/3	0	1	2	3	[ ]	[ ]	[ ]	[ ]	[ ]	[ ]	[ ]	[ ]
Identify and use secondary research data	2.2	0	1	2	3	[ ]	[ ]	[ ]	[ ]	[ ]	[ ]	[ ]	[ ]
YOUR OWN CHOICE (discuss with tutor)	Please ensure that you note the syllabus reference												
		0	1	2	3	[ ]	[ ]	[ ]	[ ]	[ ]	[ ]	[ ]	[ ]
		0	1	2	3	[ ]	[ ]	[ ]	[ ]	[ ]	[ ]	[ ]	[ ]

Figure 1.1 (cont.)

So who are your customers?

By now you will have realized that all the people you communicate with are your customers – not just the people who buy your employer's goods and services. You will, no doubt, find that you have been involved in communicating with people both inside and outside of your organization. You will have sent and received information to and from colleagues, suppliers and your firm's paying customers for a variety of reasons and in a variety of communication formats.

Who are an organization's customers?

In the traditional sense of the word, *customers* are the people who buy a firm's products. To communicate with them effectively, an organization needs to know who they are, what they want from the firm's products or services, where they are located and the most cost-effective methods of communicating with them. By doing this, it will be easier to develop effective communications, such as advertising, sales literature, packaging and product instructions, that appeal to and are understood by the customer.

The consumer/user

The most obvious customer is the consumer or person who pays for a product or service. However, the person who pays for the product may not be the user or the consumer of the product. For example, a manufacturer of toys needs to communicate with both the children who will use with the product, so they will exert pressure on parents, and the parents themselves as they will be the purchaser/decision maker.

The decision-making unit

In business-to-business marketing, it may be relevant for an organization to communicate not only with the purchaser but also with others who could be involved in the decision to purchase. The other people involved in the purchase decision are often referred to as the *decision-making unit.*

For example, a firm that supplies computer systems to other businesses needs to communicate with a variety of people who may not be customers but who may influence the decision to buy and therefore need to be communicated with.

The purchaser

A purchasing official may have sourced a new computer system and may ultimately place the order. As far as customer communications are concerned, it is important to make the purchaser's job easy, ensuring that up-to-date product, contact and after-sales information is easy to digest and that the ordering process is easy.

The initiator

The initiator or the specifier could be a member of staff or senior manager or even an external consultant, who sees the possibilities for new equipment to improve efficiency. The computer company must consider who these people might be and raise their awareness about its products, possibly via relevant trade press advertising, sales promotional material, exhibitions or public relations activities.

The user

The users in this example would be the staff who would use the computer system. These people may not influence the decision at the outset of the process but may be invited along to test equipment as part of a task group before the purchase decision is finalized. After the decision to purchase has been made, the good opinion of these people is vital if repeat business is to be transacted. The computer company could ensure good customer communications by providing clear user manuals and by providing training and helplines.

The influencer

Influencers could be the technical staff who affect the purchase decision by supplying information about a variety of suppliers or by setting buying specifications. Or they could be staff in the finance department who could block the purchase decision with financial constraints. Similar to the situation with initiators, these *customers* need to be supplied with sufficient information about the product/service via whatever channels are considered suitable.

The decision maker

These people are the most influential in terms of making the purchase decision. They may be senior managers or the managing director. It is vital to identify who these people are within a firm. The computer company's message could be communicated directly by a sales representative who might use some form of corporate entertaining to influence the purchase decision.

The gatekeeper

Gatekeepers control the flow of information through an organization and may be switchboard operators or secretaries who are responsible for dealing with incoming calls, mailshots and trade journals that arrive by post. The computer company should communicate effectively with this customer in order to be able to reach others in the decision-making unit. Sales representatives need to be able to talk persuasively to the gatekeeper to obtain appointments or pass on information to the decision makers or influencers.

Targeting via children

Nivea distributed over 1.5 million leaflets to children that offered advice about skin care and protection from the sun during hot weather. The leaflets, although given to children, were actually intended to reach parents, the children being used as an effective communication channel. The company was regarded in this instance as being very philanthropic as they were seen as contributing a health message.

Source: Adcock et al., *Marketing Principles and Practice*, 4th Edition, 2001.

Definition

Stakeholders – Stakeholders are people who affect an organization or are affected by its activities.

The stakeholders/publics

Most organizations also have a mix of stakeholders or publics, i.e. internal and external individuals or groups who come into contact with an organization or who affect or are affected by its activities. From a communication point of view they can be considered as important customers or target audiences with whom the organization must communicate.

It is important to appreciate the importance of knowing about an organization's stakeholders and why they might want to communicate with them. An organization may choose to communicate with these publics, such as the media or the local community, because it is good for its public relations image and ultimately good for business. Or it could be a legal requirement for an organization to produce an annual report for shareholders. It is often essential for an organization to form a close relationship with suppliers or distributors. Thus an organization may establish an Intranet to provide suppliers with up to date stock requirements or provide distributors with automatic access to orders to help them plan their distribution schedules.

In addition, most organizations wish to communicate effectively with current and potential employees to attract and retain the best staff in the marketplace. An organization's stakeholders might comprise the following (see Figure 1.2).

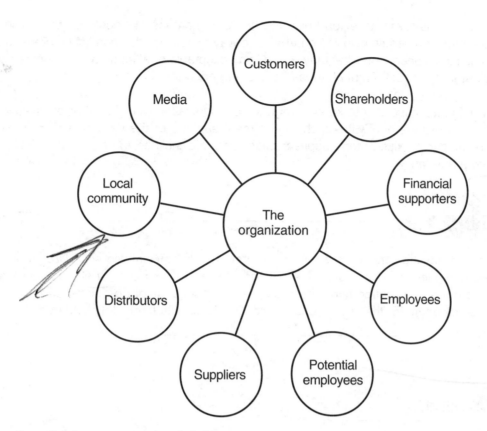

Figure 1.2 An organization's stakeholders

Let's consider the example of a small restaurant that serves food. Its stakeholders might be passing trade and regular customers who eat there. All forms of communication with them from the 'shop front', through the menu, advertisements or its website, need to be considered to ensure appropriate and effective communication with customers. The business may be a family business or part of a large chain. Whoever has a financial share in it and a say in the running of it (e.g. shareholders) are stakeholders. Again, communications with this group need to be carefully considered to ensure the successful running of the business.

If the restaurant owners have a bank overdraft to help with the cashflow then the bankers are also stakeholders. Regular communication to show that the restaurant is operating successfully is necessary to show business expertise and may be important at a later date if the bank overdraft has to be extended.

Staff and even potential staff are stakeholders. It is wise to communicate with staff and find out what customers think of new additions to the menu. It also makes sense to inform staff of changes to the menu before they occur. How will they be able to answer customer questions about a dish if they have not tasted it and do not know what is in it?

If staff are happy they tell others and encourage them to apply for positions that become vacant. A good reputation in the local community and with customers may also make future staff recruitment easy. Very few staff would like to work for a restaurant that had been prosecuted for breaches of hygiene regulations.

If the restaurant passed a local authority inspection with 'flying colours' or was recommended in a 'good food guide', or if the chef won a food competition, this could be the sort of information that a restaurant would want publicized. This could be via press or radio advertising or via the restaurant's website.

The restaurant may want to extend opening hours to increase business but this could have a negative effect on people who live nearby. One way to address this conflict of interests could be to consult local people on what they would find acceptable or at least to communicate why it is important that the restaurant changes its opening hours.

Similarly, it is also important to keep in regular communication with the other businesses that the restaurant owners deal with, such as the meat supplier or the dairy that delivers milk. If a good relationship exists, then suppliers might be more inclined to help if last-minute extra orders were needed.

Activity 1.2

Identify the stakeholders that a car manufacturer would communicate with. Use the list of stakeholders mentioned in Figure 1.2 and add to them if you can. Briefly explain what methods of communication might be used, what messages might be communicated and why it is important for the organization to communicate with these stakeholders.

Internal customers

Consider your internal customers and how important it is that there is good internal communication in an organization. Think about how sometimes you are the customer and someone else is the service provider.

For example, when you receive your payslip from the finance department, you are the customer and expect it to be correct, to be delivered on time and the salary payment actually paid into your bank account. If there is a problem, you expect to be dealt with courteously and promptly. You do not expect to have to engage in lengthy correspondence to rectify a mistake. If you do receive information from the finance department – say, for example, about a new profit-related pay scheme – you expect it to be clearly written and well presented.

At other times you could be the service provider to your colleagues or line manager, for instance, when you are asked to find out the costings of producing a sales promotion item as part of a future promotional campaign. Your internal customers will expect you to have completed the task on time, accurately, and to present it clearly at the next planning meeting.

So internal marketing is about working together with colleagues and providing them with a good service so that, as a team, your organization achieves its goals.

Internal marketing

Just as individuals have internal customers, such as colleagues and line managers, that they have to deal with, organizations have internal customers in the form of their staff.

From an organization's perspective, internal communication is vital to internal marketing, and the maintenance of employee motivation and company competitiveness. Simple methods of communication can be used to keep staff informed about new products/services, internal re-structuring or how well (or not) the organization is doing. In dynamic environments, where firms need to manage change effectively, communication needs to be harnessed to help staff adapt and become familiar to changes in their working environment.

According to Berry & Parasuraman (Berry, L. L., & Parasuraman, A., *Marketing Management*, 1992) 'A service company can be only as good as its people: if they aren't sold, customers won't be either.' The point here being that most organizations provide at least some level of customer service as part of their product offering and increasingly it is seen as a way of differentiating products in an overcrowded market. Without a culture of internal marketing and effective internal customer communications, the employees within an organization face the following problems:

- o Communication problems
- o Frustration and non-cooperation
- o Time-wasting and inefficiency
- o Stress and lack of job satisfaction
- o Poor quality of work.

All of these problems eventually lead to poor service to the external customer, which eventually leads to reduced profit in the long term.

To foster strong relationships and an atmosphere of shared values, communication and information should flow two ways. Information will obviously flow downwards from senior management to employees, but mechanisms should be put in place to ensure that it also flows upwards from employees to senior managers.

Consider the following statement and how this state of affairs can be achieved:

> *When everyone in an organization understands their role in meeting customer needs, the organization can be described as customer-focused.* (Smith. *Meeting Customer Needs* Butterworth-Heinemann, 1997)

The answer is, of course, communication. It is important for many marketers to market their department or services internally to colleagues and other departments. Problems can be raised by other people unaware of the marketing department's full range of services and the contribution it can make to the business.

Wal-Mart stores

Wal-Mart is a classic example of a company that has embraced a marketing orientation. Listed below are some quotes from a report on Wal-Mart.

'Every morning at 5.30 a.m. the previous days results for each region, store, department and merchandise are provided to the managers, who in turn pass on pertinent information to their associates (employees).'

'Stories about Sam Walton and those associates who have made exceptional efforts to please customers are told regularly. These have become the informal way to communicate expectations and behaviours to other associates.'

'Wal-Mart make the customer the focus of everything they do. The company empowers all associates closest to the customer to do whatever it takes to satisfy them. This can go beyond the normal, helpful, friendly service and can include a cashier giving a customer a price reduction based on the customer's word that the product was cheaper elsewhere, or replacing at no charge an item left in the parking lot.'

'Wal-Mart consider themselves to be "students" of customers, buying habits, demographics, wants, likes and preferences through data gathering and personal contact. They see their role as the "customer's agent" – seeking out the best products, negotiating the best price and passing on savings to customers. The policy of EDLP (Every Day Low Prices) drives the company, but price is not the sole determinant of their success.'

'The company is willing to try out many new ideas and to adjust them depending upon their success.'

Wal-Mart is a pro-active company that makes exceptional effort to please its customers. They want to make shopping a pleasurable experience and they are willing to change or adapt anything in order to remain relevant to the needs of customer.

Source: Adcock et al., *Marketing Principles and Practice*, 4th Edition, 2001.

Two-way communications

To encourage a two-way flow of information organizations can choose from a variety of methods to enable managers to hear the views and opinions of employees:

- Regular staff meetings and team briefings
- Meetings with senior managers where the overall performance of the firm and future developments are discussed
- Performance reviews/appraisal systems that enable staff to suggest how they could be empowered to do their jobs better
- Suggestion schemes where employees are rewarded if they suggest ideas that are implemented
- Work councils where staff can get involved in the running of the organization.

Future challenges for internal communications

The changing environment in which organizations operate means that it may be difficult for some organizations to communicate with staff in the traditional way, and pressures upon staff may mean that they are less inclined to be committed to the organization's values and culture.

Factors influencing change

○ The combination of downsized organizations and flatter management structures has removed layers of management and this means that employees are nearer to the decision makers and the communication process is speeded up. However, staff who are less secure in their jobs and more pressured to work faster and harder are less likely to communicate openly with their colleagues and managers.
○ The trend to teleworking, with more people working away from the office, means it is more difficult to create a corporate culture and sense of belonging where people feel happy to communicate on an informal basis.
○ The merging of companies across the UK and elsewhere in the world is creating global organizations that do not have local identities and which cross over different cultures, languages and operating systems. This can make it difficult for senior managers to communicate effectively with employees.

Communicating with the extended organization

Good customer communication goes beyond your own immediate organization. The relationship your staff has with your organization's suppliers, distributors and the like, can have a critical impact on the service your customers enjoy. For example, the Body Shop, the retail chain that sells health and beauty products, ensures that its staff work closely with the firm it retains to distribute its merchandise to its retail network, and the distributor actually has office space within the Body Shop factory. This arrangement ensures that close relationships and good communication are achieved.

A good working relationship with suppliers and other 'partners' can produce dramatic effects, such as:

○ Innovation
○ Improved performance
○ Lower costs
○ More holistic solutions to problems
○ Better understanding of the needs of all parties
○ New ways of working together
○ More co-operation.

Activity 1.3

You have been shortlisted for the post of Communications Manager at a privatized electricity company. As part of the selection process you have been asked to do a presentation on the importance of effective internal marketing and internal communications to the success of the organization. Draw on your experience to explain how some organizations improve their internal communication systems. Draft the notes that will form the basis of your presentation.

Improving customer communications

In the earlier parts of this unit, you looked at who should be communicating with whom. The next stage is to consider the ways you communicate with your customers.

The internal communications mix

Internal customer communications involve the effective use of memos, letters, reports, notices, e-mails, meetings, team briefings, telephone calls and presentations. Obviously some of these communication methods can be used to communicate externally. In this workbook we are making the distinction that external communications are those that are used to promote and sell the organization's goods and services, which we will refer to as the *external communications mix*. For guidance on using internal customer communication methods, see Unit 3 and Unit 4.

Shared values – B&Q

B&Q is a do-it-yourself retailer employing over 22,000 people spread across 286 sites. This means that communicating a consistent message to these employees is a complex yet important task, if there is to be brand consistency.

B&Q utilizes a number of different internal communications tools to undertake this task, including e-mail, team briefs and energise sessions (early morning team work-out sessions). The company has a distinct and visible personality in that it requires employees to act as brand ambassadors. There are five main values that act as the central pillar of the organization. These are:

o   A down to earth approach
o   Respect for people
o   Being customer driven
o   Being positive
o   Striving to do better.

In partial fulfilment of these values B&Q staff feature in the retailer's advertising. These show staff offering advice on tools and materials, ideas for gardening and indoor projects plus information about prices. This reflects the importance of integration because (real) staff are shown endorsing their brand and in essence challenging all customers to ask employees about a range of matters. To make this loop work, staff need to know about the product range and how products might apply to different customers. If the message transmitted by employees (the promise) is not realized and experienced by customers, then there will be disappointment, falling expectations and a failing corporate image.

B&Q recognizes that its staff are a major part of the organization's success. It also recognizes that the continuing commitment of its staff is essential, and effective internal communications are an important component in the process to gain this commitment.

Source: C. Fill, *Marketing Communications, Contexts, Strategies and Applications*, 3rd Edition, 2002.

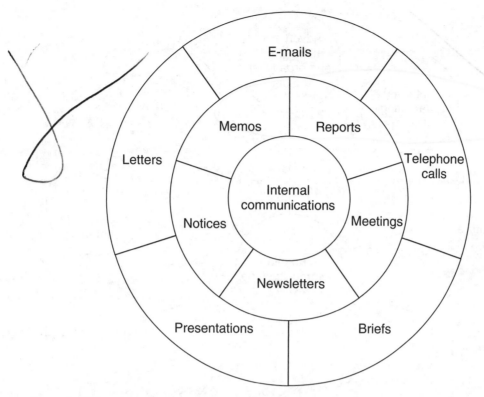

Figure 1.3 Internal communications

The external communications mix

To communicate with external customers, organizations use a range of activities that can be described as the *external communications mix.* These activities range from advertising, direct marketing and selling to public relations and the creation of a strong corporate identity. These activities are used to create brands, to inform customers about product improvements and to promote sales, and because most organizations are not interested in a one-off sale, communications are used to build an ongoing relationship with the customer. For guidance on how to use these communication activities, see Unit 4.

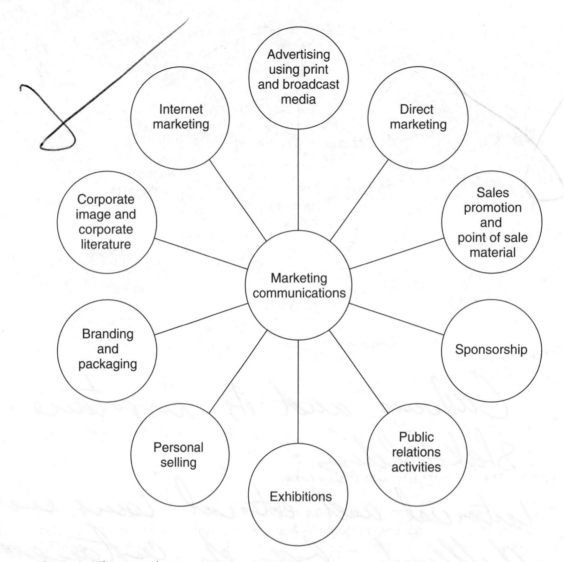

Figure 1.4 The external communications mix

Summary

In this unit you have studied the following:

○ What is meant by the terms 'customer' and 'stakeholder'

○ The range of internal and external communications that individuals and organizations use to communicate with their *customers*

○ How internal communication and internal marketing can help achieve customer focus.

Further study and examination preparation

Attempt to answer Question 2 parts (a) and (b) from the December 2000 examination paper. Go to www.cimeduhub.com to access Specimen Answers and Senior Examiner's advice for these exam questions.

Exam hint

Be prepared to answer questions where you have to identify the stakeholders or customers in a given situation. Ensure that you are able to distinguish between internal and external customers, and able to determine the appropriate communication method and message that might be relevant in a given situation. Avoid attempting to rote learn the contents of this unit. Instead, familiarize yourself with the material so that the knowledge you have gained will give you an overview of the whole subject before you cover other topics in the book.

Customer and its importance.
Stakeholders.
Internal and external coms methods
different type of customers.

unit 2 buying behaviour

Learning objectives

In this unit you will:

- ○ See how an understanding of customer behaviour can help in the development of customer communications

- ○ Examine the difference between consumer buyer behaviour and organizational buyer behaviour

- ○ Recognize the factors affecting buyer behaviour

- ○ Relate communications theory to the buying process.

By the end of this unit you should be able to:

- ○ Distinguish between different types of buying behaviour, depending on the classification of the customer

- ○ Understand those factors affecting buying behaviour

- ○ Apply communications theory when developing communications material.

Study Guide

This unit provides an overview of the buying behaviour process and an insight into how an understanding of the buying behaviour process can help in the development of customer communications. It covers indicative content 2.1, 2.2, 2.3, 2.4 and 2.5 of the syllabus. It should take you about two hours to read through this unit and a further two hours to work through the activities.

The purpose of communication

In marketing, you communicate with others for the following reasons:

- To inform or persuade
- To obtain a decision or request action
- To get something done
- To maintain relationships or respond to a previous communication.

The pressures of modern-day living mean that when you communicate in business it must be clear, accurate and efficient so that time, effort and money are not wasted. Successful communications occur when the person communicating has a clear purpose or objective that is achieved as a result of the communication.

One further factor that is crucial to successful communication, in addition to having a clear objective, is knowing who you are communicating with. Unit 1 clearly defined the whole host of customers and stakeholders that organizations encounter on a daily basis, each of whom has a key role or influence to play at different times. For our communications to be effective, we must know who it is that we are trying to aim our communications at, so as to increase our chances of getting the right message over to them in the right format.

Communications and marketing

To reinforce the importance of understanding who our customer is, we need to look to how marketing has been defined. Marketing, and the marketing concept itself, is an area of study that will be covered in greater depth within Marketing Fundamentals, however, its relevance is no less important here. The following definition is by the Chartered Institute of Marketing (CIM; http://www.cim.co.uk).

Marketing is the management process which identifies, anticipates, and supplies customer requirements efficiently and profitably. (CIM)

We won't dissect this definition too much within this unit, however, a brief discussion of some fundamental areas is worthwhile. What is key then within this definition? Without a doubt, the words 'identifies' and 'customer requirements' are crucial to understand from a marketing and customer communications perspective.

Imagine you are developing your entire marketing mix for a new product which is about to be launched – how can you possibly do this without prior knowledge and understanding of your customer? For example, how can you choose the most appropriate soundtrack to an advertisement if you don't know your customer's listening habits and tastes. Alternatively, how can you develop the appropriate range of tractors and the right specifications if you don't know what your customers want.

Relating customer behaviour to external communications

Understanding how customers behave and what influences their purchase behaviour helps determine effective and relevant communication and promotional activity. When designing and implementing communication plans it is important to consider who your customers are, what their lifestyles are, their educational background, the type of jobs they do, their income levels and their attitudes.

Influences on consumer behaviour

One approach is to consider a customer as a 'black box' with a variety of inputs that influence purchase behaviour. Some of these inputs or stimuli are SLEPT (social, legal, economic, political and technological) factors over which you have no control. However, consideration of these factors can help you to communicate with your customers. For example, at a time when the cost of borrowing money is low because of low interest rates, a financial services company might want to invite current mortgage customers to extend their mortgage. In drafting a mailshot to communicate this message to customers, you would probably want to make reference to the economic situation as part of your selling message.

Other influences that affect purchase behaviour are controllable factors, such as your organization's marketing mix offering. So, for example, the knowledge that in the washing powder market on-pack price promotions and money off influence customers to change brand (at least in the short term) may be a vital piece of information when manufacturers are planning customer communications.

There are several other buying influences that affect consumer behaviour.

Social influences
Through research into your organization's customer base you should be able to identify a profile of your target audience which enables you to develop the right messages and tone of voice in communications that will appeal to them.

The following are powerful social influences on consumers:

- o *Social class* In terms of a person's job, income, educational background and social status, which may influence the newspapers people read, where they spend time socializing with friends and the type of holidays they go on
- o *Stage in the life cycle* In terms of whether a person is single and has high disposable income or is married with young children and therefore spends large amounts on household products
- o *Culture* In terms of religion or ethnic grouping, which can affect people's food choices, the clothes they wear and the magazines they read.

Individual differences
The following are some of the influences that shape people's individual tastes/needs:

- o *Motivation* Affects people in different ways. Some people are highly motivated by status and therefore tend to buy expensive brand-named goods that are a 'status symbol'. Others are more interested in self-fulfilment and prefer to spend their disposable income improving themselves, for example, learning how to play a musical instrument or to speak a foreign language.

o   *Personality* Can affect a person's consumer behaviour. Although everyone has their own distinct personality, there are specific traits which are identifiable in some groups of consumers. For example, if you ran a travel agency that specialized in adventure holidays, then your advertising would be designed to appeal to people who could be described as having an 'independent' personality.

o   *Beliefs/attitudes* Relate to a person's opinions about things. For example, The Body Shop appeals to consumers who have strong beliefs that testing products on animals is wrong. The Body Shop communicates this message in all its advertising, packaging and in-store promotions.

Lifestyle

Lifestyle refers to how consumers spend their free time and what they spend their disposable income on. For example, if you were marketing a magazine that focused on health and fitness for men, then you would want to target men whose lifestyle was oriented around keeping fit, playing sport, being a member of a gym and going on activity holidays. This customer profile or visual image of your target audience would enable you to develop communication messages and strategies that would appeal to them.

Influencers

Ask yourself about the sources of information on fashion clothing and two major sources are likely to appear in your list. One source is the television, the other is magazines. The editors, reviewers and presenters working in these media have a significant filtering role in selecting the pieces of information that reach our decision environment (*Brandweek* 1996). What Jeff Banks says on the BBC's 'Clothes Show' will be heard by millions of potential customers. Similarly, magazines such as *Vogue* have been considered as essential reading for those wishing to keep up to date with one aspect of the fashion scene.

Similarly, the contact that the individual has with salespeople will have an influence on the decision to buy or not to buy. Why should the salesperson in an electrical goods shop offer a Sony TV in preference to a Panasonic? How the marketer communicates the benefits to the salesperson will ultimately affect the attitudes of the salesperson and their willingness to promote your product in preference to competitors' products (Sujan 1986).

For marketers the implications is that there are a range of influencers and decision makers and that all of them offer as potential target audiences when constructing communications strategies.

Source: Pickton and Broderick, *Integrated Marketing Communications*, 2001.

The relevance of customer behaviour to customer communications

Having a basic understanding of the influences on consumer behaviour can help you identify or understand your target audience when drafting customer communications material, such as press releases or mailshots, deciding what to say at an internal meeting or a sales presentation or when planning sales promotion offers.

So, for example, if you are writing a mailshot with the objective of encouraging people who enjoy surfing as a hobby to book an activity holiday in a coastal area known to be good for surfing, your understanding of customer behaviour would help you convey your message. With your understanding of customer behaviour, you would know that people who enjoy surfing tend to buy magazines and equipment related to their hobby. That would probably lead you to renting a database from a specialist retailer or undertaking a joint project with a relevant magazine.

Your understanding of stages in the life cycle and social class would help you refine your knowledge of your audience. You would also have a mental picture of your audience's personality type, what motivates them and their attitudes/beliefs.

Your knowledge and research into this target market might lead you to identifying people who are aged 18–35, with a high disposable income, who are slightly rebellious and are keen on self-fulfillment, i.e. they want to improve their surfing ability and skill. They may also have strong beliefs about pollution and be keen to visit clean beaches.

By giving consideration to customer behaviour you would have a strong starting point for developing material to communicate with this customer group. It would provide you with a focus for your message and how you should frame it.

Activity 2.1

What internal and external stimuli might affect a consumer who was considering buying a new car?

Communication objectives and the buying process

Consumers are generally recognized as going through a number of stages as they proceed from initially identifying that they have a need for something to the point of purchase (see Figure 2.1). Sometimes consumers can proceed through the various stages in a matter of seconds, when they buy on impulse. Typically, consumers are unaware that they are going through a process, it just happens subconsciously.

AIDA

Attention
Interest
Desire
Action (Satisfaction)

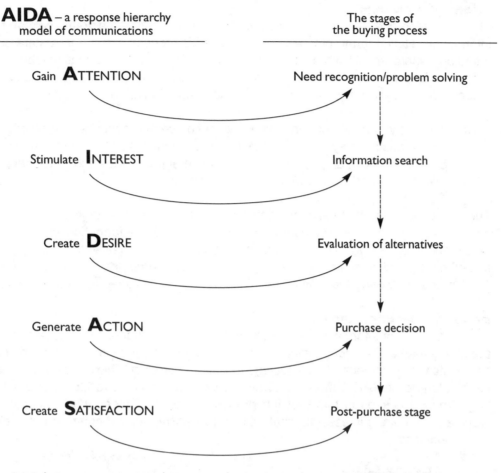

AIDA – a response hierarchy model of communications	The stages of the buying process
Gain **A**TTENTION	Need recognition/problem solving
Stimulate **I**NTEREST	Information search
Create **D**ESIRE	Evaluation of alternatives
Generate **A**CTION	Purchase decision
Create **S**ATISFACTION	Post-purchase stage

Figure 2.1 Relating communication objectives and messages to the stages of the buying process

Using the AIDA model (see Figure 2.1) you can see that customer communication strategies and messages can be tailored to fit in with the buying process that a consumer might go through.

For example, when consumers purchase a car, they will go through various 'problem-solving' stages. Communication messages to prospective car buyers therefore need to be staged to match their progression through the decision-making process.

The buying process

Need recognition/problem-solving
Consider the case of a young woman who decides she needs to buy a car as she has moved to a new job that is not convenient for public transport. She may also consider that she would like a car because all of her friends have one. At this stage she has recognized she has a need.

As far as customer communications are concerned, car manufacturers may tailor their messages to young people to trigger their need/desire to own a car. They may appeal to a young person's desire to have freedom and a good time. Knowing the attitudes and lifestyle of the target audience is key to developing communications that have appeal. This corresponds to the *attention* stage of the AIDA model. Therefore communications should be designed to grab the target market's attention at this stage.

Information search

The next stage after recognizing a need/problem would be for the young woman to search for information relating to the prospective purchase. At first she may be in a state of heightened attention, where she is more receptive than ever before to information about this product category. She will look at poster sites and magazine advertisements for cars with a new interest. She may listen to friends' conversations about their cars.

Next she is likely to undertake an active information search about different types of cars. Her sources of information may be friends/family and memories she has about various cars she has driven. She will also look at advertising, read consumer magazines and watch car programmes, talk to salespeople and even perhaps have a test drive.

The implications are that car manufacturers need to take advantage of every opportunity to communicate with prospective customers and have product information widely available in the media and in car showrooms. In addition, they need to have cultivated a strong brand image and other satisfied customers in the target market. This corresponds to the *interest* stage of the AIDA model, indicating that communications should be designed to create interest.

Evaluation of alternatives

After searching for information, she is likely to evaluate the various car models and makes that are on the market. The communications task for the car manufacturer at this point is to get the brand into the customer's 'choice set' and to want the product. This corresponds to the creating *desire* stage of the AIDA model. However, research should have identified what exactly the target market desires in terms of the product's main attributes. Having identified the most important attribute, it is essential that this *unique selling point* is communicated clearly to the target audience.

The purchase decision

Having got to the intention to buy stage, the consumer's personal circumstances, attitudes and beliefs will affect the purchase decision. But it is at this stage that customer communications, whether they are through advertising or the face to face approach from a salesperson, should move the consumer to the purchase decision. This corresponds to the *action* stage of the AIDA model.

Post-purchase evaluation

Having bought the product, consumers will either be satisfied or dissatisfied, depending on their expectation of the product and the product's actual performance. Even at this stage, communications with the consumer are important in order to foster a favourable opinion of the product. This is mainly because customers tend to discuss purchases with friends/family, and so word-of-mouth advertising becomes a powerful communications tool. In addition, a favourable memory of the product may influence a repeat purchase decision in future years. At this point it is possible to add a final communications stage to the AIDA model, creating *satisfaction*.

How the buying process relates to communications

If, for example, you were marketing nicotine supplements, such as, chewing gum, patches, tablets and fake cigarettes, as a healthy alternative to smoking and to help smokers give up smoking, you could use your knowledge of the buying process to help you produce customer information about your products.

Looking at the stages of the buying process in Figure 2.1. you see that you need information that would gain the target audience's attention, in the first stage of the buying process. This could be public relations activity to raise awareness of the health and economic reasons for giving up smoking.

The next stage is to stimulate interest when people are at the information search. Advertising in relevant magazines, newspapers and on television and radio could help at this stage to provide information about the different products that are on the market. The audience needs to know what products are available to help give up smoking and reduce the 'craving' for nicotine.

At the evaluation of alternatives stage, it is important to have plenty of material about your products at the places where purchases can be made. This could involve having leaflets on the customer counter in chemists or pharmacists. It could involve having free trial products available in health or consumer magazines or even at the point of sale. It is important at this stage that *your* product (rather than the competitors') is visible when potential customers are evaluating their options.

At the purchase decision stage, the call to action could be generated by sales promotion offers that just help tip the buyer's decision in your favour rather than the competitor's. Ideally you would have a persuasive sales person to advocate the benefits of your products but this would probably not be possible in a consumer situation. However, you could target the retailers with appropriate information so that they recommended your brand in favour of other brands.

Activity 2.2

Using the AIDA model and the model that illustrates the buying process, complete the table below to indicate which promotional tool a car manufacturer might use at each stage.

The buying process	AIDA model of communication	Promotional tool
Need recognition	Gain attention	
Information search	Stimulate interest	
Evaluation of alternatives	Create desire	
Purchase decision	Generate action	
Post-purchase decision	Create satisfaction	

Understanding organizational buying behaviour

So far, we've looked at the buying process for consumers. Understanding how an organization undertakes its buying function is just as important when designing effective and relevant communication and promotional activity as when you're dealing with consumers.

A definition of organizational buying is:

> 'The decision-making process by which business buyers establish the need for purchased products and services, and identify, evaluate and choose among alternative brands and suppliers.'

(Kotler, Armstrong, Saunders and Wong, 1999)

25

When designing and implementing communication plans it is important to consider what type of company they are, e.g. public sector or private sector, the composition of the Decision-Making Unit (DMU) and any other relevant factors.

Activity 2.3

Imagine you work as the Buyer for John Deere Tractors. What sort of factors do you think you would take into consideration when purchasing engines for your mass-produced tractors?

Influences on industrial behaviour

Like consumer behaviour, industrial behaviour too is affected and influenced by a host of different factors. The following are some that you should take into consideration.

External influences

Few, if any, organizations manage to escape the impact of external, environmental factors, which broadly consist of PEST factors, namely Political, Economic, Social and Technological Factors. These factors have the ability to affect organizations in many ways, the challenge for organizations is to somehow deal with them and develop strategies for managing the impact.

Political and legal factors Often have far-reaching affects on organizations. If the Government of the day decides to introduce new legislation for organizations, then they must comply with these new regulations, otherwise they can face severe penalties. For example, if a new law on Health and Safety was introduced stating the need to wear protective clothing in a particular job environment, then companies are under a legal obligation to make this clothing available to employees.

Advertisers too are closely governed by rules and regulations. Watchdogs like the Advertising Standards Association keep a very close eye on the 'claims' that are made by advertisers in their advertisements. This applies equally to F.M.C.G companies and manufacturing companies.

Economic factors Will have a powerful effect on purchasing behaviour within all organizations. If a company is thinking of developing a new range of products, for example when Ford developed the Ford Ka or Ford Focus, a great deal of thought has to go into areas such as interest rates, labour costs to manufacture the product, the cost of raw materials and so on.

Social and cultural factors Are perhaps those which have the least direct impact on organizational marketing; however, that does not mean they do not have any indirect effects. For example, a change in styles and fashions amongst consumers will affect what they buy, i.e. clothes, shoes, linen and furniture. Ultimately this will have an impact on those companies who manufacture these goods. Therefore, companies who supply the raw materials to manufacturing companies, for example steel manufacturers or rubber manufacturers, will be affected by these trends.

Technological factors Are a major influence within organizations. If your organization manufactures goods, they will need equipment to do so. Over the years, many new methods of manufacturing have occurred due to new forms and levels of technology. Quite often they can make manufacturing operations more efficient and effective. However, this new technology can be very expensive and those organizations who cannot afford to buy the new technology may find themselves at a disadvantage to those who can.

Insight

Transport accounted for 26 per cent of aluminium use in Western countries in 1997, and the second biggest sector was construction, using 20 per cent. It is important, therefore, that aluminium producers such as Alcan should follow usage trends very closely in those markets. In the motor industry, for example, the trend is towards greater aluminium content in passenger cars. Aluminium content was 85 kg per car in 1997 and it is expected to rise to 130 kg by 2005. By substituting aluminium for steel, the overall weight or a car can be reduced, leading to better fuel consumption, reduced exhaust omissions, improved safety with reduced braking distances, and overall allowing more scope for new, sometimes weighty features such as air conditioning (Batchelor 1998). The manufacturers of substitutes, such as steel, must also follow trends very carefully if they are to plan capacity over the next 10 years.

Source: Brassington, F. and Pettit, S., *Principles of Marketing*, p. 142, 2nd Edition, 2000, FT Prentice-Hall.

Organizational influences

There are many factors within an organization that will affect their purchasing behaviour. For example, a company's ethical strategy when it comes to purchasing raw materials. A good example of this would be The Body Shop, who probably wouldn't buy raw materials, e.g. cosmetics or the ingredients for perfumes, from suppliers who had tested their products on animals.

Another example may be a large chocolate manufacturer, for example Nestlé or Cadbury's. These organizations may object to buying the cocoa they need if the farmer who produces it uses cheap labour in a less developed country to bring up the crop.

The Buying centre – the Decision-Making Unit (DMU)

For many consumers, the decision to buy a product is made by themselves. However, we know they may be influenced by others, e.g. family, peers and friends. Within organizations, the buying decision is very rarely taken by one person alone; many or at least several individuals are normally involved, namely the Decision-Making Unit.

Unit 1 already identified the key individuals who make up the Decision-Making Unit, including buyers, users and deciders. Each of these individuals may well have a say in the purchasing decision, whether its to buy office stationery or a major new piece of mechanical equipment.

It is important to realize the roles that these individuals will play within the buying process, whether it is a one-off purchase, a straight re-buy or a purchase which is part of a long-term arrangement or project.

A campaign to communicate with the financial controllers of companies with large transport fleets was undertaken by a major tyre company. The company realized financial controllers were a key 'advisory' group and in some cases held the 'decider' role. They were primarily interested in the lowest total cost of operation, not just the cheapest tyre. They could be reached directly, and a campaign was directed at them, emphasizing areas they considered rather than issues important to the transport manager. It proved successful in boosting sales levels.

Source: Adcock et al., *Marketing Principles and Practice*, 4th Edition, 2001.

Activity 2.4

Within the Decision-Making Unit (DMU), how might people in different functional roles (for example, marketing, finance or production) participate in organizational buying?

Communication objectives and the buying process for industrial buyers

The buying-decision process for industrial buyers can often be more detailed and often more drawn-out than that for the consumer. As we already know, many factors influence the process itself. According to Robinson et al. (1967), the following stages may be involved in organizational buying decision-making.

- o Anticipation or recognition of needs
- o Determination of characteristics and quality of required item
- o Specification of characteristics and quality of required item
- o Search for and qualification of potential suppliers
- o Acquisition and analysis of proposals
- o Evaluation of proposals and supplier selection
- o Selection of routine order
- o Performance feedback and evaluation.

For example, if you were the Engineering Manager in a large engineering company that manufactured tools for a variety of industrial purposes, you may well go through this buying process. If your company was about to commence manufacturing a new mechanical tool which required a lot of steel to make it, you would probably involve several potential suppliers in a proposal situation. You would then evaluate each of these proposals from the steel suppliers on their own individual merits, bearing in mind such factors as cost, reliability and geographical location. Others who would be involved in this decision would possibly be the Production Manager, the Finance Director and possibly one of the production line operatives too. Finally a decision would be reached and, over time, the success or otherwise of this decision would be evaluated.

Insight

Velden Engineering (UK) manufactures a wide range of component parts and assemblies for various industries and applications, such as medical and aeronautical. In such sensitive areas, it needs to ensure that everything supplied is right first time, as failure can be very expensive indeed. Its customers not only expect compliance with standards such as BS 5750 and ISO 9002 but also to be supplied with finished components or tested assemblies that can go straight into the production process on a Just In Time (JIT) basis. This is a crucial factor in supplier selection.

Source: Brassington, F. and Pettitt, S., *Principles of Marketing*, p. 164, 2nd Edition, 2000, FT Prentice-Hall.

As with consumer decision-making process, the AIDA model can again be used to show that communication strategies and messages can be tailored to fit in with the buying process that industrial consumers may go through. In other words, organizational customers have to be made aware of a product, their interest has to be raised sufficiently to stimulate their desire, for example, to find out more information about it and finally, an action should result – hopefully a sale for your company.

How the organizational buying process relates to communications

If, for example, you manufactured rubber tyres, you could use your knowledge of the buying process to help you produce appropriate customer communications.

Looking at the stages of the buying process according to Robinson et al., you would need information that would gain the attention of those organizations who would buy your tyres whenever they've identified a need for the product. These organizations could be aeroplane manufacturers or car manufacturers. This could be brochures or literature that you could send to them, or they could download this information from your web site.

The next stage, i.e. stimulating their interest, involves a lot of hard work. You may need to draw on the expert knowledge and personal selling techniques of your sales team, who may either perform a presentation to key members of the decision-making unit within these companies, or they may have discussions with them at their exhibition stand. Hopefully, this will persuade the company that they desperately want to buy their rubber tyres from you, rather than any other supplier.

You must be on hand whenever your potential customers are evaluating your quote or proposal. They may well need to discuss a point further, or they may need you to supply them with further information. Personal contact is always recommended, particularly if there's a lot of technical detail to be discussed.

Finally, should your proposal be the successful one, it doesn't all end there. If you want to build up a long term supplier relationship with the company, then it takes time, effort and commitment from everyone. Hopefully, this won't be a one-off purchase. Key communication tactics can keep your company name in the buying centre of the customer for some time. For example, invite them to corporate functions, like a day away playing golf at an exclusive golf club. Alternatively, make sure your sales team are in close contact with them, so that any problems can be quickly and easily ironed out. Furthermore, send them Christmas cards or a copy of your Corporate newsletter. All of these communication strategies should help build and progress your relationship.

Insight

Chubb, an organization noted for its locks and security systems, developed a security product particularly suited to manufacturing organizations based in small factory units. Market research identified the specific target market for the product and the buying behaviour of that target.

A campaign was developed which focused on the decision-making unit (DMU). The DMU concept recognizes that buying decisions are often the result of decisions affected by many people and not just the purchaser. The DMU is the group of people (or players) who are most influential and involved in the purchase and use of the product. Four key players are commonly identified: The Buyer, the User, the Specifier and the Decider.

Research told Chubb that for their market there were, in fact, two key DMU players. One was the financial director who acted both in the capacity of decider and buyer. The other was the factory manager who acted in the capacity of specifier and user. In other words, the financial director would make the final decision about which security system to buy then actually be responsible for the purchase contract. The factory manager would influence the purchase by specifying the type of system required and be responsible for its use. The combined efforts of these two players would dictate whether a purchase would be made and, if so, which systems would be shortlisted and eventually purchased. Marketing communications targeted on only one or the other of the players would represent missed opportunities to maximize sales.

The industrial sales force has long known the value of identifying multiple points of contact within customer organizations. Users of the other elements of the marketing communications mix sometimes fail to do so. Chubb recognized the potential. They did not send a single, general communication to their potential organization customers. Chubb's campaign focused on two people within each organization. And it did so in an interesting and creative way. Small metal moneyboxes were purchased into which were put coins and some information leaflets. Each moneybox had a lid, a lock and a key. A locked moneybox and covering letter was sent to the finance director of each of the potential customer organizations. At the same time, a letter with a key was sent to the factory manager of each organization. In all cases, research had identified the names of each recipient so that the mailing was carefully targeted and personalized.

The covering letters, which gave no details of the product being promoted, requested that each finance director should contact the factory manager and that each factory manager should contact the finance director. In this novel way, members of the DMU were invited to get together to discuss what their mailings were about. Only after coming together were they able to discover the contents of the moneybox and the Chubb security system being offered. Why were coins put into the moneyboxes? Simply to ensure that their moneyboxes rattled. In this way they were more intriguing.

The campaign was a success – it was an award winner. To the delight of the company, sales targets were not only met, they were exceeded.

Source: Pickton, D. and Broderick, A., *Integrated Marketing Communications*, p. 12, 2001, Pearson Education Ltd.

 ## Activity 2.5

Imagine that you are developing a communications campaign for a new kind of pharmaceutical drug. What forms of communication do you think would be most relevant to persuade the following customers to buy your product?

1. A General Practitioner
2. A hospital.

Communication differences

Having identified the need to communicate with a number of different audiences, it would now be useful to summarize the key differences between those communications used by and targeted at consumer markets and those aimed at the business-to-business markets (see Table 2.1)

Table 2.1 Differences between consumer and business to business marketing communications

	Consumer-oriented markets	**Business-to-business markets**
Message reception	Informal	Formal
Number of decision makers	Single or few	Many
Balance of the promotional mix	Advertising and sales promotions dominate	Personal selling dominates
Specificity and integration	Broad use of promotional mix with a move towards integrated mixes	Specific use of below-the-line tools but with a high level of integration
Message content	Greater use of emotions and imagery	Greater use of rational, logic- and information-based messages although there is evidence of a move towards the use of imagery
Length of decision time	Normally short	Longer and more involved
Negative communications	Limited to people close to the purchaser/user	Potentially an array of people in the organization and beyond
Target marketing and research	Great use of sophisticated targeting and communication approaches	Limited but increasing use of targeting and segmentation approaches
Budget allocation	Majority of budget allocated to brand management	Majority of budget allocated to sales management
Evaluation and measurement	Great variety of techniques and approaches used	Limited number of techniques and approaches

Source: C. Fill, *Marketing Communications, Contexts, Strategies and applications*, 3rd Edition, 2002.

Success at Dell

A company that has successfully integrated messages across the consumer and business markets is Dell Computers. Dell has accomplished this feat by using five demand generation channels:

o   The field sales force
o   Third-party business partners
o   Retailers
o   Telechannels
o   The Internet.

Dell uses its field sales force to reach major corporations, institutional customers and governmental customers, which generate 65 per cent of their total revenue. To reach small and medium-size businesses, Dell uses third-party business partners, telechannels and the Internet. To reach consumers, Dell uses retailers and the Internet. Dell encourages the customer to place additional orders either by telephone to inside salespeople or through a special premium Internet page that Dell sets up for the business customer. The premium Internet page allows the business customer to order merchandise not normally available via the Internet.

Dual channel marketing is a key to Dell's success. Specializing its methods of reaching consumers has led to growth in sales. At the same time, Dell maintains its image across all markets: one of being a quality provider of various computers.

Source: Clow and Baack, *Integrated Advertising, Promotion & Marketing Communications*, 2002.

Summary

In this unit you have studied:

o The purpose of communication

o The buying decision process for consumers and for organizations

o The differences and similarities within the buying decision process for consumers and for organizations

o How customer behaviour and the buying process related to customer communication.

Exam hint

Ensure you understand how the stages of the buying process and the AIDA response hierarchy of communications model relate to using different types of communication to target customers effectively.

Bibliography

Kotler, P., Armstrong, G., Saunders, J. and Wong, V. (1999) *Principles of Marketing*, 2nd European Edition, Prentice-Hall.

Robinson, P. J. et al. (1967) *Industrial Buying and Creating Marketing*, Allyn and Bacon.

unit 3
the communication process

In this unit you will:

- Examine the process of communication

- Recognize the barriers to successful communication.

By the end of this unit you should be able to:

- Produce a simple model of the communications process

- Identify how and where barriers to communication occur

- Use a planning framework in the development of customer communications

- Apply communications theory when developing communications material.

Study Guide

This unit provides an overview of the communication process and an insight into how to be an effective communicator. It covers indicative content areas 3.3, 4.1, 4.2, 4.3 of the syllabus. It should take you about two hours to read through this unit and a further two hours to work through the activities.

Study tip

After reading this chapter you could identify a major item that you have purchased recently. Think about the steps you took before actually making the purchase decision and why you chose that product over others in the market. Consider how you found out about the product and any other information that you obtained about it in the period before buying it. In particular, consider what forms of communication influenced your decision and how.

The purpose of communication

In marketing, you communicate with others for the following reasons:

- ○ To inform or persuade
- ○ To obtain a decision or request action
- ○ To get something done
- ○ To maintain relationships or respond to a previous communication.

The pressures of modern-day living mean that when you communicate in business it must be clear, accurate and efficient so that time, effort and money are not wasted. Successful communications occur when the person communicating has a clear purpose or objective which is achieved as a result of the communication. To help you understand what actually happens when you communicate, here is a simple model of the communication process.

The communication chain

Communication is a *chain* of events which has *five* distinct dimensions (see Figure 3.1).

1. The sender has the need to communicate
2. The need is translated into a message (encoding)
3. The message is transmitted
4. The receiver gets the message (decoding)
5. The receiver interprets the message and provides feedback.

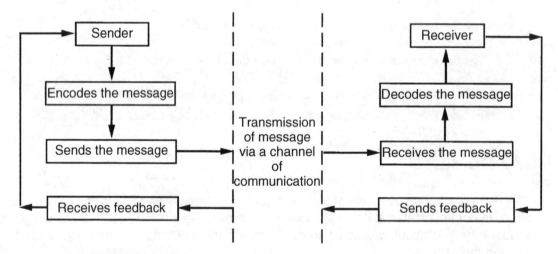

Figure 3.1 The process of communication

1. The need to communicate is *intrinsic*, but the *perception* of a message will be unique, therefore in the process of *conceiving* an idea, you will inevitably make assumptions and leave out details that seem unimportant. However, others will not perceive this in the same way, therefore you must appreciate the *needs* of your recipient, their possible interpretation(s) and *plan* your message accordingly.

2. Messages may be *expressed* in a number of different ways depending on the purpose of the communication, subject or topic to be related, the needs of the recipient and your own personal skills in communication. In the process of *encoding* you will select bits of information and organize them for transmission. The first step is to decide what and how

much to say; if a message contains too much information it is difficult to absorb, but if you do not include enough, it will not meet with the expectation of the recipient and may leave room for misinterpretation.

3. The *medium* you choose for transmission will depend on the message to be conveyed, location of the recipient, speed, convenience and degree of formality required. The usual internal methods are memo, report, telephone and face-to-face interaction.

4. Technological advances in electronic office equipment such as computer-based systems for sending electronic mail copies of documentation have made it possible to send communications from one location to another quickly and effectively.

5. *Decoding* is the interpretation of the message that has been received and will have been successful if the recipient has absorbed the message and assigned to it the meaning which the sender intended.

6. *Feedback* (or lack of) is the response that the recipient sends back to the sender and is a key element in the communication process because it enables the sender to *evaluate* the effectiveness of the message. Feedback may take the form of verbal (telephone call, face-to-face interaction, etc.), non-verbal communication or action (body language, etc.) or written messages.

Feedback is the key element that creates a *cycle* in the communication chain, enabling the information that is sent to be *reviewed* when it is received back and on this basis further communication initiatives or corrective action can be taken as necessary.

Barriers to successful communication

Distortion

It is possible to lose the meaning of a message during the communication process. This can occur at the *encoding* stage, where the sender puts their thoughts into a message. It can also occur at the *decoding* stage, where the recipient attempts to grasp the meaning of the message. This breakdown in communication can be caused by the sender not translating his message into appropriate language, with the result that the wrong message is sent or it is not understood by the recipient.

Although there may be instances where people deliberately choose to distort the message and understand only what they want the message to say, the most common reasons for the meaning being lost in the 'handling' of the message are as follows:

- o Using the wrong words
- o Using jargon or technical words that are not understood
- o Using a foreign language or an accent that is not understood
- o Using words or pictures that have more than one meaning.

Distortion can occur with an advertising message where there is ambiguity in the message, whether this is intentional or not. For instance, if the people who write and design an advertisement that is used in international marketing are from one culture and the recipients of the message are from another, there may be problems in how the advertising message is interpreted. For example, Shell's advertising campaign slogan 'To put a tiger in your tank' caused problems in Taiwan where people attach a religious significance to tigers and therefore had a different understanding of the message being conveyed.

Noise

Noise, such as distractions or the interference that occurs as the communication is being encoded, transmitted and decoded, can obstruct the transmission of the message. There are many different types of noise that can render the message inaccurate, unclear or even mean that it is not received at all.

Technical noise
Technical noise can occur while the message is being transmitted; for example, a poor telephone connection means the caller's voice cannot be heard or a fax machine breaks down.

Physical noise
Physical noise can occur while the message is being transmitted; for example, people talking, traffic or noisy machinery could render a speaker's voice inaudible during a presentation.

Social noise
Social noise creates interference in the transmission and decoding of messages. It is caused when people are prejudiced against others because they are of a different age, gender or social class. For example, a young woman delivering a presentation on corporate funding to older businessmen may be perceived to lack credibility by some of the audience who are prejudiced because of her age and gender.

Psychological noise
A person's emotional state or attitude could interfere with message transmission. A person's anger or hostile attitude can create psychological noise. For example, a customer whose goods have not been delivered may be unable to hear the reason why the goods have been delayed because he is so angry about the situation.

Other barriers
Perceptual bias Can occur where the recipient of a message makes assumptions and selects what they want to hear. This can result in the wrong message being received. For example, if a doctor has told a patient that their condition is not serious as long as they change their diet, the patient might choose to hear only part of the message and not take in the message about changing their diet.

Information overload Can occur if the recipient of the message receives too much information or information that is too technical. The result is that the key messages are not conveyed or understood. For example, when a new member of staff is given a very detailed demonstration of how several pieces of equipment work in a short space of time, it is likely that they will become confused and remember very little about what was actually said.

Contradictory non-verbal Messages can occur if the person encoding a message says one thing but their body language says something else. For example, if a person wears casual clothes and a baseball cap to a job interview in a formal business environment and says that they think they would fit into the organization, they are conveying mixed messages to the interviewer.

Language Can act as a barrier if two people speak different languages and cannot understand each other.

Case history

UK factory hosts Japanese delegation visit

A UK manufacturing company hosted a delegation from an associate company in Japan. The Marketing Manager was given the task of arranging the first day's activities, which were to include a two-hour-long presentation about the history, structure and objectives of the firm, a tour of the main manufacturing site, and lunch followed by a brainstorming session on how the two companies could forge closer links and benefit from future joint projects. However, little consideration was given to the communication barriers that arose during the visit:

- Cultural differences in the way Japanese people greet others, their degree of formality and taste in food

- The language barrier in that many of the delegation did not speak English and none of the host company spoke Japanese

- The unfamiliar technical environment and organization of the company, which meant that the jargon and abbreviations specific to the host company that were used in the presentation, made the presentation incomprehensible to most of the delegation

- The noisy manufacturing site meant that during the tour most of the visitors could not hear what was being said to them

- The lengthy presentation meant that the visitors who understood English had 'information overload'. Most lost concentration and could not take in the overall message that was being conveyed

- The delegation did not feel confident or comfortable with contributing to the brainstorming session.

For future visits the marketing manager thought of a number of ways to eliminate the communication barriers:

- Employing an interpreter

- Researching cultural differences and using this information to provide appropriate refreshments and use appropriate greetings, seating arrangements, etc.

- Ensuring that no jargon or colloquialisms are used by speakers

- Using small groups to tour the factory at a quiet time so that visitors can hear what the guide is saying

- Using a shorter presentation to prevent boredom and information overload

- Using a different presentation approach, with visual media, such as slides or video and Powerpoint software

○   Increasing interaction with the audience with question and answer techniques to check understanding

○   Providing a pack of information in English and Japanese, containing key points about the company, such as its structure, objectives and current operations

○   Avoiding the brainstorming session as it is probably too ambitious an exercise. Replacing it with a more social event where individual host managers can be 'partnered' with visiting managers and interpreters used to help exchange views in a less threatening context.

Avoiding barriers to communication

Communication barriers cause mistakes and can damage the business relationship with external customers. With internal customers, communication barriers can lead to conflict (at worst) and irritation (at best), neither of which are a good recipe for internal marketing and customer care.

To overcome possible communication barriers, careful thought needs to be put in before encoding messages so that the full message is conveyed. Gaps in messages are usually caused by making assumptions about how people will 'decode' the message.

Avoid jargon or technical words that may not be understood and try to avoid ambiguity.

Ensure that you understand your target audience as this is the key to avoiding barriers to communication. The accuracy and precision of your message is important if it is to be decoded correctly. An understanding of your target audience's needs should mean that you are able to have the same 'mental image' about a product or service that your customers have.

For internal communication with staff, you could provide training to eradicate unnecessary social and psychological noise that can be created when people make assumptions about customers or allow themselves to react inappropriately when customers make complaints.

When communicating with customers it is essential not to create information overload and to be aware that only part of the message may be heard. You may have to repeat a message many times before it is heard fully.

It is also important to establish credibility so that customers feel you and your message is trustworthy and internal customers believe in what you say.

By taking some time to consider how a communication might be received you are more likely to shape a message that will not be misinterpreted or misunderstood. In other words, by carefully shaping your message and considering the effect it might create, it is more likely that the communication will be successful.

Nike in the penalty box

In 1996, to coincide with the European Football Championship, Nike launched a new advertising campaign. This was directed at the more sports-aware segment of the market and featured many of the football stars playing in the contest. The format was of a team of devilish-looking ghouls playing against a 'good' side made up of stars that endorsed Nike products. The visual composition of the ad was visually stunning and symbolically similar to that used in horror movies. The scheduled showings were closely related to match times so that the ad would be shown throughout the afternoon and evening times.

The campaign grabbed the public's attention. The combination of sport, horror, stars and a desirable brand were just too much to ignore. Unfortunately, it was the stunning visual impact that caused the problem for Nike. Hundreds of parents complained to the Independent Television Commission, the Advertising Standards Authority and to Nike itself. Their concern was that this ad was frightening their children. As it was often being shown at a time when children's TV would normally be shown there was an altogether different reaction from some of the audiences reached by the ad.

Similar complaints in Denmark led to the ad being deemed unsuitable for viewing. In that country it was banned from being shown in cinemas. In the UK the ITC's response was to limit the broadcast times to after 9p.m., except when shown during evening matches. The ITC felt that as long as parents were on hand the impact of the communication would not be so frightening.

This example demonstrates an excellent use of creativity in grabbing the viewers' attention. It also shows how the interpretation of the message is in the control of the viewer and that if the message is misunderstood then there can be a serious negative consequence for the advertiser.

Source: Pickton and Broderick, *Integrated Marketing Communications*, 2001.

Activity 3.1

Read the following case study and identify the barriers to communication and the problems they are causing in the workplace.

Sally Strict, the office manager at XYZ, is nearing retirement and considers herself to be 'of the old school'. She likes the girls on her administration team to appear neat and tidy and to do as they are told without question.

One day they are short-staffed and the recruitment agency agrees to send a temporary administrative assistant to work for a week. Sally had asked the agency to send someone for two weeks but the telephone line had been so crackly that the message had not got through.

When Peter Patel, a young business studies student who liked to get work experience during his vacations, was sent by the agency to the XYZ office, Sally was shocked by his appearance. She wondered how a young man with dyed hair and earrings would ever be able to cope with the work done in her department.

She spoke to him in a sarcastic tone and said: 'You'd better make yourself busy – that is if you know anything about office work.'

Peter was very irritated by her hostile attitude. However, he knew that she and the rest of the department were under a lot of pressure to get work completed. He was sure the office manager would appreciate his hard work and he decided that if she did not, then he would just walk out and leave them in the middle of all the work they had to complete.

Later in the day the department received a large number of orders that had to be processed immediately and this would involve all the team staying late.

During the afternoon tea break, Sally, who had by now realized that Peter was an efficient and hard-working member of the team, said: 'So how are you getting on now?'

Peter immediately assumed that she was being sarcastic and 'having a go' at him. He smiled politely and said: 'Fine, thanks.'

Sally was relieved that he had not taken offence at their initial meeting and was glad to see him settling into the office.

A few minutes later, Peter put on his jacket and walked out of the office. He was determined that he was not going to stay at XYZ to be insulted by the office manager.

Effective communicators

Successful business communicators have the ability to transfer and receive information using the most appropriate channel. They eliminate barriers to communication and proceed without prejudice, bias and unsuitable language in line with the needs of the recipient. They possess the following attributes:

o *Credibility* They are highly believable and trustworthy in terms of the content of their communication/message with which you, as a recipient, feel completely comfortable. Indeed, this is vital for successful managers and those involved in the leadership of others.

o *Precision* This is linked to the first point. It is not only related to the ability to articulate words, sentences and phrases into a meaningful communication but also helps to create a communication experience whereby the recipient(s) share the sender's 'mental picture'.

o *Perception* A successful communicator will be able to anticipate and predict how their message will be received and therefore shape it accordingly. The reponse of the recipient(s) (which may be presented in written format, verbally or non-verbally) will then be assessed by the sender and if necessary further communication will take place to adjust for misunderstandings.

o *Control* Linked to the point about perception is the feeling that you should now be getting, which is that successful communicators are able to control their message to a great extent and also to generate (mostly) the required response, if appropriate.

o Finally, one of the most important (natural) skills possessed by successful communicators is that of congeniality – the ability to be pleasant and friendly, in written, verbal or nonverbal communication, even if the message is serious and possibly very bad news.

Wendy's misses the mark – then hits a winner

'Where's the beef?' A series of commercials sponsored by Wendy's during the 1980s featured this slogan. The commercials were highly popular and even rated as the decade's best by some advertising analysts. The phrase was so well known that one presidential candidate even asked another, 'Where's the beef (in your campaign)?' during one of the debates. Unfortunately, the impact for Wendy's was marginal. When consumers were asked who sponsored the ads, most attributed them to Burger King. The clever slogan and Clara Pellar, the elderly woman who starred in the commercials, overshadowed the message and created interference. Thus the impact on sales was negligible.

This outcome demonstrates one type of advertising noise. In this case, it shows how an ambiguous transmission device can fail to achieve a complete transfer of the desired meaning to the audience. In essence, Wendy's may have missed the mark with this ad.

In 1982, Wendy's switched to featuring its CEO, Dave Thomas, as the pitch-man. Thomas was able to demonstrate a self-effacing honesty that made his name and Wendy's nearly synonymous. At the time, the company had been drifting in a number of different ways. The food line had expanded to include breakfast; people were not sure what they were getting.

The refocus, with Thomas at the forefront, was a return to a simpler menu and a renewed focus on clean restaurants, high-quality food and reasonable prices. The approach succeeded. Thomas has since performed in over 500 commercials and has won numerous awards as the entrepreneur and restaurateur. Theresa Howard of Nation's Restaurant News summarises the success this way: 'While all things surrounding Thomas on a set are fake, he is not. His integrity, charisma and true commitment to basics continues to come through in each series of commercials'.

The theme 'quality is our recipe' drives Thomas. He believes one thing for certain – he knows how to make a good hamburger. When that burger is served in a clean store, by friendly people, at a good price, customers are satisfied and they come back for more. This quality message permeates the entire organization, and as a result Dave Thomas has carefully built a solid Integrated Marketing Communications (IMC) plan in his organization.

Source: Clow and Baack, *Integrated Advertising, Promotion and Marketing Communications*, 2002.

Activity 3.2

Explain how each of the following can create a barrier to communication and use an example for each to indicate how the impact of noise could be reduced.

1. Lack of credibility (4 marks)
2. Perceptual bias (4 marks)
3. Information overload (4 marks)
4. Contradictory non-verbal signals (4 marks).

Planning the business message

Professional communicators decide the purpose of their communication at the outset. By being clear about their intention, they then know if they have achieved their objective at the end of their communication.

Business communications tend to be planned, formal, impersonal and succinct. The degree of planning involved in the communication depends on the purpose and context of the communication. For example, you may carefully plan a sales call to a prospect, since you may need to deal with any objections that the customer may raise. However, you are unlikely to do this when you want to arrange lunch with a colleague, even though there may be several important matters you wish to discuss with him. In this situation you may not make detailed notes of the issues but your planning may extend to making a mental note of them.

A planning framework

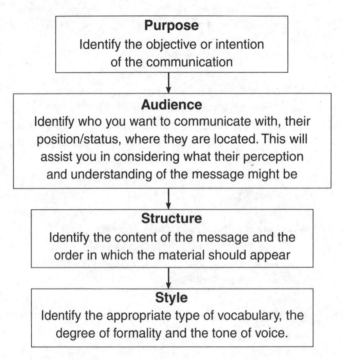

Purpose
Identify the objective or intention
of the communication

Audience
Identify who you want to communicate with, their
position/status, where they are located. This will
assist you in considering what their perception
and understanding of the message might be

Structure
Identify the content of the message and the
order in which the material should appear

Style
Identify the appropriate type of vocabulary, the
degree of formality and the tone of voice.

Figure 3.2 A planning framework

The PASS framework is an easy to remember mnemonic that you may be familiar with. To assist you in the planning of messages you should also consider the communication *mode* you intend to use, as the communication format and media you use will be important in determining the structure and style you adopt.

Identifying the purpose

There are an infinite number of reasons why you might communicate in business. Generally, in internal communication situations, you will be informing colleagues, line managers or subordinates about something, responding to a previous communication, obtaining a decision or requesting action. In external markets you may be trying to raise awareness in the media, persuading customers to buy or stimulating some other response, such as ordering a catalogue or ringing for more information.

Barker (1999) recommends that you do not confuse your document's purpose with its subject. He says that if you were writing about a new piece of equipment, you could write about it in many ways. The way you choose will depend on your purpose and what you want your document to do.

According to Barker, possible objectives of a product include:

- Justifying the cost of buying it
- Comparing it with similar products
- Telling the reader how to operate it
- Listing the options for using it
- Detailing its technical specifications
- Explaining how it fits into an existing network or system.

Each purpose will generate a completely different document. The document will only be useful if it addresses the purpose clearly.

Acknowledging the audience

For internal communications the position of the person you are communicating with and how well you know them will determine the style of communication you adopt in terms of the detail, complexity and words used. In addition, the purpose of the communication and the urgency of the matter will determine which communication format and media you will use.

In order to tell a colleague that you will not be available for lunch for another hour, you may just call into their office or telephone them. In contrast to this, you may write a memo or send an e-mail to inform staff about a change in the time and place of the weekly sales meeting.

In writing a press release to announce some important news about the company you work for you may draft two versions of the press release. One may be tailored for the national press and one may be targeted at the trade press. However, if you had a particular contact in the broadcast media whom you wanted to inform, you may consider using the personal touch and actually telephoning the contact with the information.

In developing advertising to your target market, you will need to consider the characteristics of the target audience in terms of their age, gender, education, social background and lifestyle when composing the words and deciding on the visual approach and the media you will use.

Structure

Having identified why you are communicating and with whom, you need then to consider what you are going to say and how you are going to organize the content of the message.

Business communications should be succinct, so you should be selective with the content you choose to include. Use relevant, accurate information and make sure that you do not overload the recipient with too much information.

Having selected the material for your message, you need to decide how you will organize it. The way you group material together and how you sequence it determines the shape of the message.

It may help you to structure the message if you identify the most important point and then follow with the supplementary information you need to include. If you are dealing with particularly complex material it may be helpful to present the simple information first and build up to the more complex argument or points you wish to make. You may feel it is important to present information in a chronological order, particularly if you are dealing with a series of events or a complaint about a number of issues.

Whatever structure you adopt, you should note that it is easier to read an argument that follows a logical progression and quicker for people to absorb information that is grouped together in chunks with relevant headings.

Style

The style you adopt in any message is governed by the words you use, the way you structure sentences and the tone of voice you adopt.

The way you use vocabulary is a personal choice. The English language is very rich and you may often have several words to choose from that will convey the same meaning. However, you should consider your audience and their familiarity with the words you use. It is not always appropriate to avoid jargon or technical words, especially when you know your audience is familiar with them and where it is important for you to establish credibility and common ground with your audience.

By changing the structure of sentences you can place emphasis on certain words and by altering the order of words you can produce greater fluency or flow.

The tone of any communication conveys the overall effect. You can create an overall impression of friendliness and informality with the greeting you use, simple wording and colloquial expressions. For example, the following sentence has a friendly, informal tone: 'Thanks for lunch yesterday. It was useful to go through the client list and I will make appointments to see each of them a.s.a.p.'

Alternatively, you can convey a formal tone by giving instructions, using technical wording and an impersonal tone. For example: 'The figures indicate that sales staff need to cut the cost of expenses by *x* per cent. Consequently all journeys over *x* miles should be agreed by the Sales Manager.'

By emphasizing points, by appealing to the recipient's emotions, repeating selling points, using reassuring terms and asking questions that lead the recipient to a series of benefits, you can create a persuasive message. For example, the following statement has a persuasive tone: 'How can Home Care help you? With Home Care you can be assured of quality care in the comfort of your own home. No more struggling with the cooking and cleaning.'

Activity 3.3

Rewrite the sentences below, avoiding the use of jargon and cliches, and correct any unnecessary wordiness.

1. The practicability of planning to meet possible future service requirements should be explored
2. The supplies manager has been at pains to explain that the availability of the product is diminishing rapidly
3. Inflationary land prices have rendered it an uneconomic proposition to relocate the production operation.

The mode of communication

The communication format (whether that is a written report or an oral presentation at a meeting) or the media (whether that is the telephone or electronic means or some form of advertising media) that you use to transmit your message will influence its structure and style.

In addition, when communicating internally, you will need to consider the purpose of the communication and the audience you wish to communicate with, to help you decide the correct communication format. For example, there will be some occasions when it is suitable to put a notice on the noticeboard to communicate with colleagues and at other times it will be more appropriate to send a memo or organize a face-to-face meeting.

For external communications there will be occasions when it is suitable to send a fax message and at other times it will be easier and more confidential to send an e-mail.

Where you need to raise awareness about an issue or a new product, your choice of media will influence the style you will adopt.

For example, if you were trying to raise awareness about the dangers of driving without seatbelts you could either use a press campaign or a radio campaign to communicate your message. However, the treatment of the message would be different in each case. For radio, you could use sound to communicate an emotional message of a family talking about the death of a loved one. For the print advertisement, you could go into more detail as you would not have the same time constraints as a short radio commercial. So you could include more facts and figures about the number of car accidents caused by not wearing a seatbelt. Such a detailed message would be totally inappropriate if it was read out loud in a radio commercial but could be absorbed by people reading it in their own time and at their own pace.

Figure 3.3 A print advertisement can contain more detail than a radio or poster advertisement

How the PASS framework can help in planning messages

If you needed to raise awareness among teenage girls in one city in your country, about the dangers of smoking, the PASS framework could be your starting point to help you decide what you want to say and how you should frame your message.

For example, by considering the 'purpose' of the communication task you would be clear about the message you needed to convey, i.e. to warn of the dangers of smoking.

By considering the 'audience' you would ensure that you concentrated on teenage girls. This may influence the language you use, i.e. not technical or medical language. For instance, sending text messages is very popular amongst teenagers so you could use that type of language to give your message impact and credibility.

As the style and structure of a message are greatly influenced by the communication method you are going to use, you would consider this aspect next. Assuming you were restricted to a tight budget, you may consider that posters or outdoor advertising could be an economical medium to use. However, you would also need to consider where you would place your posters. Relevant places could be community and sports centres that young people use. Or outdoor poster sites at cinemas and shopping centres or transport advertising on buses and underground trains or at 'Adshel' bus stop sites, could be used.

The next consideration would be the 'style' of the message that would suit your target audience. You would have to ensure that your style was not patronizing. You could even use a celebrity who appealed to this age group. You would need to consider the restrictions of the poster format and the best design of the poster in terms of layout, typeface, colours and imagery that could be used.

The structure would be the final consideration. This would mean looking at how you are going to convey your message. You would have to be selective with words and group the material in a sequence that is logical. In other words you would have to focus on the most important point and make that first. This could be fairly straightforward task when determining a short poster-style message.

Thus the PASS framework can help in planning messages.

The ice-cream business – Magnum

This material was originally written by Eileen Buckwald, product Manager for Birds Eye Walls.

The ice-cream market has become increasingly complex as consumers' understanding and expectations improve and manufacturers provide a variety of products to meet new segment needs.

One part of the impulse market is known as the 'personal indulgence' sector. Within this sector Birds Eye Walls with Magnum is the market leader, with Mars and Galaxy the other major competitors.

The Magnum brand received heavyweight support in the early 1990s and was positioned as the intensely personal, adult indulgence ice-cream. The positioning reflected the intensity of the relationship consumers felt towards the brand. It socialised their feelings by preventing any embarrassment and provided it with universal appeal (everyone is having this affair). The main result of this campaign was that it helped widen consumption habits.

By the late 1990s, the context for the brand had changed. It was being challenged as imitations began to erode Magnum's distinctiveness and price competition reduced added values. The brand no longer represented exclusiveness, nor was it a rule breaker any more. The brand had begun to age and impulse sales were declining.

The marketing plan for 1999 required that the brand be repositioned from one based on a one-to-one relationship to one where personal sacrifices had to be made. The theme 'Life is all about priorities' was adopted, so that Magnum be perceived as a brand for which sacrifices had to be made. Personal indulgence had to be fitted into a busy lifestyle because 'Magnum is worth it, and I'm worth it . . . so as Magnum is really special – so I deserve it.' It was at this point that the Magnum Girl became an additional feature associated with the brand (see Table 3.1).

Table 3.1 Magnum target consumers

Kids	Teenagers	Young adults	Pre-family	Family with children	Empty nesters
	Magnum	Magnum	Magnum	Magnum	Magnum
	Classic	Classic	Classic	Classic	Classic
	Magnum	Magnum	Magnum	Magnum	Magnum
	Caramel & Nuts	Double	Double	Snack Pack	After Dinner

To propel the Magnum brand to power brand status in 2000, products were developed (e.g. Magnum After Dinnner) and some were renovated (Magnum Classic). However, overall the brand range was reduced on the principle that fewer bigger brands could be more effectively supported by the media spend.

Although prices were held in 2000, the media investment of £7.5 million was designed to provide support for an integrated promotional programme across television, press, outdoor (posters) and marketing public relations. This sum represented 65 per cent share of voice and nearly 5,000 TVRs. In addition, in-store support was increased to provide for improved visibility and to cut through the own-label imitations. Also, at a time when ideas about brand 'experiences' were becoming central, Magnum became associated with the UK's first triple loop roller coaster 'Magnum Force'.

The public relations programme sought to build on the visibility of the brand and the coverage that the Magnum Girl gained. For example, Magnum became the first brand ever to appear on the front cover of the Sunday Mail magazine supplement, one which has the second highest circulation of Sunday newspapers. The Magnum Girl became the central point to the campaign, featuring on posters, television, in store and press work. Each year a competition is held to find a new Magnum Girl to front the brand, in itself a positive means of securing good public relations for the brand.

The Magnum brand grew in volume terms 147 per cent in the multi-pack sector. The brand retains strong measures of awareness and research indicates that consumers perceive Magnum in terms of 'treat', 'irresistible' and 'high quality'. However, above all else it is perceived as 'indulgent'.

Source: C. Fill, *Marketing Communications, Contexts, Strategies and Applications*, 3rd Edition, 2002.

Activity 3.4

Suggest an appropriate communication style and mode of communication for each of the following situations:

1. You work for the city council and wish to use an advertising campaign to inform motorists that tolls will be introduced on routes into the town centre.
2. You work in the research and development department of a factory that makes cleaning materials. You wish to demonstrate the prototype of a new window-cleaning product and the main findings of a financial viability study to senior management as you need their approval to proceed to the next stage of product development.
3. You are the distribution manager at a chemical company. There have been problems with deliveries from the warehouse to a number of distributors. You have collated your findings about the problems and now need to communicate them to the Sales and Marketing Director.

Summary

In this unit you have studied:

- ○ The purpose of communication

- ○ How communication occurs

- ○ How and why barriers to communication occur

- ○ How to overcome communication barriers

- ○ How to plan customer communication activities.

Further study and examination preparation

Attempt Question 4(b) from the December 2000 examination paper. Go to www.cimeduhub.com to access Specimen Answers and Senior Examiner's advice for this exam question.

Exam hint

Practise drawing a simple model of the communications process as this sometimes crops up as one part of a question on the communications process. Ensure you can apply your understanding of it to practical questions relating to communication barriers. Consider the variety of contexts where communications barriers occur, for example, in interviews, in advertising and in any written messages. Be prepared to apply your understanding of the PASS framework to the development of communication activities, for example, writing a letter, a report or an advertisement.

unit 4
the communications mix

In this unit you will:

- Extend your knowledge of the communications or promotional mix

- Examine the differences between above- and below-the-line promotion

- Understand the need for an integrated approach to marketing communications

- Appreciate what influences promotional decisions

- Briefly examine the role of Information and Communication Technology in Communication.

By the end of this unit you should be able to:

- Formulate a promotional brief

- Determine the suitability of various promotional activities

- Evaluate the appearance of corporate literature

- Devise a press release.

Study Guide

This unit provides you with a basic understanding of the communications or promotion mix and covers indicative content area 3.1–3.13 of the syllabus.

It links with the Marketing Fundamentals syllabus indicative content area 1.2.9 which is covered in Unit 7 of the Marketing Fundamentals workbook. With the Marketing Fundamentals syllabus you are looking at the promotional mix as one element of a total marketing mix; with Customer Communications this topic is the key to understanding how organizations communicate with their external customers.

The other major difference is that, with this syllabus, you not only need to know about the various communication tools but you also need to be able to use them and combine them into integrated marketing communications. For instance, you need to be able to write a press release, suggest the layout for a press advertisement or write the copy for a mailshot. However, you would not be expected to be able to make a television or radio advertisement because these are very specialized activities that would be difficult to assess in a written examination.

You need to appreciate that although some larger organizations sub-contract all their marketing communication activities out to specialized agencies, there are many smaller organizations where working in marketing is synonymous with drafting press advertisements (or at least knowing what makes an effective one) and being able to write a press release or the text for a mailshot.

Although Unit 5 focuses specifically on ICT, this unit will provide you with a brief insight into its role within the communications mix. You will look at how technology specifically affects your communication with customers.

For further information for how this material in this unit will be examined, read the Exam/ Revision Hints section at the end of this unit.

This unit will take you three hours to read through and a further three hours to work through the activities.

Study tip

This unit provides an outline of the main advertising media and their main attributes. To provide further examination of this topic you need to spend some time looking at examples of advertising using different media. For each advert you should specify the advertising objectives, identify the target audience and consider why that particular medium has been chosen.

You could undertake a similar activity looking at sales promotions. List how many different types of sales promotion you can see when you next go shopping. Consider the objectives of each promotion.

Because the speed of technological change is so fast, you should use this unit as a starting point to think about how Information Communications Technology (ICT) is changing the way you communicate. You need to extend your knowledge by accessing information outside the course book, in the quality press, specialist marketing magazines and specialist technical press.

You should also use the Internet to see how it can be used. Look up some websites that are of particular interest to you and surf the web for more information about technological developments. One of many websites that you could visit is www.net-profit.co.uk, which is in the form of an online magazine and provides information about technology developments affecting business.

In addition, look at how telecommunications equipment in your workplace has changed the way you and your colleagues do your jobs.

If you cannot access the Internet at home or at work, you could find access at your college or local library or even visit an Internet or cybercafe, where you can pay for access.

The communications mix or promotions mix

You have already looked at the various ways that individuals inside an organization use to communicate either with colleagues or others outside their organizations. The *communications or promotions mix* refers to those forms of communication that are used not on behalf of an individual but on behalf of the entire organization to promote either itself or its goods and services.

Refer to Figure 1.3 in Unit 1 for an example of the communications mix and Figure 1.1 for the target audiences that organizations may want to communicate with.

The communications or promotional mix can be categorized as *above-the-line activity* and *below-the-line activity*. (These definitions will be explained as you work through the unit.) Organizations usually use a mix of above- and below-the-line activity to communicate with their target audience.

These activities include:

- Advertising using main media
- Direct marketing
- Sales promotions
- Sales or corporate literature
- Sponsorship
- Point of sale material
- Public relations
- Exhibitions
- Personal selling
- Branding and corporate image
- Packaging
- Internet marketing.

Marketing communications – Cadbury

Cadbury is one of the best-known brands in the UK and is synonymous with chocolate. In order to communicate and develop its brand with customers and other stakeholders, it uses a variety of communications methods. Some of the main ones are as follows:

Methods of marketing communications used by Cadbury:

- Advertising
- Point of purchase
- Public relations
- Direct marketing
- Website
- Personal selling
- Exhibitions and events
- Packaging
- Sales promotions
- Café Cadbury
- Sponsorship (Coronation Street)
- Trade promotions

- ○ Product placements
- ○ Cadbury World – associated merchandise
- ○ Field marketing
- ○ Vending machines.

One recent addition to this impressive list has been the development of Café Cadbury and its entry into the expanding coffee house market. Positioned as a 'Chocolate Experience', the Cadbury cafés seek to extend the Cadbury brand even though direct sales through these outlets will be small. The objective, as reported by Mason (2000), is to keep the Cadbury brand high in the minds of the public and to maintain the quality and trust that the brand has evoked. Cadbury refers to this brand extension as part of its present marketing programme.

Source: C. Fill, *Marketing Communications, Contexts and Strategies*, 3rd Edition, 2002.

How the communications mix works

Advertising is just one activity in the 'tool box' of promotional activities that marketers can use but it is the most visible of all communication activities because it uses the main media of print, television, radio, cinema and outdoor. (You will look in more detail at the different types of advertising and other types of promotions or communications later in the unit.)

Promoting goods and services came about because as goods and services became mass-produced and supply outstripped demand, organizations realized that advertising and selling could help 'shift' items from shop windows and company shelves.

Initially the main medium for advertising was print (mainly newspapers) and it helped the owners of newspapers and magazines to cover their production costs. Gradually owners of other media appeared, such as, poster sites and cinemas. During the 1950s and 1960s in the UK, commercially owned radio and television stations also gained revenue from advertising.

Now there is a proliferation of media globally which means that people are exposed to a mass of advertising messages.

As a result of this, advertising has had to become more sophisticated to attract people's attention. A single advert placed indiscriminately in a magazine or newspaper without careful planning is unlikely to attract your customers' attention.

Nowadays you would need to consider carefully what your objectives are and who you are trying to reach before deciding which promotional activities you need to use and what approach you need to take. You would need to consider the following factors:

- ○ What is to be achieved? What are your objectives?
- ○ Who do you want to communicate with? Who is your target audience?
- ○ How big is your target audience? How can you reach them? What are their media habits?
- ○ What is your message? How can you express your message?
- ○ When do you need to communicate your message?
- ○ How much money do you have to spend?

Promotional objectives

Here is a selection of promotion objectives:

- To create an image
- To create awareness
- To inform about a new feature
- To change attitudes
- To correct misconceptions
- To reassure
- To remind
- To generate interest
- To generate response
- To encourage trial
- To prompt purchase
- To support other promotional activity.

Case history

Promoting a sports brand in Thailand

In a recent article in *The Nation* (courtesy of Lexis-Nexis), the managing director of Adidas (Thailand), Michael Wellman said: 'We are the number one sports brand in Thailand in terms of revenue and we would like to maintain the position.'

Wellman said that the company would be working on improving visual merchandising in its retail outlets, as well as promoting in-store activities such as bringing in local athletes to talk with customers to enhance their knowledge of sports.

Adidas has already launched its 'Be Better' campaign in Thailand, which is part of the firm's global strategy to strengthen its leadership as a sports brand.

'All sports fans in Thailand already recognize Adidas as a sports brand that provides genuine sports products. And we want to convey to people the terrific feeling they can get through sports and exercise,' Wellman said.

'It makes you feel good and you want to share the feeling with others and help others be better. That is what this campaign is all about,' he added.

Promoting a film in the UK

The film 'Bridget Jones's Diary' ran at cinemas throughout the UK for a fixed period. But before its release and during the period of its release, it had been heavily promoted to ensure that exposure of the film will be maximized in order to attract audiences and revenue.

Around the time of the release of the film, an extensive bus shelter and billboard hoarding campaign was mounted, showing the lead actors or 'stars' of the film. Those sited near cinemas also provided information about when the film would be showing.

To celebrate the first showing of the film in London (its premiere) the 'stars' of the film allowed themselves to be photographed, along with other celebrities invited to see the film, so that national newspapers would print their pictures and a related story to publicize the film.

Around this time, film reviewers/journalists who had been invited to a special screening of the film wrote reviews of the film that appeared in many national newspapers and magazines.

Once the film was on general release, the major cinema chains produced material in their 'free' magazines about it, to target regular cinema-goers.

Some of the film stars were interviewed on television and radio chat shows to publicize their latest movie.

If the film had been targeted at children, a great deal of merchandising material would have been produced as well (think about the remake of '101 Dalmations' and the variety of merchandising material that was produced including toys, books, posters, pencilcases, etc.) not only to generate income but also to indirectly publicize the film.

The role of integrated communications

From the case examples, you can see that organizations are aware that one advertisement on its own would be unlikely to make any real impact on people because of the amount of advertising 'noise' that exists. As a consequence, organizations repeat their message many times and in many ways to achieve 'coverage' of their target audience. These efforts are often referred to as 'integrated communication campaigns'.

Integrated marketing communications

Put very simply, integrated marketing communications is about combining all the elements of the communications mix for the maximum communications impact. It is 'a new way of looking at the whole, where once we saw only parts such as advertising, public relations, sales promotion, purchasing, employee communication and so forth, to look at it the way the consumer sees it – as a flow of information from indistinguishable sources'.

Source: Schultz, D. E., Tannenbaum, S. I. and Lauterborn, R. F. (1992), *Integrated Marketing Communication: Putting it Together and Making it Work*. Lincolnwood, IL: NTC Business Books.

So basically, by thinking about the 'bigger picture' and looking at how we can put together all the individual pieces of a communications mix in the most effective way, hopefully our communications campaigns will be better received by our intended audience(s).

Case history

Orange brand integration

Since Orange's launch in April 1994, it has maintained its brand image in both advertising and below-the-line marketing and has positioned itself as the mobile phone brand that owns the 'future' of telecommunications. As Orange was the fourth company into the market, it had to carve out a niche for itself. At the time the market was cluttered with many different and confusing messages about mobile phones. To cut through the clutter, Orange's communication had to be consistent and motivating. While everyone else was talking about mobile phones, Orange talked about 'Wire-Free Communication', in other words a clean world that is optimistic and uncluttered. This clean optimism is consistent in everything Orange does.

Wolff Olins created and has continued to develop and supervise Orange's corporate identity. WCRS are responsible for all above-the-line advertising and help coordinate activity with other agencies as new campaigns are launched. Dutton Merrifield ensures that all copy and glossary of terms are consistent through-the-line and provide customer communication leaflets such as bill inserts. Option one provides Point-of-Sale and until recently WWAV was working on the Direct Marketing. All this is managed between the agencies and also through the Orange campaigns and design team.

Since launch, Orange has created a multi-media mix to ensure that synergy is felt across all sectors. Creative consistency and media phasing create a sense of ubiquity for the brand.

Source: Philip J. Kitchen, *Marketing Communications; Principles and Practice*, 1999, International Thomson Business Press.

Another fundamental aspect of Integrated Marketing Communications, or IMC, is the focus on the customer. IMC recognizes that for the most appropriate and effective combination of communication elements to be developed, an understanding of the customer is paramount. The whole IMC process therefore starts with the customer and then the appropriate forms and types of communication methods should be developed.

Previously, or at least traditionally, marketers have treated the elements of the communications mix individually, almost in isolation of each other. It has been said however, that: 'The marketer who succeeds in the new environment will be the one who coordinates the communications mix so tightly that you can look from (advertising) medium-to-medium, from programme-to-programme event, and instantly see that the brand is speaking with one voice.'

Quoting Spencer Plavoukas, chairman of Lintas (New York), and cited in Laurie Petersen, 'Pursuing Results in the Age of Accountability.' Adweek's *Marketing Week*, 19 November, 1990.

Colgate's Integrated Marketing Communications Programme for Fresher Mouths

Colgate-Palmolive recently provided an example of an effective advertising strategy, when a new brand of toothpaste was launched. The company used a two-tiered marketing strategy to launch its new Total brand. The first tier was a campaign aimed at end users. The second tier was a trade campaign focused on the retail channel and dentists. The goal was to capture a major share of the market.

Colgate's research identified its primary target market as 'orally aware' consumers with an above-average interest in oral health. These individuals are heavy users of toothpaste and other dental hygiene, and visit their dentists more often than average patients. For these consumers, Total has an ingredient called 'Triclosan' that aids in the prevention of cavities, combats gingivitis and fights plaque build-up. It also helps control tartar and bad breath. No other toothpaste can offer all of these benefits in a single product. Not surprisingly, Total has a higher price, but Colgate was convinced that the target group for this product would be willing to pay a premium price to obtain these benefits.

Colgate invested $100 million to launch the Total brand. The money was divided among network and cable television advertising, print advertising in general-interest magazines, multiple free standing inserts in newspapers, outdoor advertising on bus shelters, and postcards distributed in health clubs and coffee shops. Colgate's sales force worked diligently to cultivate the retail channel to get favourable store displays and in-store support. Colgate used 20 per cent of the $100 million for a massive sampling push to its secondary market, dentists, with the goal of encouraging them to introduce Total to their patients.

The results of Colgate's massive integrated marketing thrust were impressive. During the first six days of sales, a projected six-week supply of the product was sold. After just four months on store shelves, Total had captured 10.6 per cent of the toothpaste market. At that point, Colgate shifted its advertising thrust from creating brand awareness to encouraging repeat purchases. Colgate exceeded its market share goal by integrating the consumer and business thrust with advertising and other promotional tools. The results could not have been obtained neither by only developing an advertising campaign, nor by only using sales promotions. To succeed, the company effectively integrated advertising into a consumer marketing plan combined with business-to-business tactics.

Source: Clow and Baack, *Integrated Advertising, Promotion and Marketing Communications*, 2002.

Key Features of IMC

According to T. Shimp, *Advertising Promotions supplemented aspects of Integrated Marketing Communications*, 2000, Harcourt Inc, 'five key features underpin the philosophy and practice of integrated marketing communications.' These five features are:

1. *Affect behaviour* According to Shimp, the goal of IMC is to *affect the behaviour* of the communications audience. This means that marketing communications must do more than just influence brand awareness or enhance customer attitudes toward the brand. Instead, IMC's objective is to move people to action. For example, McDonald's would want their customers to be aware of any special promotion they had ongoing with their hamburgers, however, what they really want is the customer to go and *buy* the hamburger.

2. *Start with the customer or prospect* According to Shimp, the second key feature of IMC is that the process starts with the customer or prospect and then works back to the brand communicator in determining the most appropriate and effective methods through which persuasive communications should be developed.

3. *Use any and all forms of contact* According to Shimp, the key feature of this third element of IMC is that it reflects a willingness to use whatever communication outlets (contacts) are best for reaching the target audience rather than pre-committing to any single medium or subset of media. So, direct-mail advertising, promotions at sporting and entertainment events, advertisements on packages of other brands, slogans on T-shirts, in-store displays and Internet pages are all potentially important contact methods for reaching present and potential customers.

4. *Achieve synergy* According to Shimp, inherent in the definition of IMC is the need for *synergy*. All of the communication elements (advertising, point-of-purchase, sales promotions, events and so on) must speak with a *single voice*; coordination is absolutely critical to achieving a strong and unified brand image and moving customers to action.

5. *Build relationships* The fifth characteristic of IMC, according to Shimp, is the belief that successful marketing communications requires *building a relationship between the brand and the customer*. A relationship is an enduring link between a brand and its consumers; it entails repeat purchases and perhaps even loyalty.

Case history

Integration – Haagen-Dazs

Haagen-Dazs demonstrated the effective use of IMC when it entered the UK market. Ice-cream was traditionally a seasonal children's food and the market had experienced little growth or innovation. The business strategy adopted was to create a new market segment, one that has become referred to as the super-premium segment.

The positioning intention was to present Haagen-Dazs as a luxury, fashion-oriented food for adults. To achieve the business goals, the entire marketing mix was coordinated: the product reflected high quality, the high price induced perceived quality, and the distribution in the launch was through up-market restaurants in prestige locations and five-star hotels where Haagen-Dazs was the only branded ice-cream on the menu.

The promotional campaign used celebrities from many walks of life as opinion leaders to create a word-of-mouth ripple effect. The quality of the media used and messages themselves reflected the same quality theme. The brand has since become firmly established and, although the arrival of Ben & Jerry's and other up-market brands has increased competition and rivalry, the brand remains distinctive and continues to use an integrated approach to its communications.

Source: C. Fill, *Marketing Communications, Contexts, Strategies and Applications*, 3rd Edition, 2002, Pearson Education Ltd

Activity 4.1

Consider a brand or product that you buy regularly. Can you think of all the different forms of communication that are used to persuade or remind you to buy the brand?

Benefits of Integrated Marketing Communications

What's the use of an excellent advertising campaign, full of creativity, if it's backed up by a second-rate website? The answer is, there is no use. The same principle applies to all the elements of the communications mix.

The key to success is synergy via integration of the individual elements of the communication mix. According to Pickton and Broderick (*Integrated Marketing Communications*, p. 70, 2001, Pearson Education Ltd): 'Integration is not easy to achieve, but when it is achieved, the 4Es and 4Cs of Integrated Marketing Communications create the synergistic benefits of integration.'

The following are Pickton and Broderick's 4Es of integrated marketing communications:

- o *Economical* Least cost to the use of financial and other resources; not wasteful
- o *Efficient* Doing things right; competent, not wasteful
- o *Effective* Doing the right things, producing the outcome required, not wasteful
- o *Enhancing* Improve; augment; intensify.

The following are Pickton and Broderick's 4Cs of integrated marketing communications:

- o *Coherence* Logically connected; firmly stuck together
- o *Consistency* Not self-contradictory; in agreement, harmony, accord
- o *Continuity* Connected and consistent over time
- o *Complementary communications* Producing a balanced whole; supportive communications.

Case history

Charities and IMC – the National Society for Prevention of Cruelty to Children (NSPCC)

This campaign, which sought to stop cruelty to children, had a number of integrated communication characteristics. The ambitious targets, range of activities and the huge number of people involved needed an integrated marketing communications campaign to make it succeed.

To start with there was a range of stakeholders involved: police, parents, teachers, businesses, agencies, the media and, of course, children. All needed to be part of the communications.

The strategy was based around two main phases. The first was a strong pull campaign directed at the public and designed to raise awareness of child cruelty and the second step was action oriented. In parallel, there was a strategy designed to communicate with businesses in order to generate funds, goodwill and support.

The overall profile of the organization (NSPCC) was also to be raised and communications needed to ensure that the integrity of the organization and those associated with it was maintained. In addition, all communications had to be consistent. The promotional mix used to create a dialogue with the public included public relations, TV, posters, field marketing, direct marketing, direct mail, telemarketing and a website.

In the first phase, public relations were used at the initial stages of the campaign, to help create awareness. Public address systems at railway stations and airports were used as a reminder mechanism.

A national TV campaign, supported by posters, broke soon after the public relations in order to raise awareness and provoke within each individual the question, 'what can I do?' The message strategy was very emotional and used strong imagery to create shock and attention.

The heavy TV campaign looked to generate 600 TVRs, 8.5 per cent coverage at 7.1 OTSs. The supporting poster campaign used 48 sheets on 3500 sites designed to deliver 55 per cent coverage with 21 OTSs. Initial enquiries in response to this wave of communications were handled by an automated telemarketing bureau.

In the second phase, the aim was to provide the public with an answer to the question that the advertising had provoked, namely to sign the pledge and/or volunteer as a donor or fund-raiser. An envelope picked up on the TV creative treatment repeating as a subdued background motif the image of nursery wallpaper with a teddy bear covering its eyes with its paws: 'Don't close your eyes to cruelty to children.' This was to be delivered to 23 million postboxes, as a doordrop campaign.

It was thought that the doordrop letter addressed as 'Dear Householder' might offend established donors. To avoid this, 160,000 best donors were sent an early warning letter in advance of the campaign breaking in order to get their support. Another million received personal letters just ahead of the doordrop. It was expected that the bulk of enquiries would come from the doordrop action and these were to be handled through personal telemarketing resonses (inbound). The website was also adapted in order that it would be able to accept pledges.

In addition to this, the campaign utilized a call-to-action weekend with volunteers manning 2000 sites around the country, including most city centres, to remind and raise cash donations.

The promotional mix used to communicate with businesses involved sponsorship, the direct mail/ information pack and the Internet. Sponsorship deals were made available enabling businesses to align themselves more closely with the campaign. Microsoft has been closely involved with the NSPCC for a number of years and it acted as a prime mover, encouraging other businesses to pledge their support. The advertising for the campaign was sponsored by Microsoft. Other sponsorship and cause-related marketing packages were detailed in a toolkit distributed to other major organizations. Direct mail was also used to encourage businesses to make donations and electronic communications to promote pledges on-line.

At this stage, it appears that the coordinated promotional plan enabled a simple yet hard-hitting message to be conveyed to a substantial part of the nation. The publicity derived from the above-the-line work and the rigorous nature of the below-the-line activities suggest that many of the objectives have been achieved. However, results declared in December 2000 showed that in its first year, of the £75 million budget, less than half was spent on child-related services, suggesting to some that the Full Stop campaign was more about brand building.

Source: C. Fill, *Marketing Communications Contexts, Strategies and Applications*, 2002, Pearson Education Ltd, Adapted from K. Goften (1999) 'NSPCC aims to convert abuse anger into cash', *Marketing*, 25 March, pp. 37–8 and J. Day (2000) 'A time for gifts' *Marketing Week*, 14 December pp. 22–5.

Above-the-line promotional activity

'Above the line' is a slightly out-of-date expression that refers to advertising on which a commission fee is paid by the media to the agency that placed the advertising. As the rules and methods for booking advertising and the whole area of remuneration has changed, it has come to refer to the main advertising media of television, radio, cinema, outdoor and press.

Television advertising

This is the most visual medium, as most people spend at least some time watching television for entertainment. Because it can reach large numbers of people, the cost of one spot or commercial break can be very high. In order that the television commercial does not look out of place with all the other professionally filmed programmes that appear either side of the commercial, television advertising requires production specialists, which adds to the cost of production. The relatively short exposure time (most commercials last for no more than 30 seconds) means that television advertising has to be repeated many times and, as the cost of airtime is very expensive, this means that it tends only to feature in the marketing budgets of the mass-market fmcg (fast moving consumer goods) brands.

Television is a very creative medium that offers:

1. Sound, movement, interesting visual effects
2. Entertainment that famous people are happy to appear in
3. Impact – you can see it in action or being demonstrated
4. Credibility to the product or service.

Television is a very transient medium that can easily be missed. This is more so since people with video recorders can fast-forward past commercial breaks in programmes they have recorded (zipping) and people with a remote control can quickly change channels (zapping) to avoid television advertising. There is also no opportunity to sample or smell a product.

Take for example the UK television advertising situation, where it is possible to buy television advertising that appears only in one of the 13 ITV regions and so target a specific area of Britain. However, it is also possible to buy national advertising airtime covering all the television regions, which makes it ideal for mass-market products or services.

Until recently, it was a difficult tool to use for targeting specific groups, except in a fairly crude way. For example, media planners could make generalizations that mothers mostly watch daytime television, the evening news is watched by upmarket business people, and teenagers watch late-night television.

With the introduction of more channels via cable and satellite television, there are more opportunities for specialist programmes, for example, about specific sports. With this comes more opportunities to target specific audiences. For example, MUTV is a channel devoted to the interests of Manchester United fans. With greater audience fragmentation comes greater opportunities for niche advertising.

Unique or not so unique?

The term 'Unique Selling Point' (USP) was coined by an American, Rosser Reeves. He used the term to represent his view that advertising works best when a single, differentiating proposition is stated – rather than confusing the advertisement with lots of propositions or ideas – and better still if that proposition is something different (unique) from what everybody else is saying. He never intended the concept of USP to represent a truly unique product. Indeed, he recognized that one of the biggest problems he faced in designing advertisements was the fact that brands were so alike. What he believed, and is followed by many others, is that advertising works best if you can find something new to *say* about the product. The concept of the USP, then, does not rely on unique products, but rather is about a single, differentiating statement about a product. The USP concept is seen by some as being founded on advertising as a strong force. This need not be the case. To the extent that USPs help distinguish brands, they do not of themselves have to operate as strong forces, they can simply be used as reminders and reinforcers of customers' original decisions to buy.

When Bold washing powder was introduced into the market, television advertising featured the product being dissolved in water and a drop being placed into a bowl of water covered with a dark, oily film. The result was dramatic. Immediately, the dark film seemed to disappear. Bold was clearly and demonstrably very effective in removing oily stains. But was Bold actually any different from other washing powders in this regards? The answer is no. Any detergent or soap powder would have had the same effect under these conditions. It is a physical reaction. The advertisers, however, had managed to present what appeared to be a USP because this sort of dramatic demonstration had not been seen before. The majority of viewers presumed that the effect was 'unique' to Bold. In this way, the advertising distinguished Bold from its competitors – at least in the short term.

Source: Pickton and Broderick, *Integrated Marketing Communications*, 2001.

Radio advertising

Radio relies only on sound. It does not therefore have the same creative impact as television and cannot show products. However, it can tap into the listeners' imaginations with the use of evocative sound effects and voices (including famous voices) to make it a very effective advertising medium.

It can reach large audiences as in the UK there are several national commercial radio stations. These stations specialize in particular types of music (from jazz to classical). In addition, most regions have local radio geared to the needs of people in their catchment area. In this way radio advertising campaigns can be targeted geographically and according to lifestyle/tastes.

Cost varies with the size of audiences reached but production costs are not as high as television. However, advertisers usually have to buy a large number of airtime 'spots' because of the transient (and sometimes background listening) nature of the medium.

Radio can be successful

With radio, practitioners recommend building up pictures in the listener's mind with words. One example of this was an advert by Feed the Children, an international distress agency. It interviewed one of its senior directors who had been in Rwanda during the crisis in 1995, and used this to convey a strong 'in the front line' feel. A picture of what it was like at that time in Rwanda was quickly built up, and this was used in the 90-second radio advert.

More than £600,000 was raised, with costs being only a fraction of this figure.

The *Practitioner's Guide to Direct Marketing* (1992) reports on a radio commercial aimed at getting blood donors to respond. A test resulted in 1041 responses, compared to 79 in a control area without a radio.

Source: A. Tapp, *Principles of Direct and Database Markeing*, 2nd Edition, 2000.

Cinema advertising

Cinema advertising has the same creative characteristics as television and perhaps even more impact because there are fewer distractions and potential interruptions from zipping and zapping. In addition, media buyers can ensure that advertisements fit the audience profile that applies to particular films. In the UK, most cinema advertising is sold on a national basis through various cinema chains and two contractors. There is some opportunity for geographic segmentation, with a small proportion of advertising aimed at purely local audiences.

Magazine launch – Glamour

When *Glamour* was launched in 2001, the new publication from Conde Nast received huge marketing communication support. This included a £4.5 million campaign featuring television, print, outdoor and cinema. In addition, public relations generated a huge amount of publicity about the A5 'handbag-sized' format.

Part of the rationale for the radically different size was not only the success experienced in the USA and Italy where the format has been successful for over seven years, but also the trends towards miniaturization (Walkmans, mobile phones) and the fashion appeal that the smaller size might represent. In addition, however, is the high impact the smaller size has, in standing out on the shelves of newsagents, amongst the clutter of the established, larger heavyweight competitors.

Source: C. Fill, *Marketing Communications, Contexts, Strategies and Applications*, 3rd Edition, 2002.

Outdoor advertising

This type of advertising covers a whole range of different types of media that can be found outdoors and indoors. It includes large roadside billboard hoardings, small poster sites on bus shelters and bus stations, underground and ground level train stations, the inside and outside of various types of transport, such as buses, trains, tubes and taxis, and even peripheral sites, such as parking meters and street furniture.

Although a poster site can have plenty of impact, it is limited to short messages with bold images. Usually there is a very short exposure time as people are moving past the advertising. (Exceptions here are people waiting at tube or rail stations.) Most outdoor advertising does not incorporate sound or movement in the message. However, there are some moving poster sites where the image changes every few minutes. There are also some well-known three-dimensional sites. For example, an airline has one in the form of an aeroplane at Heathrow and there was a famous one designed to look like a pub that sold Guinness.

Press advertising

Press advertising comprises all printed media. In the UK this covers national newspapers, local newspapers, specialist trade and technical magazines (one for almost every industry sector and job), general-interest magazines (the most popular of which are female interest magazines aimed at different age groups) and specialist magazines that cover almost every hobby and interest area, from fishing to stamp collecting.

Therefore advertising in print media can be carefully targeted at demographic and geographic segments. Quite complex messages can be conveyed because print media can be retained and seen more than once. Advertisements can also benefit from the credibility of the newspaper or magazine.

However, advertising in the print media has limited impact and there is little flexibility for creative messages compared with television advertising. Although magazines can be in full colour and quite glossy, newspapers tend to be in black and white with only spot colour.

Finding the balance – the Vegetation Society

A recent example of shocking images illustrates the tension between the desire to make a point powerfully and the need to avoid undue offence. The UK-based Vegetarian Society ran a brief press advertising campaign in 1997 which drew attention to recently published research findings of possible links between diets that are high in red meat and an increased risk of some types of cancer. Readers were recommended to reduce or eliminate meat consumption, and to eat more vegetables and fruits.

Expressed in this way, the proposition seems to be a reasonable and unsurprising communication from an organization with the aims of the Vegetarian Society. The campaign, however, attracted an adverse adjudication from the Advertising Standards Authority in December 1997, for reasons which were mainly to do with *how* the point was made, rather than the underlying proposition. The advertisements were deliberately hard-hitting in style, showing photographs of cancer operation scars and including headlines such as 'It's much easier to cut out meat'. Objectors – who included bodies such as the Meat and Livestock Commission and the National Farmers Union – claimed that the advertisements had in a number of ways exaggerated the research findings and the government recommendations alluded to in the text, and that the advertisements were shocking to those directly or indirectly affected by cancer and unduly distressing.

Most of these complaints – including that of undue distress – were upheld by the ASA. The adjudication was followed by a defiant response from the Vegetarian Society, maintaining that the evidence upon which the advertisements was based was robust and pointing out that the Society had received around 2500 telephone calls responding positively to the advertisement. Two years later, Barnardos, the children's charity, ran a press advertisement featuring a baby sitting alone in a filthy flat and holding a syringe. The advert was headed 'John Donaldson, Age 23' and the copy explained how the work of the charity sought to prevent child abuse victims from the bleak future that could await them. Protestors objected that the advertisement was shocking and offensive, but the ASA did not uphold the complaints, noting that the advertiser had behaved responsibly in researching the advert among its target audience in order to ensure that the message was understood and was unlikely to cause offence.

The purpose of these examples is not to comment on the decisions made, but rather to illustrate the complex issues that have to be weighed in these situations in marketing communications. The Vegetarian Society, Barnardos and other cause-promoting organizations are not businesses in the normal sense, but they do need to make similar broad and balanced judgements in deciding how to communicate their ideas.

Source: C. Fill, *Marketing Communications, Contexts, Strategies and Applications*, 3rd Edition, 2002.

Internet advertising

According to Kohl (*Getting attention – Leading Edge Lessons for Publicity and Marketing*, Butterworth-Heinemann, 2000) spending on Internet advertising will continue to grow despite that fact that some people consider that online advertisements do not work. Kohl cites the Forrester Research estimates that global spending for online advertising will reach $33 billion by 2004.

The Internet is a global advertising medium which uses websites, banner advertisements and streaming media as ways to target web users with information about products and services. Although it is a developing industry which is difficult to evaluate in terms of advertising effectiveness, it is still possible to compare the number of click throughs on a website after a banner advertising campaign has run. Alternatively, if a website can be used for transactions then the amount of business conducted can be measured, say after an e-mail marketing campaign.

Mixing in Internet advertising

One of the biggest challenges marketing account executives face is integrating and mixing Internet advertising into more traditional advertising programmes. Many Internet companies use television spots, designing fast-paced, high-tech, intriguing ads to market their websites.

Another potential area for Internet firms is radio advertising, which is less expensive than television. Many Internet companies have small budgets. Therefore radio is an ideal medium. Radio spots can be produced cheaply and quickly. Radio lends itself very well to the branding messages of Internet companies. Radio spots reach potential customers on their way to and from work, at work, and when they are at home on the computer. This makes radio ads ideal for both consumer and business-to-business Internet marketing spots.

As with radio, outdoor advertising is becoming a popular avenue for web companies. Amazon.com, Excite and Mothernature.com are three major users of outdoor advertising among the Internet companies. Outdoor advertising requires companies to keep messages short; therefore, many simply promote the Internet address. For instance, Playboy Enterprises has a dot.com website. The company invested $10 million in outdoor advertising aimed at younger, more Internet-savvy readers in New York, Los Angeles and Chicago. The objective was not promotion of the magazine, but rather the website address.

One growth area in magazine advertising are the many dot.com advertisements. Similar to radio, Internet companies find that magazines are an excellent medium for advertising. Businesses also see magazines as an appealing medium for establishing their web addresses. Computer manufacturing companies such as Dell and Gateway invest heavily in magazine advertisements.

Newspapers are also inviting places for Internet companies, because ads can be positioned close to the type of news provided. Thus, e-trade companies can advertise near stock market prices, sports sites can be positioned near the sports page and so forth. In addition, local companies can advertise their addresses in smaller newspapers.

The least likely outlet for Internet advertising is direct mail. 'Snail mail' stands in direct contrast to more high-tech websites. Thus, it is less logical to advertise in that way.

Internet advertising has already made a significant impact in the business-to-business sector. It now ranks sixth among the business-to-business marketing media, just behind direct marketing. Annual expenditures are almost $4 billion. The Internet is rapidly becoming the medium of choice for communications with customers and for e-commerce. All estimates are that the business-to-business marketing will continue to increase at a very rapid pace.

One question remains as to how individuals and businesses use the Internet. If individuals use it to gather information during the information search stage of the decision purchase process, then it may be difficult to measure the impact of Internet advertising. Through Internet advertising, brand awareness can be increased and so, when the time comes for a product purchase, the brand is considered in the person's evoked set. The individual or business may not have considered the brand if it were not for the Internet banner viewed. Tracing the movement of a brand from unawareness to becoming part of a consumer's evoked set is difficult. This is especially true when an advertiser used the Internet, billboards, or any other medium. It becomes unclear which ad caused the product to move to the consumer's evoked set.

In any case, it is certain that many businesses will continue to advertise on the Internet and Internet companies will continue to promote their sites in other media. Media buyers must consider this interlinkage as advertising campaigns are designed and implemented.

Source: Clow and Baack, *Integrated Advertising, Promotion & Marketing Communications*, 2001.

Activity 4.2

Look at the following scenarios and evaluate the proposed advertising media decisions.

1. Calvin Klein are considering using local newspapers to promote their expensive new fragrance 'y', which is aimed at fashionable young men and women.
2. The manager of a small hotel in Wales would like to use television advertising to attract tourists.
3. Harvey Goldsmith Entertainments sell concert tickets in the UK. They are considering using radio to advertise a number of outdoor summer concerts featuring the famous Three Tenors.
4. ASH (the anti-smoking lobby group) has identified that there is a massive growth in the number of young female smokers and is considering using cinema and teenage girl magazines like Jackie and 19 to target them in a hard-hitting anti-smoking campaign.

Below-the-line promotion

Basically, any promotional activity that does not come under the five main media mentioned above comes under the category of below-the-line promotion.

Corporate literature

Corporate literature, such as stationery, brochures, leaflets and annual reports, is a visual record of an organization's corporate identity in which branding and logos are often featured extensively. An organization's corporate literature has a vital role to play in communicating information about a company, its products/services and its annual performance to its stakeholders.

Production of literature

Unless it is specific to your job role, it is unlikely that you will need to have extensive knowledge of graphic design and print production techniques. However, you should be able to critically evaluate rough drafts that designers supply to you for corporate literature and provide layout information for items to be published in-house and by printers.

Here are some points you should look for:

Consistency
Overall, there should be some consistency in headings, margins, spacing of paragraphs, white space, text justified or ranged left/right, typefaces and typesizes. It is better that a page has unity, which can be created by a dominant headline or illustration or a combination of both, so that the reader is focused and is not confused by too many visual 'tricks' or devices. However, there is often justification for text and images to be arranged in an interesting way to encourage the reader to follow through the text.

Colour
Colour can be used to provide variety, impact, interest and even to communicate a mood. However, too many colours can bombard the reader and convey a cheap and 'tacky' feeling.

Typefaces

Typestyles are a whole area of study on their own. If you look at the various typestyles or typefaces (also known as fonts) on your computer, you will have an idea of the choice and variety available. Different typefaces convey different visual images. Some have an old-fashioned/traditional feel, others appear modern, some give an impression of formality and others appear light-hearted and would be appropriate for a party invitation.

Some typefaces are easier to read than others; others provide more emphasis for headings and sub-headings. You should ensure that there is consistency in the typefaces used in your organization's corporate literature.

Typesize is also an important consideration and you should ensure that all printed material is legible.

Activity 4.3

You work in the Marketing Department of the local chamber of commerce. An international conference is planned on e-commerce (business on the Internet). A gala dinner will launch the event. An expert speaker will make a keynote speech on the topic, and dignitaries and interested parties will be invited to attend.

Draft an invitation to the gala dinner to be printed on A5-size card. Include layout instructions for the printer.

Corporate image

An organization's image and that of its products/services are a vital way to communicate with target markets.

A corporate identity or image can be communicated by the following:

o An organization's logo
o The typeface on an organization's letterhead
o The materials it uses for correspondence (stationery, business cards)
o Corporate literature (brochures, annual reports, internal training material, application forms, internal newsletters, exhibition stand material)
o Its headquarters and offices (including signs inside and outside the building, its reception area)
o The signs on its vehicles
o The appearance of personnel (uniforms, badges) and the way they deal with people (they are ambassadors for the organization)
o Its public relations image (the way it is reported in the media and public perception in general).

However, Dolphin (2000) says that corporate image is often used as a synonym for reputation, which can be the single most significant point of differentiation between competing companies. However, he states that organizations cannot always control their image. He cites Albert and Whettan (1985) to differentiate between image and identity. If identity answers the question 'who/what do we believe we are?' then image answers the question 'who/what do we want others to think we are?'

Dolphin makes the distinction between product and corporate advertising in a reference to the Chrysler Corporation when it announced its 'first corporate advertising campaign in years'. The campaign was to concentrate on changing the company's image as a whole – rather than just selling a single car or truck brand. Post-campaign research showed that few consumers associated some of Chrysler's most successful brands with the parent company and that most people thought that JEEP was a company.

Dolphin also makes the point that corporate image is concerned with a mental impression. If a public thinks well of an organization it is more likely to wish to do business with it; and it is more likely to encourage others to do the same. A favourable image is more likely to encourage would-be investors – who are often the lifeblood of an organization.

He adds that an organization that is well regarded by its audiences is likely to do well. It is more likely to have a good foundation on which strategic success can be built and will probably to be one step ahead of the competition – its image being an added value factor.

Case history

British Airways

When British Airways decided to change its corporate image to give itself a more international feel so that it could compete more effectively in a global market, it had difficulties in persuading some parts of the British media and the British public why it needed an image change, particularly one that cost so much. By replacing the Union Flag with bold 'images of the world' on its aeroplanes, it had angered some of its domestic market but the new corporate image was in keeping with its advertising strapline 'the world is closer than you think'.

Brand image

Whereas a corporate image refers to the organization as a whole, the organization may be the umbrella for a number of different brands. For example, Virgin is an organization with a corporate image and there are a number of Virgin brands, such as Virgin Vodka, Virgin One (financial services) and Virgin Trains, each with their own brand image.

A brand can be communicated by any of the following:

o   A name
o   A term
o   A design
o   A trademark
o   A symbol
o   A logo.

With brands, consumers can be encouraged to associate certain attributes with a product. These attributes can be used to personify the brand and add value to a commodity. For example, it is much easier to promote Andrex toilet paper using the Andrex puppies than if the manufacturers could only talk about the product and show images of toilet rolls. It allows Andrex to distinguish the product from its competitors and allows the manufacturer to charge a premium price.

Corporate identity – on-line banking

Many financial services organizations have begun to offer online banking. The chance to reduce costs and reach new customer groups has been a major force behind this development. What is interesting, however, is that many have chosen to rebrand their online offering and create a separate identity.

The Halifax uses 'If', the Cooperative Bank 'Smile' and Prudential 'Egg'. Abbey National chose to use the name 'Cahoot' in order to reach a more affluent customer, one who, research shows, would not normally bank with Abbey National. The disguise of the online brand identity therefore enables organizations to use communications to be directed to particular customer segments without having to overcome the negative values associated with the parent brand.

Source: C. Fill, *Marketing Communications, Contexts, Strategies and Applications*, 3rd Edition, 2002.

Logos

Logos can be just as important as a brand name or brand image in that they can:

- Attract attention
- Create an impression
- Create recognition
- Convey information about a product or organization
- Provide consistent imagery
- Differentiate the product/organization from its competitors.

Logos can be applied to a range of products or used in a variety of situations. By using a brand in this way the credibility of the original brand can be transferred. (See Figure 4.2 where CIM's logo can be used by 'accredited colleges' and this enhances a college's credibility in the minds of potential and existing marketing students.)

Figure 4.1 The CIM logo

Figure 4.2 Adapting a logo for different purposes

Activity 4.4

Read the following extract from 'The Power of Brands: How to enhance your brand in Asia' by Paul Temporal. It has been adapted and is used courtesy of Lexis-Nexis.

The first thing to recognize when we talk about brands is that they are not just names, terms, symbols, designs or combinations of these, although it is true to say that such things can and do differentiate certain products and companies from others.

The additional ingredient that makes a successful brand is personality.

In Asia, Coca-Cola, Sean Connery, Nestlé, Sony, Batman, Mercedes and Michael Jackson are equally well known. People tend to relate to brand personalities in the same way as they do to human personalities.

Some brands appeal to the rational part of a person, to the elements of logic and good sense such as toothpaste which prevents decay, and cholesterol-free foods.

Some brands attract the emotional part of people, appealing to their feelings such as warmth, affection and belonging. Products such as Harley Davidson motorcycles and companies like Benetton with its global village branding exemplify these.

Then there is the strange phenomenon of intuition. Some companies and products are attractive to people who intuitively feel comfortable with them, because they see these brands as an extension of themselves, a good fit to their personality, lifestyle, aspirations and behaviour – companies like The Body Shop, with its environmental approach.

Brands influence consumer decisions to buy in any of the above ways or through combinations of them.

The Marlboro brand personality is a good example of how a company understands and combines the physical and emotional elements that appeal to certain customers who live or would love to live a certain lifestyle. Products such as gold credit cards, watches or prestige items help people to express themselves to others by demonstrating that they are different and have achieved something. They act as extensions of the personality, so it really is 'all in the mind' and the key to brand management and its development is a clear understanding of what benefits the customer is looking for.

Ask consumers what comes to mind when they hear the name of a big brand such as BMW or Gucci and they will reply with a list of attributes which go far beyond the physical, tangible aspects of product and delivery, but if there is one word which brings all these together in people's minds, it is value.

Brands reduce the perceived risk of purchase and consumers rely on chosen brands to guarantee standards of quality and service.

With product branding, the company gives each product a brand name and there is little or no attachment of the company relationship. Each brand has to compete on its own merit, such as Pizza Hut which normally operates without any endorsement from parent company Pepsico.

With corporate branding the company uses one brand – usually the company name – for all its products and services, as in the case of IBM. If the company uses what is often referred to as house branding, the individual products are separate identifiable brands but the overall company brand is used as an endorsement of origin and quality. This approach is often used by car manufacturers, the hospitality sector and by financial institutions.

Some brands established in the 1930s are still the top brands now. From Coca-Cola to Colgate, Kelloggs to Kodak, many big brands have defended their position in the market and they, along with other famous names, have become synonymous with their industries.

Brands can also assist moves across industries to penetrate new markets. Dunhill is an excellent example of this. Formerly based in the declining-image industry of tobacco, Dunhill is now firmly established internationally in upmarket clothing, toiletries and fashion accessories.

Pick out two brands mentioned in the article and explain what feelings they evoke in the minds of consumers.

Packaging

Aside from the functional role of packaging, which is to actually provide a container for products, packaging has a role to play in communicating with customers. It communicates the product name and the brand image. Following on from advertising and other promotional activity, this can act as a reminder to consumers at the point of sale to purchase the product in favour of a competing product.

Colour coding – Boots

Boots the Chemist uses colour to visually direct and help its customers. Its baby toiletries, for which it has 70 per cent market share, are coded such that shampoo products are yellow, bath products green and lotions pink. When the scheme was introduced it was only the caps that were coloured; now the entire plastic bottle is coloured.

Source: C. Fill, *Marketing Communications, contexts, strategies and Applications*, 3rd Edition, 2002.

Point of sale display and merchandising

Point of sale display and merchandising refers to the in-store display that can influence consumers to purchase products in shops. It involves the layout and design of the shop and the way the goods or merchandise are presented. Manufacturers can have in-store display material produced to remind customers of their products at the point of purchase. For example, manufacturers of chocolates and confectionery might arrange with shops to display special branded stands, mobiles or life-size cardboard cut-outs of characters used to advertise the chocolate brand. Similarly, cosmetics manufacturers might supply shops with hanging signs or revolving display stands. This is another tool for marketers to communicate brand imagery and act as a reminder at the point of purchase.

Powerful manufacturers that spend vast amounts on advertising tend to have more influence on retailers in terms of where their products are displayed. The most effective display areas are at 'eye level', where products are easy to see and reach for.

POP displays and beauty products

A point-of-purchase display is the final chance for a cosmetics company to convince the consumer to choose its brand over the competitors'. Almost one-third of sales of cosmetics can be linked to noticing and being attracted to a display. Many cosmetics are also, in part, impulse buys. Consequently, the design and placement of POP displays represents a key element of the promotional efforts of cosmetics and manufacturers.

Colours are one key ingredient. Colours can create sophistication, fun and various emotions. Colours are often linked with individual companies. The colours of the display should match the packaging of the product and the Integrated Marketing Communications theme the cosmetics firm presents in other places.

POP displays should lead the consumer to touch or pick up the product. Once a consumer has touched a product, a purchase almost always follows. Teenagers are more likely to pick up items with bold and bright colours and designs. Global Beauty Concepts targets 12–15 year old girls with its brightly designed Petunia range of cosmetics. On the other hand, Fine Fragrances uses simple lines and colours in the attempt to reach key 'high street' retailers and their customers.

Males prefer more neutral colours than females. Products such as razors and colognes are more likely to sell with more minimalistic POPs. Unisex products also sell better with a more subdued approach. Calvin Klein cosmetics has led the way in promoting unisex products in its displays for CK fragrances.

A more recent trend in POP displays is to make them interactive. Clairol Cosmetics pioneered the use of interactive displays. Customers use a keypad or touch screen to select more information about the company's products.

Beyond a sturdy display rank, many factors go into the design of an effective cosmetics POP display. Colour, shape, size, positioning of 'testers' and other elements of design are key ingredients in the sale of these highly profitable items.

Source: Clow and Baack, *Integrated Advertising, Promotion and Marketing Communications*, 2001.

Sales promotion

Sales promotion is another communication tool that marketers use. It is often described as 'A short-term tactical marketing tool that gives customers additional reasons or incentives to purchase.'

Sales promotions can offer temporary added value to the customer at the point of purchase (often referred to as a sales pull strategy). Manufacturers can also direct promotions to the trade (often referred to as a sales push strategy).

There are many different versions of sales promotions that are directed at consumers:

- Price reductions
- Coupons/money-off vouchers
- Entry to competitions/free prize draws
- Free goods
- *x* per cent free
- 3 for the price of 2
- Free samples
- Free gifts
- Guarantees
- £*x* goes to *y* charity if you purchase
- Reward points/tokens against a free gift (for example, Air Miles)
- Refunds or free gifts on a mail-in basis.

Sales promotions aimed at the trade include:

- Discount on bulk orders
- Free supplies
- Incentives (for example, shopping vouchers for Marks & Spencer or a free alarm clock)
- Free prize draw competitions
- Deferred invoicing
- Merchandising and display material.

The objectives of a promotion could be to:

- Encourage trial of product
- Extend existing customer base
- Prompt customers to change brand
- Generate bulk buying
- Overcome seasonal dips in sales
- Encourage trade to stock product.

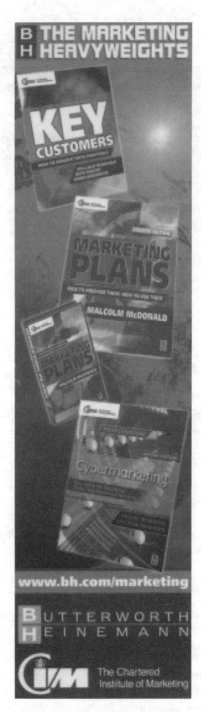

Figure 4.3 A bookmark used as a sales promotion item

Coupons and condoms

Condom use is one of the best methods for slowing the growth of sexually transmitted diseases and for reducing unwanted pregnancies. Unfortunately, far too many young people use them inconsistently (not every time) because of the embarrassment of making the actual purchase combined with the cost of the condom itself.

One recent research effort indicates that traditional condom sales promotions are not as successful as they could be. The traditional approach is a free condom giveaway in conjunction with an event, or at a booth set up by a family planning or disease prevention agency. Unfortunately, one free use does not lead to a consistent buying pattern.

To entice buyers to consider condom purchases in drugstores and other locations, they must first see the coupon and then be inspired to make the purchase. Coupons for condoms located at the purchase site (the display) are more readily noticed. The higher the value of the coupon, the more likely the coupon will be redeemed. Males are more likely to take the time to examine the coupons at purchase sites and make the purchase.

Thus, the most logical use of sales promotions, rather than giveaways or premiums, may be simply to place the coupon at the site where a person can examine it without further embarrassment. Then, by making the price less prohibitive by offering a coupon-based discount, a greater number of items may be purchased at one time, or at least the customer will return to make another purchase when needed. Such an approach may be more of a win-win solution to generating sales and at the same time preventing unwanted pregnancy and disease.

Source: Clow and Baack, *Integrated Advertising, Promotion and Marketing Communications*, 2001.

Exhibitions

In many business-to-business marketing situations, organizations have a sales force that visits the customer. With exhibitions, road shows, seminars and conferences, customers come to see the supplier. This provides organizations with a valuable opportunity to communicate with their customers and potential customers in a face-to-face situation.

These occasions take many forms.

Expo Inter

Each year around August, the Brazilian city of Porto Alegre hosts the biggest agricultural show in South America. Ranchers and breeders from Brazil, Argentina, Chile, Uruguay and Paraguay come to show their prize animals and see the latest offerings from equipment manufacturers.

The world's manufacturers of tractors and machinery are there: John Deere, Massey-Ferguson, David Brown, Caterpillar. The world's leading producers of fertilisers and pesticides are there, too: ICI, Belgo-Mineira, DuPont. For the manufacturers, it is an opportunity to show their products to potential customers from a wide range of countries who are all in one place for this one occasion. It reduces travelling time for salespeople in a part of the world where roads are not always good and where distances are vast.

For the ranchers, the show offers a chance to meet the manufacturers, to discuss the merits of the latest equipment and chemical products, and to meet other ranchers from other countries and exchange ideas and techniques. Above all, the show enables people who otherwise rarely see each other to interact and refresh their thinking about agricultural issues.

All those who attend Expo Inter agree that it is irreplaceable; in no other way could all their objectives be met, given the distances involved and the infrastructure problems in South America.

Source: Pickton and Broderick, *Integrated Marketing Communications*, 2001.

Conferences

A conference may feature speakers from a number of different organizations who are experts in various fields, and attendees pay for the privilege of attending the conference. For example, a recent conference aimed at top decision makers in NHS Trusts provided attendees with advise about taking advantage of a government scheme to allow Trusts to extend or improve their buildings. The speakers came from a variety of law firms, construction companies and architects. The conference also provided the speakers with an opportunity to promote their organization's expertise and to network with potential customers from the Trusts as well.

Seminars

Seminars are held by companies to provide customers with advice on developments in their market. At the same time, companies have the opportunity to extend their business relationship with attendees. For example, many of the larger accountancy firms provide breakfast budget briefings to discuss the implications of a new budget or taxation laws. Similarly, pharmaceutical firms arrange seminars for doctors to discuss new drugs that are available on the market.

Mobile road shows

These can be in the form of a mobile unit that goes around the country to promote goods/services. For example, the National Blood Transfusion Service attracts donors when its mobile units are placed at shopping centres or university buildings.

Trade fairs

Although there are some exhibitions that are aimed at the general public, such as The National Homes Exhibition, most exhibitions are directed at business-to-business activity.

Trade fairs are generally held in large exhibition halls where firms book a stand area and either hire a stand or pay for one to be designed. The stand and the corporate literature have to be presented in an eye-catching way to attract visitors to the stand.

Companies also have to cover the cost of staffing stands, pay for staff travel and accommodation costs and hospitality costs incurred when sales staff network with prospects and customers.

Exhibitions combine personal selling with non-personal communication activities and bring potential customers, at their expense, to a location that suits you. Nevertheless, many companies find that they usually need to undertake some pre-exhibition publicity to attract people to their stand.

Staff can make sales at exhibitions but they are usually used to generate leads that have to be followed up once the exhibition has finished.

Sponsorship

Sponsorship is another communications tool that can be used to put an organization's name across to a variety of publics and promote an image. Organizations can sponsor the arts, sporting events, individual sportsmen and women or even television programmes.

Organizations are usually interested in the type of sponsorship that either attracts publicity and media coverage or puts their name in front of their target audience in an interesting, and maybe, novel way. For sponsorship to work, it should be in keeping with the organization or its brand's image.

Sponsorship can be in the form of goods, for example, free football boots or financial reward to the sport or the individual. It could even be some kind of loss guarantee of the kind that occurs with some tennis events if they are rained off.

Sponsoring individuals can be risky if they attract bad publicity and are involved in some form of scandal. This could result in the organization's name being tainted by association. However, most organizations would withdraw sponsorship in the case of a scandal.

A good illustration of a well-integrated programme of Arts sponsorship is provided by Amex Canada, who in April–May 2000 sponsored the 'Monet at Giverny' exhibition at the Museum of Fine Arts. The integrated programme included travel savings (by Air Canad and Via Rail), and entertainment and accommodation discount tie-ins, while privileged rates at Montreal restaurants were available throughout an 'American Express Monet International Card'.

Source: Adcock et al., *Marketing Principles and Practice*, 4th Edition, 2001.

Public relations

The Institute of Public Relations has defined public relations as 'the planned and sustained effort to establish and maintain goodwill and mutual understanding between an organization and its publics'.

The above definition is a very broad one. It comprises a number of general activities, some of which you have already examined in previous units, and a number of specific activities that are devised to raise the profile of an organization or even a person representing an organization.

General PR activities generally relate to communicating with a variety of stakeholders and comprise corporate communications, community relations and customer care activities. In addition, there are a number of specific PR activities that relate to communicating with the media.

Corporate communications

Corporate communications can be defined as communications between an organization and its internal and external audiences, the purpose of which is to create greater understanding for, and perception of, the ideals and purposes of the organization. The following activities are methods used to convey corporate messages.

- In house journals/newsletters
- Annual reports
- Gifts/incentives, e.g. calendars, key fobs, desk items, etc.
- Christmas cards
- Business dinners/receptions
- Corporate entertaining, e.g. golf tournaments.

Community relations

- Scholarships or bursaries
- Charity support
- Open days for the public – for example, the fire service often has open days.

Customer care

- Customer service departments
- Complaints management
- Customer advice and help lines
- Ethical and environmental policies.

Specific PR activities

These are activities generally related to communicating with the media.

- Press conferences
- Photo calls
- Publicity stunts
- Supplying feature articles
- Open days/previews for the press – for example, some theatres have press nights
- Product launch events
- Advertorials/advertisement features (articles are written for the press but the space is paid for in the same way that an advertisement is paid for)
- Sending press releases.

PR launches a new career

The work of international publicists has rocketed Charlotte Church to stardom. In the space of less than a year, this British schoolgirl became an international singing celebrity. Her rapid rise to fame and fortune has been accelerated by the media exposure, coverage and endorsement achieved by the efforts of the numerous publicists working on her, and her record company's.

Source: Pickton and Broderick, *Integrated Marketing Communications*, 2001.

Case history

An airline company's corporate communications

Dolphin in his book *The Fundamentals of Corporate Communications* (2000) refers to the philosophy of American Airlines of working with the news media rather than against them. The company goes out of its way to make its officials available to the press, both on a formal and informal basis; and each year the communication department organizes a visit to a city served by the airline so that key executives can meet the local media.

The company puts effort into helping journalists understand the dynamics of the airline industry. It hosts an annual media day consisting of seminars and discussions on the workings of the airline and the industry as a whole.

The communication department peppers the press with position papers, consultants' reports, newspaper articles and speeches by senior airline executives, all of which reflect the company's thoughts on issues that are important in the industry.

The firm also publishes a quarterly corporate fact book that provides a wealth of statistical and analytical information about the airline's operations. The book also provides guidance to managers allowing them to talk directly with reporters in the event of an emergency.

 ## Activity 4.5

Before you start reading the section on how to prepare a press release, read the following abstract taken from a press release that was sent to a local newspaper in a farming region in England. Ignore the format but explain why the content is not suitable and suggest how it could be improved.

PRESS RELEASE FROM XYZ FARMING LTD

Dear Editor,

We believe that we can offer your readers an interesting news story and will be happy to provide fuller details if required. A new concept in dairy cow feeding has been pioneered by XYZ Farming Ltd, which is specifically designed to meet the demand of consumers for milk of higher protein content and reduced fat levels. These requirements are reflected in differential prices paid by most dairies to farmers with greater emphasis on protein content rather than butterfat: high butterfats also act as an effective constraint to the full use by the farmer of his quota allocation. In the new Granary range of compound feeds the high levels of rumen bypass starch derived from rolled wheat, is pelleted in combination with high vegetable proteins.

Press releases

Most organizations have a PR policy, which means that press releases go through a rigorous checking and signing-off procedure whether they are produced in-house or by an agency. It is a specialized job, and one that you will not be involved with unless it is specified as part of your job role.

Nevertheless you should be able to produce a draft release to show that you understand how they should be written and presented, as it could become a task that is part of your job.

You should be aware that while organizations can pay to obtain advertising space, obtaining editorial space through press releases is subject to the editorial team finding the press release interesting and usable. Even if this is the case, the space that can be given to your press release will probably be limited and they will usually change it so that the angle suits their news purposes.

It is wrong to consider that press releases are 'free' advertising, as the time and effort put into writing a good press release has a cost associated with it.

The format of a press release

A press release format should:

- o Feature your organization's logo at the top
- o Be entitled 'Press release'
- o Show the date the release was prepared or indicate when the news can be released (an embargo)
- o Have a headline that sums up the story
- o Be typed with double spacing and have wide margins
- o Only use one side of the paper
- o Indicate that more 'copy' or text follows by using the abbreviation m/f at the end of each page
- o Clearly mark the end of the release with the word 'end'
- o Contain contact details for the media to make further enquiries
- o Contain additional notes in the form of 'background notes for the editor'.

The press release content should:

- o Answer the questions who, what, when, where and how
- o Encapsulate the nub of the story in the first paragraph
- o Start with the key point at the top and add the 'bones' of the story in each succeeding paragraph
- o Contain interesting quotes that are attributed to a person relevant to the story. Be geared to the media, so you may have one version for the trade press and another for the local press
- o Use factual, not flowery, language
- o Be clear and concise
- o Relate to any accompanying photographs
- o Have a 'pic caption', i.e. a few sentences that explain the contents or name the people in a photograph
- o Usually be written as if the event has just happened (even if the presentation or the contract was won a few days ago), although some press releases inform of what will happen in the future.

Activity 4.6

See the question scenario in Activity 4.3.

   a. Assuming the event has taken place, prepare a press release for distribution to the relevant media (12 marks possible for this part of the question).
   b. State your objectives in preparing the release.
   c. Suggest which type of media you would send the release to.

Direct marketing

Types of direct marketing activity

- Direct mail (mailshots)
- Door drops (leaflets/coupons/vouchers posted through the door)
- Selling via catalogues/brochures (mail order selling)
- Direct response advertising in the press (off the page selling)
- Direct response advertising on the television (DRTV)
- Telemarketing (using the telephone to contact people to sell direct to them).

The most popular form of direct marketing in the UK for both consumer and business-to-business marketing is direct mail. Direct mail usually comprises a sales letter outlining the offer, a response mechanism and sometimes there is a separate piece which gives details of an incentive offer if you respond by a certain date.

How direct mail can be used

The principle is that organizations build a database of current customers' address details and their previous purchase history. By using this information the organization can target products/services that are tailored to suit the recipient's profile. For example, a bank will have all your financial details and could send you a mailshot promoting a gold status credit card if you fitted the income bracket and financial history for that product.

The same bank could rent a list of people with a gold card customer profile, from another organization, to send them a mailshot in the hope of recruiting additional gold card customers.

Figure 4.4 An example of direct marketing material

Figure 4.5 An example of a response mechanism

Direct marketing objectives

Direct marketing campaign objectives could be to:

- Generate sales
- Build up sales leads
- Invite recipients to visit a store
- Build the company database
- Remind people that an offer closes by a certain date.

Dear Mrs Wood,

Wouldn't it be nice if someone else paid for the fun things in life? Air Miles do just that.

Take a look at your 'Spring 2001 offers' booklet and you'll find out how. There are 2 great **NEW OFFERS**: earn mile shopping online with Yahoo1 UK & Ireland; and earn 100s of miles when you switch to gas and electricity with Scottish Hydro-Electric or Southern Electric. You could also win 10,000 miles at Sainsbury's.

But what are you going to do with all those miles? Well, for only 80 miles you'll get a cheaper holiday than you can find on the high street with 20 leading companies, or a FREE day out; and there are flights worldwide, with three ways to pay.

And remember, the more miles you collect, the more fun you could be having. So take a look at your statement and 'spring 2001 offers' booklet NOW!

Best wishes

Mary Thomas

Marketing Director

Figure 4.6 An example of a direct marketing letter from Air Miles

Writing direct mail letters

Direct mail can be a powerful communication tool but where it is sent indiscriminately it can irritate people and be judged as 'junk mail'. Wastage can be reduced if the mailshots are targeted at the right people. For example, it is very annoying for existing customers to be sent details of a new 'introductory' offer that they cannot take up because they are not a new customer.

If you want customers to respond, you can make it easier for recipients to respond by using a response mechanism (see Figure 4.5).

Although the syle of a letter is personal there are some techniques that you can use when writing direct mail letters:

- Say what you mean clearly – be clear what your key message is
- Sound enthusiastic – if you are writing with an offer, it should sound worth taking up
- Write personally – where possible use computer software that enables you to personalize letters with names and even inserting the address or a reference to the customer's current product package in the text of the letter. So for example a breakdown recovery service could write to its existing customers and in the text of the letter say, 'Now Mrs Wood, if your car wouldn't start outside 10 Acacia Avenue, wouldn't it be convenient if you had the "home start" service added to your current breakdown cover?'

o Questions can be used to good effect when you are trying to get your recipients to desire or want your product/service
o You can go into detail in a direct mail letter in a way that you cannot in an advertisement
o You can use additional pieces of materials, such as brochures or flyers to reinforce the message you are trying to convey – so the letter does not have to communicate all your messages
o In most circumstances you should use a friendly tone – but it does depend on the situation, so if you were writing about critical illness cover your tone would be more serious
o If you want a response or some form of action from the recipient, make it very clear what it is, perhaps mentioning it more than once. The p.s. at the end of a direct mail letter can be used to good effect to remind the customer what they need to do and by when. For example, you could say 'P.S. Don't forget that if you want the two free books when you join our book club you need to complete the attached post card and return it before 31 May...'

Advantages of direct mail

o Response is measurable
o You can test the copy in the letter or the design of mailshot components
o You can target precisely and therefore it is cheaper than mass-market advertising
o You can tailor messages to niche groups
o You can time the campaign precisely
o There can be short lead times in running a direct marketing campaign
o Computer technology can mean sophisticated database management.

Disadvantages associated with direct mail

o Can be viewed as junk mail
o Can be seen as intrusive
o Investment costs for establishing and maintaining a database are high.

Changing perceptions and attitudes – Land Rover

Following a brief to sell 300 Land Rovers, research conducted by the direct marketing agency Craik Jones found that the attitudes held by prospective Land Rover buyers were based on serious misconceptions about the brand. Not only did they feel that Land Rovers was essentially a rural vehicle but they also drove like a truck rather than a luxury car.

These attitudes have been developed as a result of information and perceptions of the brand, without ever having driven the car. This is typical of the order in which attitudes are formed. In order to overcome this, a direct marketing strategy was developed by the agency to encourage trial in order that attitudes could be based on direct experience. Direct mail was used to stimulate a test drive and this was followed up a week later to thank the drivers and to find out their reactions to the experience of actually driving a Land Rover. Not only were over 700 orders placed as a direct result of this campaign but the reaction and knock-on effect on the dealer network also was very positive. Direct marketing had been used as part of a pull strategy to change attitudes and increase sales.

Source: C. Fill, *Marketing Communications, Contexts, Strategies and Applications*, 3rd Edition, 2002.

Evaluating the effect of advertising

Research into the advertising process has shown that advertisements on their own do not prompt a sale. Take the example of the 'Chocco chocolate bar'. Consumers do not see an advertisement for 'Chocco' and rush out to buy it: many other factors influence the purchase decision, such as the price, taste and appearance of the product and whether it is actually available in the shop that a consumer visits. What advertising can do is to create awareness about 'Chocco' among its target audience, then convey a particular brand image and communicate the benefits (both rational and emotional) for purchasing it. In other words, advertising and promotions work on consumers to lead them to the purchase, i.e. decision-making process to a sale.

So it is not appropriate to only look at sales when you are measuring the success of an advertisement or a campaign because other factors in the marketing mix or the external environment could affect sales (in either a negative or a positive way). For example, if there was media coverage of research report suggesting that chocolate improved your IQ and reduced stress at the same time as the 'Chocco' advertising campaign then this could be the reason for a sales increase and not the effect of the advertising campaign. Or, perhaps weather conditions could affect cocoa production adversely, which could cause price rises and reduce demand for 'Chocco', no matter how effective the advertising campaign.

One way to evaluate the effectiveness of advertising is to conduct research into customer perception of 'Chocco' and identify levels of awareness or interest in the product to help set the objectives of an advertising campaign. For example, you might find out that only half the target market is aware of the new 'Chocco' bar – in which case if you set the objective of the campaign to increase awareness to 80 per cent, then use post-campaign research to identify if this objective had been achieved.

Similarly research can be carried out to assess whether a re-branding project has been successful or to judge whether a PR campaign has changed customer perception (if that was the objective of the campaign).

Another way of evaluating public relations effort is to physically measure the amount of coverage in print and broadcast media. For example, to measure the success of a PR campaign informing consumers about a new type of diet chocolate, you could count how many articles appeared in the national press and specialist press (for example, slimming magazines).

To measure the response to a sales promotion campaign that used a '20p off' coupon of 'Chocco' bars you could set up a system with retailers to count the number of redeemed vouchers.

To evaluate the success of a business to business exhibition, if the objective was to create leads for sales staff, you could count the number of contact numbers collected by the staff manning the exhibition. You could further refine the evaluation process by measuring how many calls lead to sales appointments and from there, how many appointments were converted to sales. A final sales figure could be checked against the cost of the exhibition to see if the activity was cost-effective.

Similarly the response rates from direct marketing campaigns should be evaluated and, if appropriate, a further check made to calculate how much response actually converts to sales. This way the cost of a campaign can be measured against the monetary gain from sales.

The role of the brief

In the early stages of your career you are unlikely to be developing full-scale campaigns using above- and below-the-line activity. However, one way for your organization and its advertising agency or design consultancy to determine how to communicate with customers is to write down its requirements in the form of a *brief*. A brief can also be used to help designers produce an appropriate product or packaging design.

You should be aware of the components of a brief. Below is an example of the headings that could be used in an advertising brief. However, you should note that a brief could be used to determine any kind of above- or below-the-line activity. In addition, you should be aware that every brief will be individual to the company, the product and the market concerned.

An example of an advertising brief

Client details
In this section you would include the name of the client and the name of the product.

Background information
In this section you would include whatever relevant information you had about the following:

- o The company
- o The product
- o The market
- o The competition
- o Previous advertising activity that has been undertaken
- o Any relevant research data.

Objectives
In this section you should outline the objectives of the campaign/project.

Target audience
In this section you should identify who the campaign is aimed at.

Message to be conveyed
In this section you should identify what you want to say and how it should be said. This may include the unique selling proposition (the one key benefit that distinguishes the product/service) and any substantiation for the claims being made. It should also determine the desired tone of voice and brand image that should be communicated.

Media
In this section you should specify where you want to place the message.

Timescale
Here you need to specify when the campaign is to run, its length and duration.

Budget
Here you should specify how much money is available for the campaign.

Miscellaneous information
In this section you should specify if there are any mandatory inclusions – for instance, you may have to mention membership of ABTA in an advertisement for a travel agent. You also need to include contact phone numbers or certain logos.

Case history

An airline company's corporate communications

Dolphin in his book *The Fundamentals of Corporate Communications* (2000) refers to the philosophy of American Airlines of working with the news media rather than against them. The company goes out of its way to make its officials available to the press, both on a formal and informal basis; and each year the communication department organizes a visit to a city served by the airline so that key executives can meet the local media.

The company puts effort into helping journalists understand the dynamics of the airline industry. It hosts an annual media day consisting of seminars and discussions on the workings of the airline and the industry as a whole.

The communication department peppers the press with position papers, consultants' reports, newspaper articles and speeches by senior airline executives, all of which reflect the company's thoughts on issues that are important in the industry.

The firm also publishes a quarterly corporate fact book that provides a wealth of statistical and analytical information about the airline's operations. The book also provides guidance to managers allowing them to talk directly with reporters in the event of an emergency.

Activity 4.7

You work for a charitable organization that has been established to promote health and safety issues in the workplace. You would like to run a marketing campaign highlighting health and safety hazards in the workplace and the potential financial damages that companies could incur. You also want to send a poster featuring health and safety hazards to a list of companies that are held on your database.

Draft a brief for your Marketing Officer that indicates the objectives of the campaign, target markets and any other details that you consider the Marketing Officer should have.

20 marks available

Exam hint

You do need to have a basic understanding of how organizations communicate with their external customers. You need to have lots of examples of the whole range of promotional activities from your own experience to put into answers where appropriate. So ensure that you do this type of research well in advance of the examination.

Areas that could have questions relating to how logos, branding and corporate image are used to communicate with customers.

Although it is unlikely that you would be asked a question where you just need to regurgitate facts about various media, you could be given a scenario and asked to suggest relevant promotion activities that could be used in that situation.

Alternatively, you might be asked to write a letter or a memo in a situation relating to exhibitions, sponsorship or whatever, so fundamental to the question might be your understanding of the promotional activity that relates to the context of the question.

You need to have a basic understanding of the importance of layout, typefaces and design so that you could either evaluate the effectiveness or produce a draft of an advertisement, leaflet or some other printed material.

You should be able to write an effective direct mailshot, press release or text for a press advertisement or some other promotional material and know how to monitor or measure the effectiveness of a promotional activity.

Finally, you should be able to draw up a brief that would assist an external supplier, such as, a design, PR, or Sales Promotion consultancy or advertising agency, to do their job of designing or writing for products or services in a given context.

Although this section cannot comprehensively suggest all the areas that might be examined, it does highlight that you will not have to regurgitate the material in it to answer questions, but will need to be able to apply your knowledge in questions that cover this topic.

You will not be asked questions on how computers work, the history of the Internet or about jargon connected with technological developments. However, you should be prepared to explain how technological changes are affecting the way that people and organizations do business and communicate.

Be prepared to answer questions that are set in a context of new media and technology but test you on other areas of the syllabus.

Summary

In this unit you have studied:

- The communications mix

- The role of various promotional activities

- What to look for when evaluating corporate literature

- How branding works

- How to write a press release

o   How to write a direct mail letter

o   How to measure the effectiveness of various promotional activities

o   The role of the brief

Further study and examination preparation

Attempt Questions 5(bii) and 6(a) on the June 2000 examination paper and Questions 1(a) and 5 on the December 2000 paper. Also attempt Question 6(b) on the June 2000 examination paper and Questions 3 and 7 on the December 2000 paper. Go to www.cimeduhub.com to access Specimen Answers and Senior Examiner's advice for these exam questions.

unit 5
the role of information communication technology in customer communications

Learning objectives

In this unit you will:

- ○ Examine technological developments in the field of communication

- ○ Look at the impact of the Internet and e-commerce on customer communication.

By the end of this unit you should be able to:

- ○ Explain how technological developments are affecting customer communications

- ○ Appreciate the principles of web design

- ○ Know how to use e-mail effectively

- ○ Understand how technology can be used to build databases

- ○ Be aware of the steps involved in an online shopping transaction

- ○ Describe developments in telecommunications and digital technology.

Study Guide

This unit provides an overview of technological developments and trends in communications. This unit covers indicative content areas 3.14 and 5.6 of the syllabus. This links in with 1.5 on the Marketing Fundamentals syllabus which is covered in Unit 11 in the Marketing Fundamentals Coursebook. In Marketing Fundamentals you are looking at how Information Communication Technologies (ICT) affects all the elements in the marketing mix, whereas with Customer Communications you are looking at how technology specifically affects how you communicate with customers.

For further information for how this material in this unit will be examined, read the Exam/ Revision Hints section at the end of the unit.

The unit will take you three hours to read through and a further three hours to work through the activities.

Study tip

Because the speed of technological change is so fast, you should use this unit as a starting point to think about how Information Communications Technology (ICT) is changing the way you communicate. You need to extend your knowledge by accessing information outside the course book, in the quality press, specialist marketing magazines and specialist technical press.

You should also use the Internet to see how it can be used. Look up some websites that are of particular interest to you and surf the web for more information about technological developments. One of many websites that you could visit is www.net-profit.co.uk, which is in the form of an online magazine and provides information about technology developments affecting business.

In addition, look at how telecommunications equipment in your workplace has changed the way you and your colleagues do your jobs.

If you cannot access the Internet at home or at work, you could find access at your college or local library or even visit an Internet or cybercafe, where you can pay for access.

How communication with customers is changing

Technological developments in communications are making massive changes to your personal and working lives. They are changing the way you shop, find out information, communicate with others inside and outside your organization; they are affecting the way organizations promote their products/services and even changing the way organizations do business with suppliers and distributors.

The introduction of computers has transformed the way information is handled and communicated. Data in a digital format means that when a document is typed any mistakes can be quickly corrected before it is printed out and information such as invoices, forms and previous letters can be indexed and retrieved easily.

Electronic point of sale (EPOS) systems allow retailers to record and monitor sales data. Linked to 'smart' card purchases, EPOS data provides organizations with detailed profiles of customer preferences and purchasing habits. Databases can be used to store information about customer purchase history so that mail-merged documents can be sent to customers with offers tailored to their needs.

Even the way you use the telephone has changed. Mobile telephones mean you can be constantly in touch with colleagues and customers even when away from the office. People can leave voicemail and fax messages at any time, without having to rely on others to take the information down correctly. Businesses can deal speedily with massive telephone response through voicemail and automated processes. It is also likely that videophones will gradually be introduced, which will change the way you communicate on the telephone, because your body language and facial expressions can be observed.

Even office equipment such as the photocopier has been digitized, so that now you can make multiple copies without ever having to queue at the photocopying machine again.

In addition to mobile telephones, laptop computers mean that you can work away from your desk or while on the move and still access or send information to your colleagues at the office.

The advent of electronic communication has probably had the most impact, and e-mail in particular has become so popular that for many people it is the main way they communicate with others.

The ability to use the Internet has had a massive impact on the speed at which you can communicate, either accessing information on websites or transacting business online.

You can also produce vast quantities of text, sound and picture information and store it on CD-ROM or in DVD (Digital Versatile Disks) format which is an extremely versatile and interactive way for customers to access information.

And, finally, you can also use computer software that allows you to use graphics, animation and sound to make a presentation highly polished, impactful and professional.

Business strategy and new technologies – Blockbuster

The development of broadband technology demonstrates the impact that the digital evolution can have in terms of channel structure and the strategic shift that organizations need to make in order to remain competitive.

Films are traditionally marketed first through cinemas, then through video releases and finally through television (as video on demand, then pay-for channels and then terrestrial services). The full financial potential is realized through this channel structure. The development of digital technologies and Internet facilities offer certain advantages to film studios but it is not necessarily to their advantage to cut out these intermediaries. For example, not all films are successful and it is sometimes necessary to go 'straight to video' in which case the video rental store plays a significant part in the marketing channel.

Broadband services enable people to see films online, whenever and wherever they want. For organizations such as Blockbuster video rental stores, this development posed a major threat. With 65 million cardholders and 6300 stores worldwide (Oliver, 2000), the company needed to anticipate the changes in supply and demand. Blockbuster's response was to change the fundamental purpose or mission of the organization to be an overall entertainment provider for the home. The development of e-commerce facilities has been a key part of their strategy.

Central to this strategy was the non-exclusive digital download and video streaming rights agreement with the film studio MGM and independent film operator AtomFilms. This enables Blockbuster to showcase selected films on its website (www.blockbuster.co.uk). (This first step may lead to agreements with other studios and may well prove attractive to other entertainment-based companies that might enter into partnership deals.)

The website also enables people to purchase CDs, DVDs, games as well as the core product, videos. In addition, Blockbuster has used interactive technologies to provide a higher level of customer personalization in the services they offer. For example, its 'Blockbuster Recommends' facility suggests films to customers based upon their previous selections or a list of films rated *I hate it* or *I like it*. Another example of the personalization approach is the facility to suggest films to match the mood of the viewer. For example, if someone is feeling depressed then it may suggest a Gene Wilder film. All of these changes have been supported with a substantial offline advertising campaign to inform current customers of the changes and to remind them of the Blockbuster proposition and values, to attract and persuade potential new customers to visit the site or a local store, and finally to reposition the brand by differentiating it from its previous position and its main competitors.

Effectively, the company has revised its strategy to accommodate changes in the environment, implemented the necessary changes to its offering and then rebranded itself to reposition itself in the home entertainment business.

Source: C. Fill, *Marketing Communications, Contexts, Strategies and Applications*, 3rd Edition, 2002.

The evolution of e-business

By 1997 there were 1.55 million Internet account holders and 0.8 million corporate Internet accounts in the UK; by 2000 these figures had grown to 7.49 million Internet accounts and 13.7 million corporate Internet accounts. In other words the business world has taken use of the Internet to its collective heart. The way the Internet is used in business can be described in three ways:

- E-commerce is the trading of goods and services using digital media
- E-business is the term used to describe applying digital and Internet technologies to business functions
- E-marketing is the application of the Internet and related digital technologies to achieve marketing objectives.

Global uptake in using the Internet is rising dramatically too. Total commerce over the Internet is over $1trillion (business to consumer). By 2002 it is estimated that over 88 million people between 2 and 22 years of age will be online in the USA and Canada.

In a recent survey conducted by Nielsen/Net Ratings, a New York-based Internet rating company (information courtesy of Lexis-Nexis), South Koreans spent the most time surfing the web at home (16 hours and 17 minutes per month), followed by Canada (10 hours 48 minutes) and the United States (9 hours and 46 minutes). Other countries emerging as dominant in the

Internet market are Hong Kong, Japan and Taiwan and it is predicted that Chinese will become the number one web language by 2007.

Table 5.1 Percentage of households with Internet access via a home personal computer: Asia–Pacific, January 2001.

Country	% of households with Internet access
Hong Kong	49.5
Singapore	48.4
South Korea	45.5
Taiwan	42.9
Australia	40.0
New Zealand	39.9
Japan	24.1

Source: Nielsen/NetRatings

Table 5.2 Time spent online at home: Asia–Pacific region, January 2001.

Country	Time spent per month (hours:minutes:seconds)	Page views per month per person	Average number of sessions per month per person
South Korea	16:17:16	2008	21
Hong Kong	9:46:20	877	16
Japan	7:56:48	779	16
Australia	7:07:38	446	12
Taiwan	6:57:60	737	12
New Zealand	6:28:05	423	14
Singapore	6:05:17	569	11

Source: Nielsen/NetRatings

Auction houses – eBay: the world's biggest car boot sale

A US firm called eBay is a good example of an auction house: the traditional auction model of consumers bidding against each other, only here it's on the Internet.

Desperate for an 'original' Buzz Lightyear? Keen to get hold of a used baby carrier at low prices? If neither of these particularly appeals, don't worry, eBay has nearly 3 million items for sale, to be captured by the highest bidder.

EBay is the world's biggest online auction house, and one of the secrets of its success is that however much you may feel what you are selling is junk, there is always someone somewhere for whom it is exactly what they are looking for. The key once again lies in the unrivalled ability of the Internet to match supply with demand.

EBay charges a small fee and this is its main source of income. Unlike many other Internet start-up companies, it has already started to turn in a profit.

Source: A. Tapp, Principles of Direct and Database Marketing, 2nd Edition, 2000.

Using ICT to improve customer communications

Database marketing involves using computers to capture and store data relating to customers' past purchase history. For instance, if a mail order company sells clothing in its catalogue, each customer file is computerized so that contact details (name, address, postcode) and purchases (type of item, size, colour preference, price, etc.) are stored. This information can be accessed quickly and cheaply by all the departments in the firm. For example, the accounts department may need to access it to chase payment and the marketing department could use it to target offers to customers. So customers who buy clothes for people under a certain height would only be sent information relating to the 'petite' range of clothing based on their past purchase behaviour.

Loyalty schemes work on a similar principle: the large supermarkets can use their EPOS not only for stock control purposes but also to target offers that are relevant to customers. For example, a customer who regularly buys dog food would not be sent money off vouchers to keep the customer 'loyal' for cat food.

Customer relationship management systems can work on a similar principle. The key idea is that each customer is treated as an individual, and in particular, organizations can use computer software to identify the most profitable customers and 'cherry pick' them because of their customer lifetime value (CLV). For example, basic current account holders are not particularly profitable customers for banks as those with (or potentially wanting) loans, mortgages, insurance business and pensions are much more profitable. The idea behind CLV is to spend marketing time and effort on those customers who are the most valuable.

Computer software can also be used in call centres where staff are handling high volumes of calls. For example, when credit card customers ring a call centre and quote their postcode or account numbers, customers' file details quickly appear on the call handlers' computer screens, enabling them to deal with a query or make a transaction.

Database systems can also be used to improve internal communication as a way of creating a 'knowledge management' system. For example, a firm of accountants can have all their customer files in a centralized database so that staff have access to the 'company's shared experience' of how deals and projects have been managed by others within the firm. It also works when the firm want to cross-sell their services to a client. It is much easier if details from the client's dealings with the 'taxation department' are easily accessible by another accountant who might be advising the client on business acquisition for example.

Data 'mining' is when sophisticated systems are used to track customer/client files in order to identify products/services that could be targeted in the future. They can also be used by managers to monitor sales team performance and help administrative staff improve communications by using them to send e-mails, meeting notes, telephone messages and to plan meetings around people's diaries.

Levi-Strauss & Company: Building relationships through database management

To be effective, a company's database must be more than a collection of names and addresses. Levi-Strauss & Company, when threatened by a combination of market forces and image problems, was able to respond by developing a strong database marketing programme. Old Navy, Calvin Klein and other brands had made inroads into the marketplace, just as Levi's had become associated with the older generation, possibly not hip enough to suit the younger consumers.

Levi's reacted by emphasising the concept of *relationship marketing*. This meant trying to understand what the consumers want, and giving them a voice to be heard by company leaders. To meet these objectives, the firm identified five consumer groups for a pilot programme using a major survey. Using the database that was already in place, the company contacted various shoppers and enticed them to fill out questionnaires. Totally, nearly 100,000 consumers completed questionnaires, which were distributed at stores, colleges, the Lilith Fair, via customer service lines. Levi's carefully recorded the 'doorway' each respondent used and tied it to other information, which eventually yielded the five major groups of shoppers. Each of the five groups expressed differing needs when it came to jeans.

Next, Levi's targeted the groups individually. Promotions were structured to match the nature of the customer profile that emerged. For example, one group known as Valuable Shoppers were individuals willing to spend $60 or more on a pair of pants. These patrons were sent thank-you gifts following purchases of custom-fit jeans. The gift was a planter with flower bulbs and a card signed by the clerk who took the fitting. Responses from this group were impressive. A Valuable Shopper who received a gift, purchased on average, 2.3 more pairs of jeans within the next two weeks.

On-line shoppers, who largely came from a group identified as Echo Boomers, or persons aged 15–25, were not sent this type of premium. Instead, this group was enticed with fashion messages. The goal was to match the promotional approach with the buyer group's characteristics.

By contacting consumers through questionnaires, gifts, promotions and service lines, Levi's believed it was able to establish a two-way, more intimate form of communication with its clientele. This, in turn, helped the company combat declining interest in its products. The key to success started with having a fairly well-established database to begin the programme, enhancing the database and listening to what the consumers had to say. Any organization that is willing to utilize the talents and programmes made available from an effective database management team may be in the position to reap similar rewards.

Source: Clow and Baack, *Integrated Advertising, Promotion and Marketing Communication*, 2001.

The Internet

The Internet allows people from all over the world to communicate with each other via a global network of computers. Since 1991, restrictions that prevented people from using the Internet to make a profit have been removed. This has led to a massive growth in the number of websites in the world and in the number of people connected to the Internet. Many people use the Internet to communicate with others via e-mail.

The Internet can be used by organizations to do the following:

o Promote and sell products/services
o Provide information 24 hours a day to people all over the world
o Enable two-way communication via e-mail
o Capture contact information when people register details on websites
o Build ongoing relationships (through e-mail marketing or adding services/benefits to customers who use a firm's website)
o Improve the way businesses do business with each other.

Websites

Internet software is required to access the Internet, and once you have gained access you can visit an address on the world wide web. A famous website address is www.bbc.co.uk but you will see thousands of others on business cards, on product packaging and in advertising. Any organization or person can set up their own website. A website might contain information about the organization or about a person's particular interest or hobby. Information can be communicated using a combination of text, image and sound.

Websites that you may wish to access to help you with your studies are:

o www.ebusiness.uk.com
o www.tbcresearch.com
o www.asiasource.org
o www.marketresearch.org.uk
o www.nielson-netratings.com
o www.streamwave.co.uk
o www.broadvision.com

Interesting websites that you could access to see how the web can be used are:

o www.Indya.com (one of India's top three Internet portals)
o www.penang.net (about the island of Malaysia)
o www.markwarner.co.uk (easy to use, innovative, well-designed, clear and informative also won a 'best travel site' award in 2000)
o www.cityorganiser.com (helps busy business travellers find out about hotels, car hire, restaurants, healthcare and leisure options also with bookable services).

Website design

In designing a website you should consider what you are trying to achieve with it and consider who your audience are, what they will be interested in and what sort of equipment they are likely to have.

Although attractive design with sound and graphics can bring a site to life, you need to consider if your audience will have the latest equipment and a large screen to enable them to benefit from these facilities. One way to deal with this issue is to have an alternative version of your website so that those not using a conventional desktop computer can still access it without the sound and graphic effects.

It should be easy for visitors to get around or navigate your website. It also helps if it is easy to access and has a fast response.

The contents need to be designed in a non-linear format because unlike a book, where people start at the beginning, a website can be accessed from any page. Books are also generally printed in a portrait format but websites are in a landscape format, where the width of the screen is greater than its height. Consequently, websites should be designed with a landscape format in mind.

Good web design also creates a directory structure for the information and establishes links between every page throughout the website. Hypertext will allow users to jump to other pieces of related information on the same site or to other sites anywhere in the world. It is also helpful if key words are highlighted and menus of information on the site are listed in bullet points for easy reading.

The contents of a website can start off quite simply with some company and product information. However, it is important that the content and quality is updated. The website could be incorporated with an organization's corporate video and music to make it more interesting.

Websites are developed all the time, so the published word, the animated graphic, the broadcast picture, digital video clips and voice messages can all be presented and interconnected.

Websites should also be interactive and allow for an organization to build up a database of customers. One way to get people to register with their details is to restrict access to certain pages until details are registered. Another way is to build in some form of response such as a 'freebie' if visitors to the site leave their details. For example, one law firm allowed visitors to their website to register their details if they wanted to receive an advent calendar highlighting areas of the law that companies could fall foul of. This allowed them to establish a list of firms interested in receiving legal advice that they could target with information.

For many companies it is not just about the number of 'hits' on the site but the way a site can generate leads or actually convert people to business when visiting the site. For example, the easyJet site is designed to allow people to make online bookings and the company measures the success of its website by the level of sales.

Website costs

These can vary from a very simple website that would cost around £1000 to set up to those costing tens of thousands of pounds which can handle on-line shopping. An average brochure-type site currently costs around £5000 to be designed and set up.

One aspect that many organizations forget is that once the site is set up, it needs to be monitored to measure response and maintained so that its contents are not outdated.

If the website is the tip of the iceberg, what lies below the surface? How fulfilment companies can bring database marketing and the Internet together

Internet growth has led to a new breed of one-stop shop communication firms that help businesses deliver their Web-based operations. In October 1999, the company Dataforce launched I-Force, a new venture which offers website design, database management, and links these with payment processing, storage and packing, parcelforce deliver and follow-up marketing using direct mail. I-Force promises to have its business customers up and running with e-commerce in just 12 weeks. Perhaps the key to the success of the operations is the efficient linking of apparently separate events like capturing and recording customer data on one hand, with picking and packing goods on the other.

Companies like Dataforce are building on the already established skills of the direct marketing supply sector, which specializes in the complicated businesses of fulfilling a customer order efficiently and in a high-quality way. This after all is the direct/database industry's core service to the customer – and, as every marketing student knows, customer service is vital to the long-term profitability of the company.

Source: A. Tapp, *Principles of Direct and Database Marketing*, 2nd Edition, 2000.

Electronic mail

Electronic mail or e-mail is a method of sending text files from one computer to another which allows you to send messages across the world in seconds. One way to send and receive messages is to set up an e-mail account with an Internet service provider (ISP).

If someone named John Smith set up an e-mail account, his e-mail address could be jsmith@tesco.net.co.uk. To send him an e-mail message, you would connect to the Internet and opt for the 'compose message' facility. You would then complete the various parts of the e-mail and compose your message. Your e-mail message to John Smith would then show who the message was from (your e-mail address so that he could reply to you), the subject of the message and the message itself.

A company can have a corporate mailbox, with each employee having private access to their own little part of it. For example, if you worked at Tiger Tours and your name was Mary Smith, your address might be msmith@tigertours.co.uk.

E-mail is like having a postman living inside your telephone who can deliver post anywhere in the world at the speed of lightning. However, it is more than a messaging service because text, graphics, video and sound can be sent and received across the Internet.

The information is stored in the computer until the recipient retrieves it. It is usually cheaper than other forms of communication because it only incurs the cost of connection to the ISP.

Cost comparison of e-mail with other forms of communication

Table 5.3 shows the approximate cost of sending a 10-page document from the UK to the USA.

Table 5.3

Cost	Communication method	Time taken to receive message
£1.56	First class post	5–7 days
£2.00	Fax	5 minutes
£30.00	Courier	2 working days
15p (cost of local call)	E-mail	Almost instant

E-mail etiquette

E-mail can revolutionize the way you communicate because it is so quick, easy and cost-effective. It is also paperless unless you decide to print out the message or the document attached to the message.

Because most e-mail messages are simply text files, the usual conventions connected with letter writing, such as letterheads, typesizes, typestyles, justification, layout, paper quality and signatures, are ignored. This lack of convention encourages people to be less formal than they would be if they were writing a memo or letter on headed paper.

The medium also encourages brevity, which can make you more productive in dealing with and sending messages. However, it can mean that messages sound curt to the extent of rudeness if you are not careful.

In addition, because it is easy to copy a message to everyone in your office with the click of a few buttons, it can encourage you and your colleagues to saturate people with more information than they really need.

You should also be aware that your employer owns e-mail messages sent from your workplace and has the right to monitor the e-mail you send using their computers.

Legal firms advise companies nowadays that they should guard against e-mail abuse by writing to staff about the perils associated with e-mails:

- o Instruct staff not to include any statements or other material that could be held to be abusive, racist, constitute sexual harassment or be threatening or defamatory
- o Point out that someone other than the intended recipient may receive the message and that both individuals and the company could be held liable for anything contained in it
- o Advise them to use password-protected documents for confidential information.

Many firms also attach a legal disclaimer to the bottom of every e-mail sent out from the firm.

Advantages of e-mail

- o Local call costs to anywhere in the world
- o Easy distribution to one recipient or many
- o Speedy delivery – almost instantaneous
- o No time zones to worry about – e-mail works while your recipients sleep
- o Can be addressed to a specific person
- o Will be delivered even if the recipient is out
- o No messy paperwork lying around
- o Messages sent and received can be stored for future reference
- o Security passwords restrict access of your mailbox to you.

Intranet

An intranet allows you to communicate on the Internet in a local network that is not publicly accessible. Many organizations use intranets to distribute internal documents.

However, it can be used outside the organization to allow nominated people to share documents, expertise or opinions anywhere in the world. The network would be protected to ensure that only nominated people could access information, thus keeping the network secure.

The most common form of intranet is where corporate information is published on an internal website, with hypertext links to related documents, enabling enormous amounts of time to be saved searching for information.

For example, a law practice that merged with another firm in a town forty miles away, used the intranet to create an internal 'who's who' of staff, including photographs. It then developed to include internal phone directories, which could be updated without continual re-printing costs, practice guides on word-processing house styles, the staff handbook, and even what was being served in the staff restaurant that week.

Eventually it went on to be used to produce practice-wide know-how material and legal precedents. In other words, it became a giant internal library with easy access to staff from inside the firm.

The benefits of intranets

- o Reduced costs in printing and distributing documents
- o Publishing information without delay
- o No physical filing – saving time and space
- o Ability to find information quickly.

Extranet

An extranet is an intranet extended to key players involved in your everyday business processes in order to achieve total collaboration. This may include dealers, suppliers or business partners.

For example, when General Motors started using their extranet to enable purchase orders to be made by their dealers using an electronic form process, the cost of the transaction went down from £35 to less than 10p.

Activity 5.1

Look at the CIM website www.cimeduhub.com. As a student member you can access the private qualifications extranet area and see what information you can obtain there.

E-commerce

Of course, you can visit websites to do your online shopping for CDs, books and clothes. But for many people who like to shop for clothes and books in the centre of a big city, where they can see and be seen, the idea of online shopping is unattractive.

However, those same people may not be so happy to make the same boring weekly shop for routine food items on a busy Saturday morning. So big retailers like Tesco and Sainsbury have grasped the opportunity e-commerce gives them to help their customers save time by enabling them to automate routine purchases (that are only changed by exception) and have the goods delivered as well.

Online shopping transactions

It is very easy to do your shopping on the Internet. The most common way is to access a computer that connects to the Internet through an Internet service provider (ISP). This is usually done through a telephone cable using a modem. You would then access the online store through a website browser, usually by the website address (URL) of the on-line store. For example, you could connect to the online bookstore website www.amazon.co.uk.

If, you wanted to purchase a pair of jeans and you connected to an online clothes shop, you would pull down the menu to choose the style or cut of jeans, the colour and the size of the item you require.

You would then complete an onscreen order form where you would provide payment and address details. You would then need to wait for credit card verification from your bank or credit card company. Once authorization was given you would just need to wait for dispatch of your order from the online store.

E-commerce – the bubble about to burst?

According to this opinion piece, e-commerce is a 'retrogressive step dressed up as modernism'. 'If in the dark ages they'd invented the idea of shopping by staring into a glass icon and looking at foggy images of things you'd like to buy, picking them up, and then waiting for a messenger to bring them to you, today we'd be excitedly welcoming the dawn of walk-in shops, where you can see the goods, feel and touch them and walk out with them.'

Morris describes e-commerce as 'no more than glorified catalogue shopping' (mail order) and extols the joys of spontaneous supermarket shopping in which the customers make any number of on-the-spot decisions about purchases based on what they pass in the aisles. Morris believes that the computer will become a place where only the basics are bought online, while we go shopping for the 'interesting stuff'.

The conclusion is that neither e-commerce nor high-street shopping will dominate. The likely end-game is a sensible, genuinely progressive amalgam of online and real shops, or 'clicks and mortar'. Then at last, as US e-commerce experts put it, the letter 'e' can return to its rightful place as the fifth letter of the alphabet.

Source: A. Tapp, *Principles of Direct and Database Marketing*, 2nd Edition, 2000.

E-business

It is a mistake to think of the Internet and e-commerce (doing business on the Internet) as only using websites to sell goods. E-commerce changes the way you interact with suppliers and organizations and the way they do business with you. For many organizations the key benefit from e-commerce is to use it to provide in-depth customer information. It can also be used to canvass feedback from customers.

Banks are using the Internet to add value to the service they provide to current customers. With some banks you can transfer money from one account to another and find out your bank balance.

Your local doctor may soon be able to improve their service to you by allowing you to order repeat prescriptions via the Internet. This will not only save you time but also free up busy receptionists to deal with people waiting in the surgery.

The Internet is also a fantastic resource for obtaining information and so is an ideal tool to assist distance learning. You can access news and weather sites, and there are many that you can visit just for fun. If you are interested in helping your children find out about space exploration, then you could visit the NASA site.

Utilities and other large organizations with many customers will be able to save time and money by producing automated account and billing information, and allowing customers to make online payment.

Some firms are using the Internet to improve communications with potential staff. On-line recruitment information can enable people to have a virtual tour of offices with a 360-degree photograph and 'hot spots' can be clicked on to enable them to go into the still image in more detail.

Electronic data interchange (EDI)

For many organizations the Internet will enable them to source parts, reduce waiting times for stock, cut the storage area they need for stock holding, and will mean cheaper distribution costs.

For example, a network of franchised garages had their purchasing organized centrally using the Internet. This now means that if a franchise operator uses an exhaust from stock, this information is automatically communicated through EDI to the exhaust manufacturer, who can then re-stock the garage automatically. Business process and business communication is also transformed so that there are fewer telephone calls and less paperwork, which has a great impact on the efficiency of the organization.

EDI is also used to keep track of inventory. For example, FedEx have opened up the 'back room' to business customers so that they can order courier service and track a package. This adds real value to their business relationship with customers. It also means that staff are not tied up with routine queries about the whereabouts of a package but have more time to spend dealing with orders and more complex forms of enquiry.

EDI can therefore improve a company's ability to work with others in terms of sharing documents and other information, which improves strategic partnerships on a worldwide basis.

E-marketing

There are lots of good examples of companies using the Internet as part of their promotional mix. For example, the Adidas website can be accessed in several different languages and provides information for sports enthusiasts, whatever sport they are interested in. It provides information on athletes, major sporting events, has links to other relevant sites (spotlights on various football clubs) and of course contains extensive product information via a vast online catalogue, more extensive than you could see in one shop. In addition you can buy online.

Banner advertising space can be purchased on portal sites or individual websites of other companies to promote your firm and its products/services. For example, Virgin's recent banner advertising campaign for personal and stakeholder pensions generated so many e-mail requests for information that the whole sales force was booked up for one month after the campaign ended.

Websites are useful means to deliver detailed information before purchase and after-sales support, which is particularly useful for big purchases where people need to look around for information in their own time and at their own pace. For instance, to sell cars, it is very useful to be able to allow potential customers to access detailed information that they request in the comfort of their own home and then have the option to book a test drive. The flip side is that they can also shop around for the best price in an international market.

Brand building through websites is still in its infancy but it could prove to be highly profitable in youth marketing. It is no coincidence that the soft drink manufacturers and sports goods suppliers have been pioneers in developing high-quality interactive sites.

For websites to work, it is essential that they are promoted by the following activities:

- o   Relevant offline advertising
- o   Banner advertising on other relevant websites
- o   Links to other sites
- o   Sending details of sites to large search engines
- o   Using website address details on all stationery and advertising.

The best e-marketing websites are those that really do add value by providing information that people want, and are updated regularly. So, for example, a car breakdown service company could provide an online traffic information service in return for users registering contact details. If they also set up the registration process so that users could opt in to receive further information to be sent from the company, it would be a good way for the company to extend its database. By asking the right kind of questions, the registration process could enable the firm to tailor future communications such as mail shots or e-mail marketing activity based on where the recipient lived or the type of car that they own.

E-mail marketing

E-mail has become a useful medium for organizations wanting to market their services. For example, the UK currently has 13 million people with Internet access in the home, of whom 95 per cent use e-mail and so it is a viable medium.

Table 5.4 UK e-mail penetration by age

Over 54	11%
45–54	17%
36–44	24%
25–34	25%
Under 25	23%

Table 5.5 UK e-mail users by socio-economic group

AB	35%
C1	36%
C2	16%
DE	13%

'Push' technology means that marketers can post direct electronic mailings to potential customers' online mailboxes rather than paper mail through their front door. This technique has been used by Dell Computers but has been blasted by critics for its intrusive 'junk mail' status. Dell say that they use it to target mail only at people who have requested information and it means that they can use their database to segment targets and send messages that are closely tailored to the recipients' needs.

However, many companies recognize that if they want to win or retain business they must take care of their customers and offer specialized information targeted to individual needs.

One training company started using fax marketing to generate qualified sales leads and then went on to devise an e-mail marketing campaign. They worked with a specialist business-to-business e-mail list broker and rented a specialist list of people who had opted-in to receive information on specific types of training. They combined the e-mail message with an interactive 'how do you measure up in the workplace?' fun-type quiz, which was linked to a competition. To enter it to win a Palm Pilot, website visitors just had to register their contact details. The website also included a telephone number that linked visitors to sales staff via an online discussion. This was a very innovative and successful campaign that resulted in 10 per cent of visitors to the website converting to serious sales leads.

Advantages of e-mail marketing campaigns:

o Well-targeted, personalized and direct communication method with no gatekeepers (even many relatively senior staff still open their own e-mails)
o Easy to receive and quick to respond to
o Convenient – waits in mailbox until recipient is ready to open it
o Can engage rich media content such as colour pictures
o Quite cheap compared with conventional direct marketing methods
o Recipients can opt in for further information without going through to sender's website
o Can offer more conventional response methods, such as telephone number if recipients want to speak to someone
o Can be used to send offers to existing customers on new prospects
o Can be a good way to follow up recent purchases, for example, to check whether customers are satisfied with a recent personal computer purchase and to see if any of them need help/assistance
o Can be a good way to get customer feedback and research customer opinions
o Can be used to send conference or seminar invitations to specific markets
o Ideal for rapid reactive campaigns, for instance where a company has a special offer this month – for example, if a football club wants to sell corporate boxes at the last minute for a rearranged match
o Can be used to drive click-throughs to websites and generate opt-in requests for more information.

Although people do not want to be 'spammed' (sent unsolicited information), e-mail campaigns where recipients have opted in for information can be very successful as they are a tremendous opportunity to send a message directly through to a relevant decision maker.

Signposts for the future

The way people use the Internet is opening up all kinds of possibilities. You might study for a course using an interactive video tutor. If you are considering moving house, you could see if your current furniture would suit the new house without ever visiting it but by viewing it online. If you are fixing your car, you could access a DIY guide and then change sites to order parts online. If you find that this does not work, you could then access the services of an online mechanic.

Other developments include faster speeds for surfing websites, improved safety for credit card transactions, improved graphics cards to view websites and more use of firewalls to protect information from being grabbed by hackers.

Merging web-based business and database marketing

Data factors is a company which specializes in ticketing sales for sports concerns. Established in Suffolk, it began life installing ticketing systems for Ipswich Town, the local football team. However, the company is shifting its focus and building an Internet front end to its systems so that supporters book tickets through the web. Data factors sees its future as an e-commerce portal advertising its clients' available tickets while allowing them to collate data about their supporters. The sports franchise then has a growing list of potential buyers of merchandise, now a lucrative part of the business of sport, and also a growing source of market information in the form of a transaction database.

Source: A. Tapp, *Principle of Direct and Database Marketing*, 2nd Edition, 2000.

Activity 5.2

How is the Internet being used to communicate with existing customers and prospects?

Telecommunications

There have been massive developments in the field of telecommunications.

Automated switchboards are now within the reach of even the smallest firms. This enables customers to leave a message for a particular person or department through voice mail. This facility also enables the organization to pre-select the response, so that if the customer requires information they are put through to department 1, for example, and if the customer wants to order goods, they are put through to department 2 and so on.

Voice mail can enable companies to cope with large volumes of calls and should mean that customers are dealt with more efficiently and effectively. However, automated customer-handling systems do not always improve customer communications. Customers become irritated and angry when they have to go through several button-pushing processes and still end up waiting a long time before their call is answered.

The other issue for customers is that if they have a non-standard problem or query, they often find it extremely difficult to speak to a real person who can help them.

ISDN

An ISDN line allows your computer to connect to other computers much more quickly and enables much faster transfer of large documents than a normal telephone line. This technology has been successfully used in teleworking, where homeworkers can source information from the office fast and effectively.

ISDN can also be used for:

- ○ Sending information with graphics
- ○ Video conferencing
- ○ Broadcasting
- ○ Telemarketing/call centres.

Mobile phones and m-Commerce

Mobile phones are getting smaller and more powerful. They can be used to access e-mails. The newest Nokia Communicator is not much bigger than a mobile phone but opens up into a keyboard mode. It doubles as a mobile office with Internet access, e-mail and telefax, and can receive pictures from digital cameras.

Communication methods are now converging so that text messages, telephone calls and video images can all be sent on the Internet. WAP (Wireless Application Protocol) mobile phones can be used to access the Internet on a limited scale. This technology has encouraged m-commerce which means that people can shop online on their mobile telephones or access their bank accounts.

The introduction of 3G (third generation) mobile telephone technology means that the equipment will be even more powerful and will be able to download pictures. These mobile telephones are likely to have bigger screens and will be used for videophone calls, to send e-mails with photographs attached, play online games with much better picture quality and conduct shopping and banking transactions more easily.

More organizations are likely to be sending e-mails and text marketing messages straight to consumers' handsets. Mobile network operators, such as BT Cellnet and Orange already use text messages to send customers information about new tariffs, services and promotions. So, for example, an airline operating from a regional airport could send text messages to people in that region saying there were 50 seats left on a flight to a holiday destination at a certain price.

However, mobile phone marketing could result in a consumer backlash if telephones ring at inconvenient times. At the moment an EU directive forbids companies operating automated calling systems to target customers without their consent. In addition, a new industry body has been set up in the UK – the Wireless Marketing Association, supported by Orange, Vodaphone and BT Cellnet – which has established a set of self-regulatory rules to govern use of marketing by mobile phone companies.

Although it could offer marketers the ultimate, personalized time- and location-sensitve method of communicating with customers, it could be seen as an unwelcome intruder. It is one thing leaving relevant messages on a business mobile telephone during a working day, but if the recipient was relaxing on holiday that would be seen as something entirely different.

However, in a fragmenting media marketplace, companies are keen to find new ways to get their message across, particularly to a youth market (the most avid users of text messaging) and particularly using a medium that is measurable.

Companies, including Coca-Cola, are pulling back from TV advertising and ploughing resources into marketing which 'adds value' to consumers' lives: music, sport and entertainment sponsorships and initiatives which allow the consumer to interact with the brand.

Mobile marketing is predicted to be huge but marketers have to learn how to create concise mobile advertising campaigns with only 160 characters to play with. The main issue for marketers appears to be not to inundate people with messages but to get them to give their permission and provide interesting and relevant advertising that requires a response such as ringing a telephone line or looking at a website.

Text messaging

Text messaging, which involves sending text messages to other mobile phone users, is becoming more popular than e-mail, particularly with the youth market. A new informal language is developing with no punctuation and abbreviated spelling. Although it is not particularly suited to business situations, here are some examples:

- B = Be
- C = See
- Cu = See you
- CuL8R = See you later
- B4 = Before
- NE = Any
- NE1 = Anyone
- R = Are
- RU = Are you
- 2day = Today
- F2T = Free to talk
- Ic%d mEt U @7 = I could meet you at 7
- tb = Text back
- 1t = Want
- y = Why
- msg = Message
- 1t2 = Want to
- :C = What
- :) = Smiling
- ;-/ = Confused
- :-(= Sad face.

Digital technology

Increased bandwidth for electronic communications is a general trend and has resulted in the introduction of digital radio and digital television.

Digital radio

The main benefits of digital radio will be improved sound quality and the ability to send additional data with radio signals. This means that text messages and even pictures could be sent as you listen to the radio. While the idea of having pictures on a radio might seem inherently daft, it could be simply used to have the name of the artist visible as a record is being played. Digital radio will probably be interactive, with 'tell me more' buttons that can be used for people to find out more information if they want it. This will mean it can still retain the benefit of being a background medium (when required), so people can listen to it at the same time as doing other things.

Digital television

Digital television will allow for more channels and two-way communication. It means that information can be sent in the background and be accessed by choice. The implication is that you can find out more about an advert if it interests you. This will lead to television advertising becoming more direct response driven.

The technology involved in digital television will mean that people can view programmes in real time or not, as they prefer. If they do not view in real time, they will be able to filter out things they do not want to see, such as advertising. This may lead to more programme sponsorship.

The knock-on effect of the technology will be that viewers can programme the technology to tailor viewing to suit their TV habits, which will result in a 'Channel You' type of programming.

The impact of more channels will lead to audience fragmentation, with more segmented channels. The implication will be that sports goods manufacturers like Adidas will advertise more on channels like MUTV than on traditional television channels.

The threat of e-commerce on traditional high street retailers and the effect on television companies of declining viewing share and advertising revenue will see changes in the way advertisers communicate with customers.

In addition, digital television technology has dramatically reduced entry costs for new broadcasters. Broadcast technology is also converging with the Internet, which is creating new hybrids between companies operating on both platforms. These issues, combined with the fact that exising television audiences and revenue streams are fragmenting, mean that a number of retailer and television companies are becoming involved in alliances as a means to maintain market share and appeal to specific target markets.

For example, the Wellbeing Network has recently been launched in the UK. It is a joint-venture website and television channel from Granada and Boots the Chemist which will air programmes on digital satellite, terrestrial and cable channels. It will mainly feature discussions of health problems, parenting forums, medical phone-ins, interviews and live product-testing. It is this kind of medium that many marketers will want to use as traditional broadcast media changes.

However, the kind of direct-response television advertising that is emerging will cause problems for many advertisers because often they do not plan for the peaks and troughs in handling large scale audience response.

Cancer Research UK in DRTV fund-raising push

Cancer Research UK, the largest independent cancer research body in the world, is unveiling its first direct marketing campaign since it formed in December.

The campaign, through WWAV Rapp Collins, uses direct response TV supported by a one million-strong mailing. The ad urges viewers to call the freephone number and pledge £2 a month.

It marks the first wave of fund-raising activity for the charity, which was formed following the merger of Imperial Cancer Research Fund and The Cancer Research Company.

The ad features people who have lost family members and close friends to cancer. As they look into a mirror, an image of a loved one suffering from cancer appears. In one ad, a mother sees a reflection of her sick daughter in the mirror but the ad closes on a positive note, with the child, who has successfully fought the disease, appearing fit and healthy.

The approach is in line with the current above-the-line advertising through Abbott Mead Vickers BBCO which uses family photographs and home video footage.

The DRTV ads air on Channel 4, Channel 5, satellite and cable stations in 90- and 60-second versions.

Source: Marketing, 21 Feb, 2002, p. 12.

How to deliver on a DRTV campaign: For companies that use DRTV, a reliable contact centre is a must for success

In the past few months, ITV's Pop Idol has whipped the nation into a frenzy. The reality TV show is currently attracting an average audience of eight million, with up to three million viewers calling-in to vote for their favourite contestant.

This kind of feedback highlights the effectiveness of DRTV. Providing a hotline number with an invitation to interact, buy a product, enter a game show, or donate to charity, can generate, on average, as many as 100,000 calls, the vast majority within the first twenty minutes.

Planners have to decide whether to provide live operators or handle calls automatically via interactive voice response (IVR).

An advantage of automation is that it bypasses the need to recruit and teach operators, which means that it can be implemented more or less immediately. Faced with the foot and mouth outbreak last year, the UK government set up a hotline, but this was swamped by calls from anxious farmers. It then appointed IMS Response, which had an operation up and running within hours.

But IVR would have been an inappropriate response for many of the hotline callers, and by the next day the bureau had in place a 30-strong team of operators able to provide help and reassurance to those most obviously at risk.

That dual approach is also adopted by MM Group when handling the response for the National Canine Defence League, which advertises over Christmas. Last year's spot generated a high volume of calls, although being shown exclusively on cable and satellite made this manageable. According to donor recruitment manager Mary Anne Partridge, the priority was to make it easy for callers to donate.

DRTV is not just about responding to calls, but also collecting data to feed back into marketing campaigns, making it a complex but extremely valuable tool.

Source: Marketing, 24 May, 2001, p. 18.

Activity 5.3

Explain how developments in ICT have changed the way that people communicate with internal and external customers. Provide examples of how the Internet is being used to add value, improve customer service or change the way business is being carried out.

Summary

In this unit you have studied:

o   The role of Information and Communications Technology in communications

o   How communication with customers is changing

o   How e-business is evolving

o   How ICT can be used to improve customer communications

o   What makes a successful website

o   How to use e-mail and e-mail marketing

o   How intranets and extranets can improve customer communciations

o   The role of e-commerce, e-business and e-marketing

o   How telecommunications and digital media are changing customer communications.

Exam hint

You will not be asked questions on how computers work, the history of the Internet or about jargon connected with technological developments. However, you should be prepared to explain how technological changes are affecting the way that people and organizations do business and communicate.

Be prepared to answer questions that are set in a context of new media and technology but test you on other areas of the syllabus.

Further study and examination preparation

Attempt Question 6(b) on the June 2000 examination paper and Questions 3 and 7 on the December 2000 paper. Go to www.cimeduhub.com to access Specimen Answers and Senior Examiner's advice for these exam questions.

unit 6 effective communications

In this unit you will:

o   Appreciate how non-verbal cues can add to or detract from communications

o   Understand how to be a better listener

o   Build on your telephone communications knowledge.

By the end of this unit you will be able to:

o   Use non-verbal communication effectively in a variety of situations

o   Be a better listener in all face to face interactions and when using the telephone

o   Make and receive telephone calls in a professional manner

o   Deliver effective presentations.

Study Guide

This unit covers indicative content areas 4.1, 4.4 and 4.8 of the syllabus. It provides you with a basic understanding of the role of non-verbal communication and active listening and extends your knowledge in the areas of telephone use and the delivery of presentations.

It will take you a minimum of two hours to work through this unit and a further two hours to complete the activities.

Communication skills in marketing

Effective verbal, non-verbal and listening skills are essential in marketing as there are so many face to face and telephone interactions when you need to use good oral skills and be able to listen to verbal and watch for non-verbal cues.

Verbal communication

When speaking with customers, whether face to face or on the telephone, it is important that what you say is perceived as helpful, welcoming and appropriate to the situation. It is easy for a culture of internal orientation to become established in an organization. This is evident when staff become so focused on internal procedures that they do not respond appropriately to customer queries or requests. They may answer customers in such a way as to irritate or annoy customers because they feel that their custom is not valued.

Sentences that drive customers away

'I'm in the middle of something' or 'x's busy – could you call back?'

'There's nothing we can do – it's company policy.'

'We're closing – you'll have to come back tomorrow.'

'You'll have to give me your account number before I can help you.'

Activity 6.1

Change the following phrases so that they demonstrate customer care.

1. 'I don't know.'
2. 'That's not my job.'
3. 'I don't think we have that in stock.'
4. 'You'll have to call back.'

Tone – how you say things

The tone that you use can be either intentionally or unintentionally inappropriate and can infuriate customers. An apathetic, droning or listless tone of voice can convey the message that you don't care or are not interested in the customer and their problem/query. A rushed tone can make you sound impatient with the customer. In fact different tones of voice can change the meaning of the same words. By changing the inflection in your voice, you can say the words 'Your statement is ready now' in an angry way, sarcastically, apologetically, shyly and even in a humorous way.

Customers obviously want to be greeted or spoken to by someone whose tone of voice sounds interested, helpful and patient and, if appropriate, sounds apologetic and sincere if they have been treated unfairly or a mistake has been made.

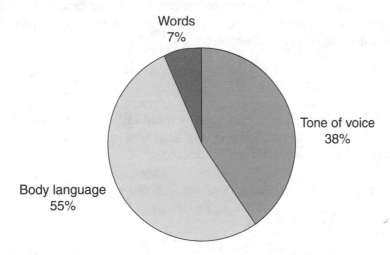

Figure 6.1 How we receive messages

Voice characteristics

Consider the expression 'Oh, that's just great'. A different message can be conveyed depending on how the voice is used to express the words. For example, said in a friendly tone of voice when someone has received something they are pleased with, it conveys a friendly, grateful message. If the same expression is shouted at someone, it could be a sarcastic message that in fact they are not pleased with something and things are not in fact 'great'. The same words said quietly in a deep and husky voice in an intimate situation would convey a completely different message. So the tone of voice, volume and pitch that are used can affect the message being conveyed.

Non-verbal communication skills

Non-verbal communication consists of:

o   The body language you use, such as eye contact, facial expression, posture, gesture and physical space
o   The impression/atmosphere you create by your punctuality, hospitality, manners and personal appearance
o   The voice characteristics you adopt – tone, pitch and volume.

Non-verbal communication can convey messages without words or add meaning to whatever words are being used.

Eye contact

The look in someone's eyes can have a variety of meanings. In a romantic scene, the way an actor looks into the leading lady's eyes conveys a very different meaning to the way a person can stare in defiance or in a challenging way. In a business context, avoiding eye contact can convey disinterest or shiftiness but making positive eye contact while you are delivering a presentation shows that you are relating to and connecting with your audience.

Facial expression

Your facial expression and coloration can convey various meanings. A flushed face can indicate embarrassment, while the colour draining out of your face can indicate shock. Pursed lips can reveal your irritation at something, a frown can show disapproval and a smile can indicate happiness, approval or a welcome.

Posture

If you adopt an upright posture, it can show you are attentive and the opposite can show you are disinterested. If you were lounging in your seat when your Managing Director walks past, it could indicate that you do not respect the individual.

If you sit hunched up in your seat in a group, it could either indicate a lack of confidence or hostility.

Gesture

Your gestures might include a clenched fist to indicate anger, or a shrug of your shoulders to convey that you do not really care, or you may tap your fingers and, without knowing it, indicate that you are impatient with the person or the situation you are in.

Physical space

Sitting on a big chair behind a big desk so that people who enter your office have to sit on a lower chair opposite you, with the desk as a barrier, can communicate your authority and the level of formality you expect from others. Alternatively, you can achieve informality in meetings by using a horseshoe-shape layout.

Physical space also refers to the invisible line that surrounds people and is referred to as *personal space.* By breaching someone's personal space you can intimidate them and be perceived as overbearing and insensitive.

An accepted move into someone's physical space in Britain is the friendly handshake. In Europe and other countries, kissing on the cheek may be acceptable. Different countries and cultures have different norms.

The impression/atmosphere

You can create a favourable impression in a business situation with a smart appearance in terms of your clothes and personal grooming. If you are punctual and use the appropriate greeting, for example a formal handshake, particularly when meeting new business contacts, this can influence whether you are seen to be acceptable by conforming to the norms of business behaviour.

Similarly, your hospitality can be judged not just by the words you express but if you are seen to be helpful and considerate to visitors. This can include taking their coats, checking that they are warm/cool enough, whether they need a drink and ensuring that your body language is positive, for example, smiling rather than looking at your watch as if you are in a hurry to get rid of them.

You can create a different impression with different types of body language. Consider the difference between a nervous cough, a bored sigh and a snigger. You can also use your body language to indicate that a meeting has finished by edging out of the door, getting up from your chair or gathering up your paperwork.

Using and interpreting non-verbal communication

You can use non-verbal communication to your advantage in meetings, interviews, negotiations and presentations to do the following:

o   To create a positive impression
o   To show that you fit in with the culture of an organization
o   To convey enthusiasm and confidence.

By recognizing the messages intrinsic in the non-verbal communication displayed by others you can do the following:

o   Recognize other people's true feelings
o   See potential problems
o   Read situations better and modify your message accordingly.

Negative body language

By using inappropriate body language you can make your customers angry. For example, if you give a customer a blank stare because you are preoccupied with a personal matter, the customer will probably feel that you are intentionally making them feel uncomfortable or that you are not interested in what they want.

By holding your head down and avoiding eye contact or being busy talking with colleagues, you will also convey the message that you are not interested in the customer.

Similarly, if you are talking with a customer and fidget in a distracted way, such as drumming your fingers on a desk or playing with a pen, this could also give the impression that you are not interested in dealing with the customer.

If a customer asks you a question and you shrug your shoulders, this could indicate that you do not know the answer and that you do not care.

Positive body language

You can also use body language in a positive way. Simply by making eye contact with customers you show interest in them and what they have to say. A friendly smile can make you seem approachable, and simply by moving in the direction of a customer with a slight inclination of the head you can indicate that you are available to help, without actually saying anything.

International body language

Even though body language is common to everyone, there are still cultural differences and language sub-groups which, if you operate in the global marketplace, you should learn.

Here are some examples of cultural body language differences:

- Southern Europeans and people from the Middle East stand close together when they are talking whereas people from Britain stand at arm's length and people from Oriental cultures stand even further apart. So don't be offended if someone from another culture appears to 'invade your personal space' or be backing away from you. Accept the difference and do not step back/forward (depending on the situation) as this could cause offence.
- Even if your gaze is meant to be sincere, avoid staring into a Japanese person's eyes. In Japan long stares are regarded as bad manners and people prefer to keep their gaze fixed on the neck.
- Never wink at anyone in Hong Kong as it is considered to be impolite.
- In the Middle East and Far East always present things to people with the right hand and do not use your left hand for eating as it is regarded as 'unclean'.
- Japanese people bow rather than shake hands.
- Nodding your head means 'no' in parts of Greece, Yugoslavia and Turkey and shaking your head means 'yes'.
- Never show the sole of your shoe when you are in an Arab country as this is considered to be a grave insult. However, eye contact is important in the Arab world.
- Do not blow your nose at a business meeting with Japanese people and always present your business card with both hands.

Activity 6.2

You are responsible for internal communications within an import/export company with offices around the world. The firm has recently moved to team working within departments, which means that managers hold regular briefings with their teams. Write a memo to managers giving guidance on the importance of appropriate body language when briefing teams.

Listening skills

Good listening skills are important in marketing, simply because you will use them during meetings, interviews, negotiations, other people's presentations and when you are in a selling or briefing situation.

You need to work at your listening skills so that you possess all the necessary and relevant information, avoid wasting time and maintain good relations with both internal and external customers. Listening skills are particularly important if you are dealing with a customer who is trying to air grievances.

Many people imagine that listening is something that just happens. However, it is important that you distinguish between hearing and listening. *Hearing* is what might happen when you have the radio playing in the background whilst you do something else. *Listening* means engaging your mind and your memory, and you are active in selecting information, organizing, interpreting and storing it.

Listening skills are a vital part of customer care. By using effective listening skills you can obtain all the necessary and relevant information you need to find out what customers want or what they are not happy with. Listening is an active, not a passive activity. By checking what a customer has said and paraphrasing it, you can check that you have understood exactly what they mean. This avoids confusion and wasting time.

In many situations where you are dealing with unhappy customers, listening skills are very important to understand the problem. Often customers will go into great detail about a number of things that they are not happy with. However, it is usually one thing in particular that they want rectified. A good listener can select the most relevant information and decide what can be done about the situation.

Barriers to listening

Your thought processes operate four times faster than most people speak, and as a listener you may become bored and allow your mind to wander. You may regard what is being said as dull or irrelevant and close your mind, thus missing vital pieces of information.

You may have prejudices or fixed ideas about things and, if you are listening to something with which you disagree, you may react by pretending to listen but 'tuning out' to the message or becoming angry and distracted from the message that is being communicated.

You may be listening to someone who is talking about something technical that you do not understand, with the result that you stop following the conversation and may become too embarrassed to ask questions.

You may be listening to a great number of facts and figures and lose track of what is being said because of information overload.

How can we be better listeners?

1. Through active listening you can actively concentrate on what the person is saying and make a conscious attempt to understand. You could even make selective notes of the key points that have been made.
2. By being a patient listener and letting the person speak without interruption.
3. By being open-minded and guarding against prejudice and stereotyping so that you do not 'tune out' from the message.
4. By seeking clarification you can check with the person what they have said, paraphrasing in your own words.
5. By being sympathetic and showing empathy, particularly if you are listening to a complaint. You can demonstrate this with appropriate body language, such as making eye contact, nodding your head in agreement or making encouraging sounds/ statements, such as, 'mm-hmm', 'that's interesting' and 'I understand'.
6. By being helpful, particularly in a complaint situation. You need to resist the temptation to argue and look for solutions to the problem instead.

Activity 6.3

A colleague has been promoted and will have to interview staff in future. He lacks interview experience and asks for guidance on listening in interviews. Suggest four ways in which he can be an effective listener in interviews.

Using the telephone

Advantages of using the telephone

With all the various methods of communication available to people, the telephone remains a popular tool for the following reasons:

- It provides quick, easy access over long distances (even if the recipient of the communication is not available it is usually possible to leave a message either with a colleague or on an answer machine/voicemail system)
- It is a relatively cheap means of communication
- It is interactive (it provides a two-way form of communication)
- It is possible to protect the time of others by deciding whether or not to put the caller through
- It is easier to hide your emotion on the telephone if you wish, because people cannot see your facial expression and body language
- It is much easier to terminate a conversation with someone on the telephone than if you are in a face-to-face situation with them.

Disadvantages of using the telephone

- There is no permanent record of the communication and it is therefore difficult to verify the contents of a telephone call unless you record it.
- There is no opportunity to judge body language, which can make negotiation situations difficult. Equally, some customers may not feel confident doing business this way, particularly with important or complex financial decisions, such as buying mortgages or pensions.
- You can become involved in a 'telephone tennis' situation, where messages go back and forth and the caller never actually gets to speak to the person they want to communicate with.
- The truth of a situation, whether someone is actually in a meeting or not, is difficult to gauge.

Planning telephone calls

The most effective approach in using the telephone in terms of saving time and money is to adapt the PASS planning framework, to ensure you make effective and efficient telephone calls.

Purpose

Plan your call and be sure of the purpose of your call. This will guide you in deciding what you have to say. Have all the relevant information to hand, such as the correct telephone number. And, for example, if you were trying to arrange a meeting, you would need your diary. If you were ringing to query an invoice, you would need the original letter with the quote and the invoice that you received.

Audience

Consider who you are contacting, as this will influence what you say and how you say it.

Structure

In planning your message it may be helpful to make a checklist of points you wish to make as a reminder for use during the telephone conversation.

Style

When making a business call you may adopt a different style to the one you use for personal calls. The style you adopt is made up of the words you use, the way you order sentences, your pronunciation and your tone.

You may indeed adopt a telephone voice that close friends and family do not recognize. You do not need to do this but you should communicate in a clear, organized and succinct way. You may need to spell out words, using other words to indicate the letter you mean where there may be confusion. For example, you may say 'F' for foxtrot, not 'S' for sierra to distinguish like-sounding letters. You may also group numbers together, if you are communicating a telephone number or reference number of some sort. For example, you may read out a telephone number as zero, one, six, one, and then pause before reading out the rest of the number.

In business calls, you should avoid slang or words that are over-familiar, such as 'OK', 'yeah', 'ta ra then'.

You should be confident when making a business telephone call, or at least sound confident. One of the advantages of telephones (at least those that are not videophones) is that the recipient of the call cannot see you. When someone is slightly nervous on the telephone, they sound hurried and use careless speech. Consequently you should speak slightly more slowly than your usual pace. This is also important because the recipient of the call cannot lip read, so it is important that you pronounce words clearly.

The tone of voice you use in telephone conversations is very important, as your body language cannot be seen (see Figure 6.2). You can overcome the barrier of not being seen by adopting the tone of voice that is relevant to the message being communicated (see Voice characteristics in the section on Non-verbal communication skills in this unit). You should also vary the tone of voice you use, as a relentless monotone can give the impression either that you are boring or that you are bored with the conversation.

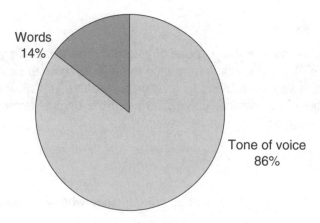

Figure 6.2 How we receive messages by telephone

Guidelines for making effective telephone calls

Once you get through, greet the person who answers, identify yourself, your company and ask for the person you wish to speak to. At this point you may have to give a brief outline of the purpose of your call.

Having made sure that you are speaking to the right person, make your call in a courteous, clear and concise way. You should be prepared for the person you need to speak to not being available and be able to give a shortened version of the message you wish to communicate. Alternatively, if it is not appropriate to précis your message, you should politely ask for the recipient of the call to ring you back.

Guidelines for receiving calls

Organizations have their own procedures for answering the telephone, so you will find that this section provides some guidelines which may have to be amended to fit in with your own organization's system.

Whatever procedures are set down for staff to follow, it is essential that a friendly and efficient image be conveyed to anyone who contacts the organization.

Callers should not be left waiting while the telephone rings. Some organizations stipulate how quickly the telephone should be answered. It is inappropriate for a caller to be left waiting for several minutes while information is being retrieved. It is equally unacceptable for a caller to be passed around several departments or to be made to feel as if they are an unwelcome interruption. Good telephone technique is vital for the maintenance of good public relations.

Putting a customer on hold

Ideally, customers should not be left hanging on the line. If you consider it is going to take some time to get the right person on the line, it is better to take down the relevant details so that the right person can contact the caller later. If, however, you do need to put the customer on hold, then you should ask for their permission first and briefly tell them why you need to do this. If you have been finding out information while the caller was put on hold and you go back to them, it is only good manners to thank them for holding.

Callers are rarely asked if they mind being put on hold. What usually happens is that when callers draw breath at the end of a sentence, they are summarily sent to telephone limbo and forced to listen to music, while the person on the other end of the line tries to transfer them or consults their files.

Transferring a call

Customers become intolerant when they are transferred over and over again, and particularly when they have to explain their situation several times.

The best approach, if it is possible to do so, is to explain why the call needs to be transferred and to whom. You should also ask if the customer minds being transferred. Before you hang up, make sure there is someone to pick up the call. Before the customer talks to the person they have been transferred to, you should briefly outline the nature of the call, so that the caller does not have to repeat details again.

Taking messages

It is very important to get the details of a message right the first time. This is where your listening skills will be very useful. It will mean taking the time to clarify the caller's name, company, telephone number, the nature of the call and the action required.

You need, therefore, the right equipment, such as a pen and message notepad, at hand. Most organizations have pre-printed pads where you complete the relevant boxes with a tick to indicate the action required. Always print your name on the message pad so that the recipient of the message can come back to you if they need to clarify any details.

Answering calls

The circumstances may vary:

- *Answering your telephone extension where calls come in through a switchboard operator* The caller knows the company they have reached and you only need identify yourself by giving your name. For example: 'Good morning Andrew Kelly speaking, how can I help?'
- *Answering the telephone on behalf of a department* You could give your name and the name of the department. For example: 'Good morning, Technical Support, Andrew speaking, how can I help you?'
- *Answering the telephone on behalf of the company* The caller needs to be given the company name and perhaps your name. For example: 'Good morning, Pine Box Productions, how may I help you?'

The greeting should be used to demonstrate friendliness. The telephone should be answered within a certain number of rings; three to five is normal.

You need to be prepared with the right equipment so that you can deal with the enquiry or instructions given to you during the telephone conversation. This will vary depending on your circumstances but usually comprises at the very least: pen, message pad, company extension list, notepad and diary.

General guidelines for using the telephone

- Answer the telephone promptly
- Smile when you first pick up the telephone
- Begin with an appropriate greeting
- Identify yourself/your department or the organization
- Establish the caller's needs
- Speak clearly
- Speak slowly
- Avoid jargon
- Be courteous
- Be concise
- Take messages accurately and pass them to the appropriate person where necessary
- Listen carefully and do not interrupt the customer
- Show empathy and understanding
- If dealing with an angry customer, do not argue with the caller or offer lame excuses
- If you undertake to do something for a customer during a telephone conversation, do it, don't just hope they won't come back
- Give the caller a name, department or extension number to enable them to pursue the matter if they need to call back at a later date/time
- End the call effectively so that the caller knows what action is to be taken, what has been agreed or when someone will come back to them
- Close the call politely with an appropriate greeting and thank the caller for calling.

Conference calls

The technology exists to have several different people in different locations talking to each other at the same time. While these conversations lack the impact of a face to face meeting, they can be a convenient and relatively inexpensive method of getting people together for instant feedback.

However, it can be difficult to avoid situations where everyone speaks at once and the conversation flow is often inhibited by the lack of non-verbal cues.

Activity 6.4

Effective use of telephones

You are the Marketing Manager for a chain of hotels. Write a memo for circulation to all reception staff about the effective use of telephones. In particular, you should focus on the appropriate way to deal with incoming calls, the transfer of calls and message taking.

Presentation skills

Types of presentations

For most marketers it is an inevitable part of their professional career to give speeches or presentations. In the early part of your career you could be asked to give an informal briefing to colleagues on a recent training course or a demonstration on how a piece of equipment works. As you become more established you may find yourself going through the results of a campaign to a group of managers, giving colleagues a progress update on a project, putting forward your proposals to a client or even delivering a sales pitch.

Planning an effective speech or presentation

As with all communications, the PASS framework is a relevant planning framework and will help you plan the content and delivery of your presentation.

Purpose
The planning of the presentation begins with objectives. Consider the purpose of the presentation, why you are delivering it and what you hope to achieve. At the end of the presentation you should be able to determine if you have achieved your objectives.

Audience
To help you decide on the message you want to deliver and how you should deliver it, you should consider who is your intended audience. Consider what their needs are in terms of what they need to know, how long you have with them, the size of the group and the type of room they will be in.

Structure
Knowing what your purpose is and what your audience's requirements are will help you decide on the structure of your presentation. You should decide on the key points, the order that they should go and how you will link the material together.

Style
To determine the style of the presentation you will have to decide the level of formality and involvement that is appropriate. For a small group, you could deliver a presentation on a complex matter in a fairly informal way with a high level of participation from the audience. You also need to decide if you are going to use visual aids.

Composing the message

Decide what you are going to say, having first, if necessary, researched your topic. List the points you *could* include and select those that you *must* include. Allocate time to each point and develop a sequence.

You should try to make your presentation conversational rather than trying to learn hundreds of words off by heart. One way could be to write out your talk in longhand, reduce it to shorthand notes and reduce that to crib cards. Your delivery should then be based on the crib cards.

Another approach is to imagine that your audience will get your message from a picture. Once you have an outline picture, then you can take people into the detail by creating a series of smaller pictures by breaking down the argument more simply.

To develop this approach you could use a mind map. The idea is that you draw a circle with your topic heading in it and from that draw branches that are labelled with four or five key areas. Then draw a branch off each of these branches to indicate other detailed points. For example, if you were giving a presentation about the opening of a DIY store, your mind map might look like the diagram in Figure 6.3. You could then use prompt cards to remind you of the key areas and sub-points from your mind map.

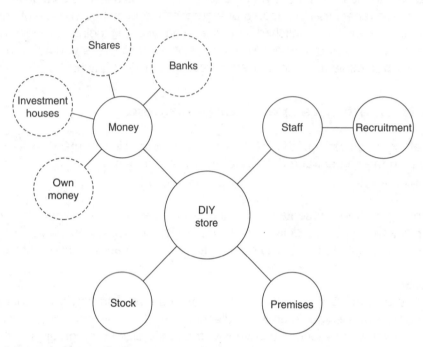

Figure 6.3 Example of a mind map

Whatever method you use to compose the content of your message, you should plan your talk so that it has a beginning, a middle and an end. A well-known quote that describes this approach is as follows: 'Tell them what you are going to tell them, then tell them, then tell them what you told them.'

Preparing for the talk

You should ensure that you have prepared the stage management aspect of the presentation. If it is a large, organized conference that you are speaking at, then this will be done for you. If not, then you need to check the following:

o The layout of the chairs and tables (for a small group a horseshoe shape is often better than lining people in rows)
o That there are enough chairs and tables for the audience
o That you will be visible from where you are going to stand
o That there is a lectern or table for your paperwork
o That the equipment for visual aids works
o That the lighting is adequate
o That the room is tidy and has adequate heating/ventilation.

Delivering the talk

A good presentation can be broken down into message, body language and voice. According to Eileen Sheridan in an article in *The Guardian* (2001), 93 per cent of our communication with others is non-verbal. What you actually say makes up only 7 per cent of the picture.

Body language

The nerves that some people feel before delivering a presentation are usually connected with having to stand up in front of an audience that is totally focused on you. You should try not to be seen to be nervous by having control of your body language. You should aim to do the following:

- Don't look tense – relax your jaw muscles and smile (be careful if you are delivering bad news, though)
- Stand upright with your shoulders relaxed
- Do not fold your arms across your chest
- Don't hunch up/bend your head down to read from your notes – just refer to them occasionally
- Maintain eye contact with the entire group – don't stare at one individual or one section of the group. This can be difficult if you arrange the group in a horseshoe shape
- Avoid gesticulating wildly or other distracting mannerisms, such as jangling change in your pocket or scratching.

Voice

Except in specific circumstances where you might need to use an authoritative tone, you would normally use a friendly tone to deliver a presentation.

You should consider practising your talk to calculate how long it takes you to get through it. One problem to avoid is an attack of nerves that tempts you into the 'racehorse' syndrome of getting your head down and charging through to the end of the presentation. Take care to consciously slow yourself down.

You can use pauses not only to slow down the pace but also to place emphasis on important points. You also need to give people time to absorb the information in any visual aids you use.

Try to vary the pitch of your voice. Another technique for slowing yourself down is to modulate your voice. If you make your voice rise and fall, as you do when you tell a joke or a story to others, you are less likely to end up with a fast monotone that sends the audience to sleep. This will enable you to put emphasis on certain words or parts of your speech. You also need to sound energetic and enthusiastic to convince people that you are worth listening to.

Use of visual aids and technology

Visual aids, such as overhead projector slides or acetates, pictures, slides of still photography or flip charts, can be used to give variety and impact to a presentation, particularly when you are presenting lists or numerical information. However, they should be produced to a high standard or they can give rise to a negative reaction.

If you are using visual aids, you should be careful how you use them. Check that you have pens to use on the flip chart or that the stand works. Check that you can focus the overhead projector. Always check that all the audience can see visual aids.

When you use visual aids, do not stand in front of them and obstruct the audience's view. Do not read from them verbatim – it is better to talk around the issues that the visual aid encapsulates. When you are finished with the topic, remove the visual aid so that it does not distract the audience.

We work in an age of specialized software such as Powerpoint, video walls and a plethora of acoustic equipment that can enhance a presentation. Used sensibly, these tools can bring clarity and add impact to a presentation. But it is essential to remember that technology is an aid, not a crutch. Unlike a brief television commercial, a successful speech is rarely a triumph of style over content. If you do not get the words right, your audience will quickly lose interest.

Tutor day task	We need 7 groups – so if 20 people could be 6 groups of 3 and 1 group of 4.

Tutor day task

In your group analyse the candidate answer
▪ to identify the positive & negative aspects
▪ to suggest suitable teaching strategies to overcome common problems shown in answers

We need 7 groups – so if 20 people could be 6 groups of 3 and 1 group of 4.
You have 30 minutes to look at a question, so if you are group 1a, analyse the candidate's answer to q1a on last session's paper and identify the positive and negative aspects of the answer and suggest suitable teaching strategies to overcome the problems shown in the answer.
I'd like to stress that these are fairly common answers…
Could you use flip chart paper to put down your main points and appoint one person to be scribe and another to present on behalf of your group.
After the half hour is up we will come back for a plenary session to see what all the groups have to say.

Figure 6.4 A slide and the speaker's notes

The use of video walls at conferences is growing as companies want their brands and the people speaking on their behalf to appear larger than life. Unfortunately for presenters, it means that every nervous lick of the lips and gravy stain can be seen in close-up. They can also have an unfortunate effect on people's clothing. Clothing with big patterns, very bright colours and glittering jewellery can blur and produce a strobe effect. The presenter can also blend into the background, if the colour of their clothing is the same as the background.

Always assume that the technology you plan to use for your presentation is going to fail. If your speech does not stand up on its own without the technology, you should question whether the script is good enough.

Verbal skills

To help you decide on how you should deliver your talk, you should consider how people listen and take in information. People tend to take in information at the beginning and at the end and only snippets throughout.

So it is a good idea to pepper a presentation with devices that bring the audience back to you. You can do this with metaphors or analogies (comparing something to something else that everyone is familiar with; for example, the business was an acorn but has now grown into an oak tree) and anecdotes or examples (stories from real life). These can be very effective tools, but do not over-use them or you might confuse your audience.

As a general rule, use punchy sentences and avoid unnecessary jargon. Beware of jokes. They can be hard to carry off as they require excellent timing. Also, you risk offending your audience.

You need to connect with your audience, so use vocabulary that fits in with them. You can add emphasis by using the following devices:

○ Repetition, for example, 'This campaign has increased our turnover by £500,000 – that's right, half a million pounds!'
○ Rhetorical questions, for example, 'You may ask me what are we going to do about it but I am asking you "What are you going to do about it?"'

o   Quotations, for example, 'As Martin Luther King said: "I have a dream"'
o   Statistical evidence, 'A dissatisfied customer tells nine other people about their dissatisfaction'.

Questions and feedback

The great advantage of presentations is that they are interactive. You can sense how your message is going down with your audience and even get instant feedback. However, you may find it very disruptive to handle questions during your presentation. If this is the case, you should say that you would be happy to answer questions at the end. You should then leave time at the end for questions and comments from the audience.

Techniques for handling questions/feedback

o   Repeat any questions so that the audience can hear and be involved in this part of the session
o   If the question or comment is relevant, then either answer the question directly or thank the person for their contribution
o   If the question is rambling or unclear, try to clarify and retrieve one simple question from the narrative
o   If the question is irrelevant, you could say that it is outside the scope of the presentation
o   If the question is hostile or you don't agree with the points made, accept as much as you can of the points made but do not get drawn into a long argument
o   If you cannot answer the question, admit that you cannot but enlist the help of the audience, or you could say that you will get back to the person once you have had a chance to look into the matter.

Evaluating objectives

At the end of the presentation, consider whether you persuaded people to do something or make a decision about something, or did you sell something, clarify something, change people's minds about something, inspire people to think about something in a different way – in other words, did you achieve your objectives?

Summary

In this unit you have studied:

o   The role of communication skills in marketing

o   How to use and interpret non-verbal communication skills effectively

o   How to be a good listener

o   Why the telephone is an important marketing tool and how to use it appropriately

o   How to deliver dynamic presentations.

Further study and examination preparation

Attempt Question 2(a) and 5(b) from the June 2000 examination paper and Question 4(a) from the December 2000 paper. Go to www.cimeduhub.com to access Specimen Answers and Senior Examiner's advice for these exam questions.

Exam hint

Do not rote-learn the body language section but be prepared to apply your understanding of it in questions that are set in a variety of contexts, such as managing staff, in interviews, dealing with customers and delivering presentations. Be prepared to answer questions on the use of listening, telephone use and presentations that apply your knowledge to marketing situations.

unit 7

communicating in meetings, interviews and negotiations

In this unit you will:

o   Develop your understanding of why meetings take place

o   Look at the different types of meetings that occur

o   See how to manage meetings effectively

o   Become familiar with meetings' terminology

o   Examine meetings' documentation

o   Understand the role of interviews and negotiations in communicating with others

o   Appreciate the different stages of interviews and negotiations

o   Recognize different negotiation techniques.

By the end of this unit you will be able to:

o   Manage and lead meetings effectively

o   Prepare appropriate meetings documentation

o   Lead and contribute to interviews and negotiations

o   Demonstrate good questioning skills

o   Demonstrate appropriate interpersonal behaviour in negotiations.

Study Guide

This unit covers indicative content area 4.4 and 4.6. The first part of the unit develops your understanding of meetings, how to lead them effectively and the documentation associated with them. The second part of the unit covers the topic of communicating in interviews and negotiations. The unit will take two hours to read and a further two hours to complete the activities.

Study tip

Use any opportunities at work where you attend meetings to take notes on how they are managed and how people interact. Develop your skills at meetings by asking a colleague or supervisor to evaluate how you lead and contribute to meetings.

Meetings

Meetings are an assembly of people for the purpose of discussion. They occur face-to-face or remotely by using satellite communications or video conferencing. Meetings are an extremely useful means of communication but while they present good opportunities for obtaining immediate verbal feedback and demonstrating or observing non-verbal feedback, they can present problems if they are not organized and planned for.

The advantages of meetings are that information can be exchanged and an immediate response can be had. Any feedback or questions can be dealt with immediately. With traditional face-to-face meetings, body language and tone of voice are very much evident and people can interpret these signs or use them to add to the communication process. Sometimes non-verbal communication and tone of voice can be distorted when using communications technology to have a meeting.

Meetings can be informative, can help build teams and can improve motivation. Meetings are also a good way to convey sensitive and confidential information.

However, if people have to attend too many meetings and/or attend meetings that are badly organized and do not achieve their objectives, they can be jaded by their experience and will resent the time spent, which they may feel they could have used more productively.

Reasons for meeting

In Marketing, meetings can be used to do the following:

- Reach decisions after discussion
- Convey information, e.g. to update people about the progress of a project
- Obtain formal approval of decisions or make group decisions
- Exchange of ideas, e.g. about how a campaign should be developed
- Discuss marketing plans
- Review an advertising campaign
- Plan corporate events
- Review the progress of new product development projects.

Types of meeting

Meetings range from informal discussions to formal meetings and can be about any number of matters.

Informal meetings

Informal meetings could just comprise two or more colleagues talking in the course of their work or as they go about their business but can be extremely fruitful in terms of conveying information and even making decisions and co-ordinating work.

Examples of informal meetings:

- Team briefings or departmental meetings
- Meetings with clients to present work or provide an update on work
- Meetings with prospective clients
- Task group meetings to plan projects, decide on who does what and make decisions.

Formal meetings

In formal meetings people are appointed to specific roles, such as chairperson and secretary, follow a particular procedure for conducting the meetings and use specific terminology about the proceedings. Formal meetings have a written agenda which participants follow, involve circulating minutes after the meeting as a record of what has occurred and tend to have a formal seating arrangement with the Chairperson at the top of the table.

Examples of formal meetings:

- Company board meetings or annual general meetings (AGMs)
- Large union meetings
- Social club meetings with a constitution, e.g. a tennis club
- Branch membership meeting, e.g. local branch of CIM.

Managing meetings

Meetings require careful planning and organization. Problems can occur if people arrive at a meeting with different objectives about what is to be achieved. If the meeting is not well organized and run to time, time can be wasted and people can become demotivated, even hostile. Information should be clearly conveyed before, during and after the meeting so that there are no misunderstandings. If contributions to the meeting are not handled properly – ensuring everyone has a chance to contribute but the discussion is kept within the parameters of the agenda – then it will lead to aimless discussion and/or a small minority dominating the meeting.

There are several ways to ensure that a meeting goes well:

- Consider whether the meeting really needs to be held
- Establish clear objectives
- Draw up a list of relevant participants and invite them to attend
- You may need to invite participants to provide you with items for discussion and/or draft a list of matters to be discussed in the form of an agenda

- Ensure participants are clear about the following: the meeting's purpose, the date, start and finish time and venue
- Distribute the agenda (you will read more about this later in the unit) and any additional material to participants in advance of the meeting
- Decide who will lead or chair the meeting
- Decide who will keep a record of proceedings
- Visit the venue before the meeting to check the layout and facilities
- Ensure that the meeting starts and finishes on time
- Ensure that there are no interruptions
- The chairperson should follow the agenda and take control of any conflict in the meeting
- The chairperson should summarize the key points or decisions made as the meeting progresses and keep the meeting moving from item to item
- The chairperson should also notice when people want to contribute and encourage quieter participants to contribute
- The chairperson should put any decision to the vote
- The meeting should be closed formally to ensure that participants know that it has ended
- After the meeting, accurate and impartial minutes should be circulated to participants and other relevant people.

 ## Activity 7.1

In your absence your colleague is to lead a product development meeting to check the progress review of product x. Your colleague, who is a very quiet person has asked for some guidance on how best to lead this informal project meeting.

Constituting a formal meeting

A formal meeting is only properly constituted if it is convened (called) according to a set of regulations (statutory or otherwise). The main issues are as follows:

1. A meeting must have a chairperson who oversees the conduct and progression of the meeting
2. A meeting must have a quorum, i.e. a minimum number of persons who are physically present, as stated in the regulations.

Formal meetings are completely different from informal meetings in their organization and procedure. A set of strict rules and conventions is followed, and formal documents are required before the meeting takes place.

Formal meetings procedure

Formal meetings are usually organized according to specific procedures and conventions.

Motions

A motion is a proposal put before the meeting in order that it can be discussed and relevant decisions made. However, not all items on an agenda are proposals which must be voted on. An agenda item may just be information that needs to be communicated to the rest of the meeting. If the motion is approved or *carried* by the meeting, it then becomes a *resolution* or decision. The procedure for dealing with a motion means that the proposer must speak first on the matter, followed by the seconder. Discussion against the motion usually follows, but the *right of reply* means that the mover (person speaking for the motion) has the last say before the item is put to the vote.

Rules concerning motions mean that they should be feasible and not *ultra vires*, i.e. outside the power or scope of the meeting. Motions need to be worded so that ambiguities do not exist. For example, a motion stating 'That a ban on smoking be introduced' is too vague because it does not state exactly where the ban extends to and when it should take effect.

A motion may be put forward to the meeting and although participants or members of the meeting may agree with it in principle, they may want to change the wording slightly so that it is more precise. Alternatively they may believe that the fine detail of the proposal should be changed. If this is the case, then an *amendment* or change may be put forward. If it is seconded the amendment will be voted on. There may well be several amendments and these will all need to be voted upon.

If enough people vote for an amendment, it becomes a substantive motion. At this point it is voted on again and becomes a resolution if it is carried. Even then a resolution can be changed slightly by the inclusion of extra words, referred to as an *addendum* and a *rider*.

Procedural motions can be made and are aimed at making meetings more effective. So if a speech is going on too long, the chairperson may use the procedural motion 'That the question be now put' to hurry business along.

If the motion 'That the meeting proceed to the next item of business' is carried, the meeting stops discussion on that item and goes on to the next item on the agenda. Often this happens because agreement on the subject seems unlikely and so it seems better for the matter to be left for the present.

An item on the agenda can be postponed with the motion 'That the discussion be adjourned' and if it is adjourned 'sine die', no date for when the matter should be discussed again is specified.

Points of order
Points of order are interruptions in the meeting, voiced when participants feel that the regulations are not being adhered to. For example:

o The meeting is not *quorate* There are not enough people present as stipulated in the rules to form a quorum
o The speaker is not *speaking to the agenda* That the item being discussed is not on the agenda
o The subject is *ultra vires* Outside the powers of the meeting
o The speaker should *address the chair* All remarks should be addressed to the chairperson rather than allow a situation where discussion occurs between other participants at the meeting.

Voting

Decisions are made through voting, usually by a show of hands (open voting), or by a general voice vote, where it is judged whether yes or no is said the loudest or even by secret ballot.

The results of voting may be declared in the following way:

- o Passed *unanimously* Everyone voted in favour
- o Passed *nem con* No one voted against but only a few have voted for the proposal with the majority abstaining
- o *Lost* The majority voted against
- o *Casting vote* The chairperson is given an additional vote to break the deadlock of an equal number voting for and against a proposal.

Terminology of meetings

There are a number of vocabulary items that are often exclusive to meetings, such as the following:

- o *Proposer* Speaks about the statement/argument that they have proposed
- o *Seconder* Supports the proposal
- o *Quorum* The minimum number of people that must be present at a meeting, according to the rules
- o *Motion* A proposal to be considered at the meeting
- o *Amendment* To the proposal which will have to be voted for and, if carried, accepted
- o *Collective responsibility* A rule by which all participants agree to be bound by a decision
- o *Casting vote* By the chairperson if there are an equal number of votes on either side of an argument
- o *Adjourn* This means that a meeting will be held over to another time or date
- o *Constitution* A set of rules by which the members of a group are expected to abide
- o *Ex officio* An individual given rights and powers by reason of the position he or she holds
- o *Mover* An individual who speaks on behalf of a motion
- o *Opposer* An individual who speaks against a motion
- o *Point of order* Drawing attention to the breach of rules or procedures
- o *Proxy* This means on behalf of another person, e.g. proxy vote
- o *Resolution* A motion that has been carried.

Meeting documents

The main meetings documentation comprises: the notice, the agenda and the minutes. These are used for formal meetings and sometimes also for informal meetings.

The notice

The notice will be prepared and circulated before the date of the meeting, according to the constitution of the company and any other regulations with which the organization may have to comply.

If a large number of participants are to attend, it may be impractical to communicate with them all individually, therefore notices of the meeting may be placed on notice boards as a main channel of communication, especially if these are regularly accessed by potential participants.

Where individuals can be contacted directly, the following channels of written communication may be used:

1.   An invitation printed on a card or note
2.   An internal memorandum
3.   A personal letter.

If the agenda (described below) is already drawn up and available for circulation, it is usually included with the notice to enable the participants to study its content before the meeting.

The minutes of the last meeting (also described below) may be attached to the notice so that any issues in respect to the points made can be stated in advance of the meeting, especially if the minutes of the previous meeting have to be approved as a matter of procedure. Figures 7.1 and 7.2 give examples of notices.

NOTICE OF ANNUAL GENERAL MEETING

Notice is hereby given that the Annual General Meeting of Anyone Limited will be held at the Anyplace Hotel, Anywhere Road, Anywhere on 10 June 200X at 10.30 am for the following purposes:

1. To receive and adopt the Reports of the Directors and Auditors and the Accounts for the period ended 31 March 200X.
2. To declare a final dividend.
3. To re-elect Mr J Sugree as a Managing Director of the company.
4. To transact any other business.

By order of the Board
Mr B Keating
Company Secretary

Figure 7.1 Notice of a formal AGM

MEMORANDUM

TO: The Marketing Task Group.

FROM: Roy Keane

DATE: 19 September 200X

The next Marketing meeting will take place on Thursday 25 September 200X at 2:30 pm in the board room at head office.

As usual meeting will be reviewing current marketing projects and will also be discussing matters relating to developing the company's marketing plan, so please forward dates to me in advance of the meeting which indicate when you can be away from normal office duties for a 3 days block. In addition, if you have any other items you would like putting on the agenda please contact me on 0161 448 7212 no later than Monday 21 October 200X.

Figure 7.2 Notice for an internal meeting

The agenda

This is the schedule of 'things to be done', i.e. the subjects to be discussed, which is prepared by the secretary after having enabled all participants to propose items for the agenda. Although an agenda is not an obligation for the conduct of a meeting, it is a useful tool for guiding the discussion and ensuring that the full scope of the meeting is covered.

Once the agenda has been set, it is then discussed with the chairperson in terms of suitability of subject matter and order of items which the meeting will follow.

The agenda will then be distributed to all the participants so that they are aware of the subject matter of the forthcoming meeting and the order of proceedings, together with any supplementary material that needs to be considered and the minutes of the last meeting. This communication process enables the participants to prepare themselves in advance and also to decide whether their presence is necessary for the full duration of the meeting.

Copies of the agenda are either sent out with the notice of the meeting or distributed to participants as they arrive at the designated location.

A special agenda is prepared for the chairperson, which contains more details than the document circulated to the participants and the names of any particular participants making a special contribution (e.g. presenting a report), with space for the chairperson to make notes on the meeting for personal reference.

Agendas normally contain the following items:

1. Apologies for absence – announced by the chairperson once the meeting has been officially opened and the time and date recorded by the secretary.
2. Minutes of the previous meeting – the chairperson will ask members whether the minutes represent an accurate record of the previous meeting and if so, he/she will sign them as such.
3. Matters arising is an opportunity for participants to declare views or report back on developments since the last meeting.
4. Correspondence from parties outside the meeting may be read and considered.
5. The main agenda items are then opened and discussed in turn, with the chairperson trying to keep the meeting moving ahead (particularly if a time constraint was imposed at the start) and aiming to reach a consensus on the main points. The types of items discussed will reflect the nature of the meeting, which may be to produce plans, solve organizational problems, deliver reports or feedback, debate proposals or reach decisions.
6. Any other business (AOB) is stated and discussed. If an item is of relevance to the general discussion or appropriate for the meeting, it may be raised under this section. If the issue is considered unimportant or unsuitable for the present meeting, it may be carried over to another or a separate meeting is called.
7. Date of the next meeting is discussed and agreed and the chairperson closes the meeting by thanking the participants for attending the meeting.

Finally, agendas will vary from meeting to meeting and may be a reflection of the following:

1. Degree of formality required for the meeting, which will determine the style of layout in the agenda and state the procedures to be followed
2. Length of the meeting, which will be determined by:

   o The number of subjects to be discussed
   o The complexity of the subject matter.

Snack Attack

The Quality Sandwich Delivery Service

MARKETING MEETING

AGENDA

19 September 200X at 2:30pm
in the boardroom at head office.

1. Apologies for absence.
2. Minutes of the last meeting.
3. Matters arising.
4. Evaluation of radio advertising campaign.
5. Update of database software.
6. Discuss product development for Winter hot soup range.
7. Motion: 'That the company purchases two new delivery vans before the Christmas period'. Proposed: Paul Rapaporte Seconded: David Surinam
8. Company Marketing Plan Arrangements
9. Any other business.
10. Date of next meeting.

Figure 7.3 An agenda

The *chairperson's agenda* is different to the one described above in two respects:

1. Each item on the agenda has additional notes which are pertinent to the discussion that will take place in the meeting and for which the chairperson should be suitably prepared with background information or sensitivity in handling material presented and discussed or points raised
2. A right-hand margin, which is wide enough for the chairperson to make notes during the meeting, is incorporated into the layout of his/her personal agenda.

The *duties of the chairperson* are as follows:

1. Keep the meeting to the agenda and in good order so that the business can proceed smoothly
2. Be unbiased and fair in allowing the members and participants to make their contribution without taking too much of the meeting's time
3. Allow only one person at a time to address the meeting and take a decision on the sequence of speakers if more than one wishes to make a contribution
4. Ensure that all issues and points of debate are addressed to the chairperson, thereby avoiding the deterioration of the meeting into fragmented groups or arguments
5. Conduct the system of voting if this is deemed necessary during the meeting or at its conclusion
6. Keep an overall sense of the meeting according to the original agenda and the logic of the discussion.

The minutes

These are a written record of the transactions that took place and should be as accurate as possible, reflecting the duration and general tone of the meeting.

The minutes are usually taken by the secretary, who should have them typed and distributed as quickly as possible after the meeting as they are an important channel of communication and source of reference.

The style or format used to present them, i.e. narrative or structured in some way, should reflect the type of meeting and needs of the participants.

There are three types of minutes:

1. *Resolution minutes* These are minutes where only the resolutions are recorded and therefore do not reflect the tone of the meeting or specific points made leading to the resolution
2. *Narrative minutes* These are a brief summary of the meeting which led up to the resolution (decisions) and include the comments made by the participants which have gone on record as their judgement of the arguments preceding the resolution
3. *Action minutes* These minutes indicate the specific courses of action that need to be taken as a result of the resolutions made in the course of the meeting and the individuals responsible for the action items.

Research and Development Group
Minutes

Minutes of the Meeting held in the 'Panelled Room' at 'Building Headquarters', Bromley, Kent on October 15th 20XX at 4 pm.

Present: T. Stones (Chair), A. Peters (Secretary), L. Simons, K. Andrews, J. Clarke

1 Apologies for absence.
   Apologies for absence were received from J. Thyme, L. Young and P. Ankers.

2 Minutes of the last meeting.
   The minutes of the last meeting were taken as read and signed as a true record.

3 Matters arising.
   Further to item 2, the Chairman has received a report of the new innovation currently in prototype stage and will circulate a copy to all members before the next meeting.

4 Proposal to cut the budget by £I million to be phased in over a period of three years.
   All members present argued for a strong statement to be issued to the M.D. on the consequences for new and existing projects as a result of this budget cut and seek clarification if jobs are also to be lost in this process.

5 New Product Development.
   Len Simons and Ken Andrews presented a visual report on the new products to be commercialized by the end of the financial year.

6 AOB.
   Jane Clarke raised the need for a new laser printer. Angela Peters will receive literature and circulate this to members of the group before the next meeting.

7 Date of next meeting.
   The next meeting of the R&D group was scheduled for January 10th 20XX at Building H.Q.

   Signed X   T. Stones (Chair) Director R&D. Date Nov. 10th 20XX

Figure 7.4 Resolution minutes

ITEM 7: The task group discussed the proposal to purchase two extra delivery vans.

JD felt that the business development work in the two new industrial estates in the East of the city had resulted in several new contracts that would be coming on stream in the next few weeks and this would put undue pressure on the current vans.

HG also admitted that the run up to Christmas would be very busy and extra resources would be needed.

GW complained about the extra cost and suggested buying one van as an interim measure. By a majority of 5:1 it was agreed that two additional vehicles should be purchased by the end of the month.

Figure 7.5 Narrative minutes

However, if the discussion went another way then action minutes might look like Figure 7.6.

Item No	Topic	Action
7.	Proposed purchase of two additional vans. It was agreed that the purchasing manager should look into the costs of leasing compared with purchase.	SW to cost options.

Figure 7.6 Action minutes

Activity 7.2

You have been asked to participate in your company's management training programme. Prepare for the first topic 'Effective Meetings' by drafting explanatory notes on the following:

1. The role of meetings
2. The different types of meetings which occur in business situations
3. Leading meetings
4. The documentation used in meetings.

The role of interviews and negotiations

Interviews tend to be planned and usually have objectives. Negotiations are often quite a formal process in which two or more parties come together to form an agreement.

At present you may not interview or negotiate with people (in the formal sense of these activities) as part of your job. However, it is very likely that in the course of your work or private life you will be interviewing and negotiating with people in an informal and almost subconscious way. For instance, when you arrange a social event with colleagues or discuss a quote with a supplier, you are often indirectly and informally negotiating about matters in order to come to a suitable agreement. Similarly when you need to obtain an update on a project or discuss a problem with a colleague you are often informally conducting an interview.

This unit looks at the more formal aspects of the interview and negotiation process, as these are activities that you are likely to become involved with in your dealings with customers, colleagues, subordinates or suppliers as you progress through your marketing career.

Purpose of interviews

Interviews are a good way to exchange information and obtain an immediate response. Interviews are generally one-to-one communication situations where you can usually determine if the information you have communicated has been received or you can deal with questions and objections immediately.

In this respect there are fewer opportunities for misunderstandings or for communication barriers to exist than in other situations. It is usually easier to appreciate the underlying message being communicated and easier to read body language in face-to-face interviews.

Interviews are also useful opportunities to adopt appropriate body language to convey your message and to convey a range of emotions, from sympathy and support to enthusiasm and trustworthiness. In an interview, you can use various questioning styles to gain a better understanding of what is being said.

Face-to-face interviews are good for improving working relationships between clients and suppliers; hence the phrase 'It is nice to put a face to the voice.' Interviews provide opportunities to develop the social side of business communication that makes doing business easier and more pleasant.

However, because interviews involve complex communication processes and require both interviewers and interviewees to demonstrate good communication skills, there are plenty of opportunities for interviews to be less effective than they might be. Common problems relate to insufficient planning, inappropriate body language, not controlling the content, the pace, the tone, the atmosphere and the timing of the interview, not asking the right questions and not listening sufficiently.

Types of interviews

There are various types of interviews used for different purposes.

Selection interviews

Interviewers use selection interviews to find out if job applicants are suitable for a job. Interviewees will also want to use the opportunity to find out about the job, the organization and the terms and conditions on offer.

Interviewers will usually prepare for the interview by familiarizing themselves with the job applicant's curriculum vitae or application form, the job description and the person specification. On the basis of these and other documents, the interviewer will draw up a list of questions.

Staff are usually trained in an organization's 'house style' or approach to selection interviews. To get the best out of the selection interview situation various issues need to be considered:

○ Candidates should be given a favourable impression with an appropriate welcome, for example, offering refreshment, showing them around the workplace, introducing them to other staff, explaining the procedure for the day
○ The physical layout of the room where the interview will take place is appropriate – perhaps without the physical barrier of a desk between interviewer and interviewee
○ The process needs to be fair, so that all applicants get an equal chance and that interviewees are given a chance to ask questions
○ The interviewer should adopt the right tone in terms of putting candidates at ease and asks open questions that encourage candidates to talk freely
○ The pace and duration of the interview should be controlled and appropriate notes taken to help with the selection process

Appraisal interviews

These are used to give feedback on an individual's performance and to identify training needs. Interviewees may wish to find out how they are doing, in order to improve their performance and raise issues about their job role. Sometimes, appraisal interviews are used as the basis of a salary review.

Because appraisal interviews deal with the sensitive issue of appraising performance they can be difficult for both interviewer and interviewee. They work best where the organization has a set procedure and trains both parties in how the process should be managed.

Issues to consider from a communications perspective relate to the interviewer's skill in preparing appropriate questions and comments for the interview, being objective rather than showing bias in favour of the interviewee or being unduly critical. The tone will depend on the situation. If the appraisee's performance is poor, then a firm but supportive tone is appropriate. The interviewer needs to be constructive and indicate clearly how the appraisee can improve performance.

Interviewers will need to be able to ask appropriate questions, listen carefully to answers and also make brief notes of salient points in order to be able to complete any necessary documentation at the end of the interview. This means the interviewer has to be focused and concentrate carefully to ensure that the interview is effective.

If the appraisee disagrees with the performance assessment, the interviewer needs to be careful that the interview does not degenerate into an argument. This requires control and careful preparation of strategies before the interview for dealing with negative responses.

Counselling, grievance and disciplinary interviews

Unless properly trained as a counsellor, most managers who counsel employees do so as a first stage to identify and resolve personal or professional problems that may hamper performance. Most managers would try to use the situation to offer support and encourage a subordinate to seek help and guidance from appropriate professional sources. Sometimes, counselling is the first stage before an organization deals with an employee's performance through its disciplinary procedure.

Most organizations have set procedures which provide a clear set of instructions about what managers should do if employees have a grievance about how they have been treated. All grievance interviews need to be treated seriously and time should be taken after the interview to investigate the problems raised. A follow-up interview is necessary to help resolve the situation.

Disciplinary interviews are used to take action against an employee who is habitually late, has a poor work performance, breaks workplace rules, such as health and safety regulations, or refuses to do work as instructed.

The first stage of a disciplinary interview may be to establish facts and investigate an incident. This may be followed-up by a second interview to discipline the employee. Disciplinary interviews are also potentially sensitive occasions which can become unpleasant. In conducting them, the interviewer has to be clear on how the interviewee's behaviour has to change and what will happen next if this does not happen. Interviewers should remain objective and anticipate that the interviewee may be resentful about being disciplined.

The interviewer needs to be authoritative without being an authoritarian, should have the full facts with supporting evidence and should be objective and fair.

Customer interviews – complaints handling

Handling complaints can be difficult when customers are frustrated and possibly angry. (See Unit 6 and Unit 10 where there are relevant sections on handling complaints and effective non-verbal communication.) In some situations complaints may arise in an ad hoc way as part of a normal day – in others, you may be dealing with someone by prior appointment.

With ad hoc situations, although there may be a variety of things that customers could complain about, you should be able to anticipate the main categories and to develop certain strategies and approaches for particular situations.

Before an appointment with a customer, you should familiarize yourself with the case and be prepared to deal with the complaint, whether that is to make clear that there is no substance to the complaint or to put things right if there is.

As with all interviews, the advantage of face-to-face communication with a customer is that you will be able to deal with questions or objections immediately and be able to use the situation to diffuse an angry situation. You will need to use your skills of diplomacy and tact to calm a customer at the same time as being objective and calm. As long as you are trying to be genuinely helpful you should be able to resolve the situation.

Your tone and your ability to read the customer's body language and use your own to good effect should enable you to communicate effectively and sympathetically. The interview situation will also mean you can clarify exactly what the problem is and sometimes this is only apparent after careful questioning.

In certain situations, you may not be able to resolve the situation there and then. In that case, you need to be clear about when the customer will hear from you and you need to make sure that you have the person's complete contact details so that you can indeed contact them.

Planning the interview

The key to success in conducting interviews that are efficient and constructive comes from being in control throughout the event and this is largely a function of careful planning.

1. Before the interview, spend a suitable amount of time thinking about the purpose and aims of the interview, whether this is to select an applicant, solve a problem or negotiate for a contract or pay claim and so on.

2. You should reflect on the nature of the discussion to be facilitated in the interview process and draw up a list of points which will help to guide the interview proceedings and ensure continuity and completeness.

3. The discussion should largely go backwards and forwards from the interviewer to the interviewee so that the interviewer maintains the position of controlling the proceedings.

4. The interviewer also has the responsibility for setting the general tone of the interview, which will reflect the relationship of the parties and the nature of the discussion.

5. The interviewee will have a general purpose for attending the interview, i.e. to obtain or pass information. However, they may also have a personal agenda in attending the interview which is not explicit and, whilst it may be wasted effort to speculate on this issue, it is useful to consider the possible reaction of the interviewee to the discussion that will take place during the interview and to plan further points of action, if appropriate.

6. Choose an appropriate location and time and collect all necessary background data that will set the structure for the interview.

7. During the interview, listen carefully for facts and feelings expressed by the interviewee. This will help you to make an assessment of the real issues under discussion and the personal qualities and judgement of the interviewee, which may be significant in appreciating the overall value of the interview.

8. You should also make notes on critical issues during the course of the interview and close with a summary of the main points raised, highlighting any further action to be taken. If possible and suitable, finish on a positive note.

9. After the interview, spend a few minutes making additional notes that may be useful for reference later, whilst the meeting is still fresh in your mind. This may also be the best time to draft a short response in the form of a memo or letter to the interviewee, to thank them for attending the interview and enclose a summary of the discussion and outcome, if applicable.

Your final task is to put into action any items that needed to be resolved as a result of the interview.

The interview process

There are five generally accepted stages to the interview process.

Preparing for the interview

The approach that will be taken during the interview should be planned beforehand. This will mean setting the objectives of what should be achieved and considering the needs of the interviewee as well. However, a skilled interviewer should be flexible enough to respond to questions and input from the interviewee as well as sticking to your 'interview plan'.

You should review all available information in preparation for the interview and have all necessary paperwork in hand and in good order for easy reference during the interview itself.

You should make any necessary physical arrangements, such as organizing seating arrangements for the interview room, refreshments, waiting areas and timings so that there are no undue delays or overbooking of rooms.

Opening the interview

At the beginning of the interview you should ensure that you set out the purpose of the interview so that the reason for it is clear and the interviewee is made aware of what is to be achieved.

You should set the pace and tone of the interview at the outset. For instance, if you are dealing with a grievance interview where an employee is making serious allegations about another member of staff, then it is in keeping with the gravity of the situation to commence proceedings in a serious tone of voice. If it is a complex situation, such as a series of complaints about different aspects of the service your organization provides, then you could deal with each complaint at a fairly slow pace so that you can check that you have a proper understanding of all the matters being discussed at the outset.

Conducting the interview

It is important that the interviewer adheres as much as possible to the interview plan to ensure that the original objectives are achieved. This means retaining control over the information gathering and giving process whilst also being flexible enough to respond to situations and information that arise in the course of the interview. For example, in an interview situation you may need to ask more probing questions to find out exactly what was involved in the interviewee's last job; or in a disciplinary interview, you should respond appropriately to an interviewee's admission that they are suffering from a serious illness which has led to poor work performance.

The interviewer should also ensure that the interview does not go over the time set aside. It is also important that you adopt and interpret body language appropriately. Non-verbal cues can indicate an interviewee's feelings, such as irritation or enthusiasm. For example, in an interview where a member of staff is raising a grievance and appears to be getting angry, you could interpret their body language to forestall an angry outburst in order to keep the interview on a calm and professional level. Similarly you may need to use non-verbal signals to show your empathy or desire to hear more where an interviewee may appear to be hiding information or seems reluctant to give you all the facts.

An important interviewing skill involves listening in order to evaluate the interviewee's responses. Active listening means paying special attention and deliberately making an effort to understand what the interviewee is trying to say. Although there will certain things you need to say in an interview, usually more time should be spent listening to the interviewee than speaking yourself. It is particularly important to keep an open mind and guard against prejudice to avoid 'tuning out' of the message being communicated. You may also need to check your understanding of what is being said by paraphrasing what the interviewee is saying. Although you may want to make a note of certain points, keep your concentration on the interviewee rather than your notes.

Your questioning skills are an important aspect of the interview. You should use different questioning styles for different purposes.

You can use closed questions. However, because these require a 'yes' or 'no' response they do not encourage the kind of free flowing conversation that is usually required in most interview situations. So, although you are getting a response, you usually have to ask several follow-on questions to get any depth of information. For example, 'Is it true that you want to move across to the sales section?' will only give you a 'yes' or 'no' response, which you should investigate further.

Although there are occasions when you need to ask a closed question to verify information, it is often much better to use open questions that encourage the interviewee to frame responses in complete sentences. Open questions tend to start with words like 'why', 'what', 'how', 'when'. For example, 'Why are you interested in moving across to the sales section?'

When you have received a response to a question, there are times when you need to get further clarification or probe deeper to find out what the interviewee really means or if what they are saying is accurate. If the response to an open question is fairly bland such as, 'Because the work looks more interesting', you can obtain more evidence to back up what is being said, with a probing question such as, 'What in particular do you think is more interesting about the work?'

Two-part or multiple-part questions such as 'Have you got any sales experience and if so tell me about the kind of clients you dealt with and your approach to them?' can be confusing. While this question can be used in selection interviews to give interviewees focus about the direction you want them to go in and tests their ability to handle large amounts of information under pressure, it often leads to the interviewee forgetting the original question and digressing onto other subjects. It is often better to keep questions fairly straightforward and follow up with supplementary questions to lead into subjects you want to discuss. Multiple questions would certainly be unsuitable in a disciplinary interview.

You should guard against leading questions in selection interviews that guide the interviewee to agree with you or give the answer you want to hear. For example, asking 'Don't you agree that working in sales would be a more interesting proposition than working in the finance department?' will not supply you with a meaningful answer.

However, you could use a leading question to encourage an interviewee to see your point of view in a disciplinary situation. For example, 'Can you see that by being late every day, you are leaving the rest of the team to do your work?'

Closure

You should control when the interview closes. If the time available has run out or you have reached your objective or it is obvious that you are unable to achieve all the objectives on this occasion, then you should signal the close of the interview.

You can do this by summarizing what has been achieved or the 'state of play' and provide any decision or information about what is to happen next.

In some instances you may need to use your body language to signal that the interview is coming to a close. As you thank the person for their time and explain what you are going to do next, you could gather a few papers together, or you could shake their hands and start to show them out. This is important in interview situations where you can see that the interviewee is not sure that the interview has come to an end.

Follow-up

After an interview you will need to spend some time considering the information that you have obtained. You may need to make notes or organize the notes you made in the interview. At this stage you should decide any action to be taken and implement your decision.

Types of questions

1. Open-ended questions allow interviewees to express themselves in detail, as they are able to form opinions and explain these, for example asking a panel survey of customers: 'What do you think about our new products that were launched last week and you have tested in the home?'
2. Closed-ended questions require short answers or simple 'yes', 'no' or 'don't know' type responses. For example: 'Have you acquired our latest catalogue and price list?'
3. Probing questions tend to follow open questions, when the interviewer wants to find out more about what the person has just said. Often a good way to get interviewees to justify what they have said
4. Restatement questions enable the interviewer to check that they have:

   o Not misunderstood a piece of factual information given in response to a question
   o Informed the interviewee correctly.

For example, 'You stated that you do not use our executive lounge because it is always overcrowded. Is that correct?'

Activity 7.3

An airline company is holding an open 'recruitment' day and is hoping to attract customer service staff for its call centre. Managers from various departments will be holding first stage interviews.

1. Write a memo that provides managers with a checklist outlining the five stages of an interview process. Briefly explain what each stage involves
2. Explain the benefits of using open and probing questions.

Negotiations

Negotiations are interviews designed to achieve agreement that is acceptable to both parties. In situations of this nature, the mutually acceptable deal often involves the agreement to provide a product or service at a particular time, at a particular price and in a particular way. Negotiation is not supposed to be about winning or losing.

Forsyth (*The Negotiator's Pocketbook*, Management Pocketbooks, 2000) says that negotiation has many purposes, for example in:

o Persuasive communication and selling
o Purchasing
o Dealing with staff
o Arbitration
o Many business or personal transactions, from buying a computer to agreeing when and where to meet for dinner.

Forsyth believes that everything is negotiable – everyone is a negotiator.

Negotiation phases

Negotiation often occurs in a 'selling' context and can involve several distinct phases:

- o   Opening the sale
- o   Identifying customer needs or problems
- o   Demonstrating or presenting the product or issues
- o   Handling objections
- o   Negotiating
- o   Closing the sale.

Planning to negotiate

Negotiations often require careful planning about the following:

- o   What are your objectives?
- o   What are the objectives of the person with whom you are negotiating?
- o   What do you know about the person and the organization that you are negotiating with?

Concessions

You should identify:

- o   What is to be achieved and what can be given up, i.e. what is the bare minimum required for a satisfactory outcome? This is sometimes referred to as the fall-back position
- o   What should be achieved, i.e. what is the optimum outcome?

What can be given up are referred to as variables or concessions. These could include price, discount, delivery, payment terms, documentation, follow-up service, timing, schedules, guarantees, conditions and options.

Managing negotiations

In conducting a negotiation you should:

- o   Know your authority – i.e. your negotiation limits and those of the person you are negotiating with
- o   Know your opposite number's needs – i.e. if you know what they really want you are in a better position to negotiate a deal that will satisfy
- o   Be prepared to barter and make concessions that are meaningful to the customer in order to clinch the deal.

Negotiation styles

There are a number of different negotiating styles:

- o   You can take a proactive direction – making suggestions, giving information and promoting your position
- o   You can take a reactive direction – asking for suggestions and checking you understand the other side's position

- o You can adopt a 'hard' approach – where there is no movement on your position which must be accepted
- o You can adopt a 'soft' position – where you accommodate the other person's position.

Negotiation seeks to narrow the differences between parties in order to achieve a satisfactory result for both sides.

Outcomes

Outcomes to negotiation can vary:

- o Lose/lose, which means neither party has achieved its objectives and the negotiation has failed
- o Win/lose, where one party achieves its objectives and the other party does not. The negotiation has failed because both parties do not find the situation acceptable
- o Draw, where both parties achieve some of their objectives, but not all
- o Win/win, where both parties achieve their objectives.

Techniques to keep ahead in negotiations

- o Use silence
- o Summarize frequently
- o Keep track of complex negotiations, particularly about concessions offered on either side
- o Promote a good feeling
- o Read between the lines about what is really being said
- o Think on your feet but hold your fire when necessary.

Interpersonal behaviour

- o Good negotiators listen carefully and do not allow themselves to be distracted
- o Ask questions to keep the negotiations open
- o Ask probing questions where necessary
- o Look for signs of open minded body language, e.g. open hands
- o Look for wariness, e.g. arms across chest
- o Look for signs of confidence, e.g. 'steepling' of hands, or territorial dominance, such as hands behind head and leaning back
- o Look for signs of nervousness, e.g. clearing throat, perspiration, fidgeting, avoiding eye contact.

 Activity 7.4

You are the Account Manager at a PR agency and have been asked to re-negotiate your firm's contract with a client. Your assistant is interested in the negotiation process and asks you the following questions:

1. What is meant by the term 'negotiation'?
2. How could you use effective body language in a negotiation?

Summary

In this unit you have studied:

o Why and how meetings are used in marketing

o When documentation is needed and how it is used in meetings

o How to lead and manage meetings effectively

o How and why interviews and negotiations are used in marketing

o How to improve your interview technique

o How to be successful negotiator.

Further study and examination preparation

Attempt Question 5(a) from the June 2000 examination paper. Go to www.cimeduhub.com to access Specimen Answers and Senior Examiner's advice for this exam question.

Exam hint

You need to know whether a meeting or informal discussion is required in a given situation. If it is the former, you may be asked to explain the steps that need to be taken to plan and hold the meeting. It is therefore important that you are conversant with all aspects of meetings, notably the issuing of a notice, setting the agenda and producing minutes. You may be given a fictitious scenario and out of this asked to set an agenda and/or issue a suitable notice – all settings will have a marketing context and you may need to rely on your knowledge from other parts of the Certificate course to place suitable details in these documents. You will be expected to know the general rules and guidelines in the planning of interviews and to explain these in the examination. You need to be aware of the different types of interview that can take place in business and how to plan and contribute effectively to negotiations in marketing. You should be aware of the different types of questions that can help you to solicit the required information. You should also expect to comment on any body language, speech and listening skills as important tools in meetings, interviews and negotiations for successful communication.

unit 8 using statistical data and visual information

Learning objectives

In this unit you will:

- ○ See the relevance of interpreting, analysing and presenting data in marketing

- ○ Understand how to interpret and summarize data

- ○ Appreciate the value of using graphs, tables and charts in the visual communication of marketing information

- ○ Study a range of graphs, tables and charts and understand when they should be used

- ○ Appreciate how information can be distorted.

By the end of this unit you will be able to:

- ○ Analyse and interpret oral, written and graphical information accurately

- ○ Be selective with data that you include in reports

- ○ Produce a range of graphs, tables and charts from raw data.

Study Guide

This unit provides you with the underlying knowledge and understanding to be able to deal with data that occurs in the compulsory question in Part A of the Customer Communications paper and covers Section 4.5 of the syllabus.

In this unit you will examine how to analyse and interpret information and look at the ways in which information can be communicated using a variety of visual presentation techniques. This unit will help you when you tackle Part A questions because as part of the compulsory question, candidates are regularly asked to read narrative material and examine statistical data or visual data. They are then asked to interpret the data and are often asked to convey the key points in some communication format or other (often a report). In addition, they are often then asked to use some part of the information on which to base a chart or graph.

Consequently it is important that you familiarize yourself with the format of the Part A questions asked in previous years (go to the back of the book for the last two papers), and you will see that this unit directly relates to answering these type of questions.

It will take you a minimum of two hours to read through this unit and a further two hours to do the activities.

Study tip

To put this area of the syllabus and this unit into context, you need to appreciate why it is an important aspect of your marketing studies.

As a starting point write a list of the types of visual and number or statistical information that you have come across in your personal and working life in the last month.

For instance, you may have watched the news on television and seen a feature about employment figures, crime rates or trends in tourism. If you had, you would probably have noticed that the presenter did not go into great detail, explaining every possible figure and percentage that the report was based on. It is much more likely that the he or she would have given you a 'snapshot' view with some key, pertinent points that summarized the overall situation. Any figures would not have been shown in a long list of numbers but would probably have been presented in a visually appealing and easy to understand format, using graphs, charts, maps and possibly including graphical symbols in a pictogram format or even moving images to attract your attention.

Similarly in your working life you may have attended a sales and marketing presentation or meeting where market share and sales turnover figures were discussed. The presenter would probably have manipulated the data so that it could be presented in a user-friendly format such as handouts, slides or a PowerPoint presentation.

These are just two examples. Now, using your own experience before you start reading the unit, you should be in the correct 'mindset' to read this unit and appreciate why this is an area of significance when you are studying Customer Communications.

Why is data relevant to marketing?

If you work in marketing you will find that you often have to use information to make decisions and may need to convey it to internal and potential or actual external customers. The information you deal with could range from market size, the number of brands in a range, to pricing and distribution information, or information about promotion activities, media spend, sales levels or market share.

The information can be in one of the following 'formats':

o   In a raw 'data' format (facts that are not organized in any particular way), such as market research data or sales figures

o   In an 'information' format, where the information has been selected and sorted or analysed for a purpose, such as showing sales of one brand compared with that of another

o   In an 'intelligence' format, where the information has been interpreted and analysed, for instance where figures show that sales have increased compared with competitor brands over the period of a special promotion.

Data can be in the form of narrative prose or consist of a series of numbers or percentages. It can be very detailed and there can be too much of it to make sense of in a short time. In situations like this, it is necessary to be able to select the most important data, summarize the key points and where appropriate use visual presentation techniques to make the information user-friendly.

Numerical and statistical information is used in a variety of ways in business:

o   For record keeping

o   To provide progress updates on advertising and promotion campaigns

o   For budgeting to compare actual with forecast figures

o   As evidence to support proposals

o   To show trends in sales revenue for different brands or to indicate labour turnover or absenteeism

o   To demonstrate proportion and show market share.

Interpreting, selecting and summarizing information

When you communicate information you rarely convey all the facts and details that you have. For example, if you are asked the question, 'What happened in the Manchester United game against Bayern Munich?' your answer would probably be to give the final score but not a detailed account of every pass of the ball and attempt on goal.

Similarly, when dealing with marketing information and communicating with colleagues and customers, you need to be able to select the relevant information given in the circumstances and to make some sense of it. For instance, in the football game example, rather than listing every single attempt on goal and every foul you might want to sort the raw data to make the information easier to digest. For example, you might want to say that there were four fouls and two yellow cards given to Bayern Munich players and five attempts each on goal. You might also want to summarize what happened in the general flow of play, for example, Bayern Munich attacked well although their defending left a lot to be desired but Manchester United played with flair and were unlucky not to score another goal.

Now, look at these survey findings and note the process used for summarizing this information for part of a brief market research report.

300 out of the 500 female customers questioned in a postal survey said they would be interested in the x company home shopping service. Their catalogue was judged to be appealing and to feature the kind of products that shoppers find difficult to track down, especially when parents had young children to accompany them on shopping trips.

> *Due to the large numbers of people who were interested in the home shopping service, the x company is looking into the possibility of expanding its retail operations to include a home shopping service.'*

o Firstly, the original material is read thoroughly to identify the main facts and how the ideas are developed

o Then the information in the whole report is grouped into different categories under main headings

o The main points in each paragraph are selected and this key information is interpreted to give it meaning. If necessary, it is expressed differently to give it impact and/or make it more understandable

o The material should be expressed in the third person, i.e. 'it has been shown' or 'the figures show that'

o Now look at how the information has been summarized for the report:

> *'Sixty per cent of female customers who responded to the survey said they would be interested in a mail order service provided by x company. Because the majority of customers would use such a service, the mail order option will be further investigated.'*

o Any summary of information should be checked to ensure the main points are covered and that the key points link together with some continuity.

Activity 8.1

You have recently joined Robinsons, a grocery chain with 96 outlets in the north of England. Following a survey which was carried out by the magazine *'Food Retailer'*, you are required to analyse the information given below and deliver a presentation to senior management. With use of an overhead projector, draft out the visual information you would include on three acetates/slides.

Prepare a brief report on the main findings from the perspective of the senior management at the Robinsons' grocery chain, to be handed out at your presentation. (For more information on report formats go to Unit 9.) You should be selective with the information you use and summarize the main findings. Ensure that you interpret the statistical data where you can.

Table 1 How often do you shop for groceries not including the times when you have forgotten something?

	%
More than twice a week	7
Twice a week	17
Once a week	60
Every two weeks	11
Every three weeks	1
Less often	2
Miscellaneous	1
No response	1

Table 2 On what day or days of the week do you usually do most of your grocery shopping?

	%
Monday	12
Tuesday	4
Wednesday	8
Thursday	24
Friday	40
Saturday	31
Sunday	6

* Results add up to more than 100% because respondents could choose more than one day.

Table 3 What is the main reason you do your grocery shopping on that day?

	%
Most convenient time	45
Fits in with pay-day	30
Good day for special offers	26
Habit	19
Not crowded	8
Stock up for the weekend	7
Leaves weekend free	6
Run out of food on that day	6
Better selection of groceries	3
Miscellaneous	13

Table 4 At which one store do you shop for groceries most often?

Top UK retailers	%
Sainsbury	11.2
Tesco	10.4
Co-op	6.9
Asda	5.7
Safeway	4.7
Robinsons	4.5
Fine Fare	4.5
Gateway	4.4
Spar	4.2
Kwiksave	3.2
Others	40.3

Table 5 What are the reasons for shopping at (name of the shop) most often?

	%
Convenient location	42
Special offers/low prices	38
Good meat	25
Carry all brands	22
Friendly assistants	20
Quality of fresh produce	17
Good display	14
Adequate parking	12
From habit/miscellaneous	47

Table 6 What are your reasons for not shopping at the other stores?

	%
Prices too high	45
Too far to travel	27
Slow check-out	22
Prefer the shop I go to	17
Very few special offers	17
Poor selection	15
Unattractive store	7
Too small	7
Too overcrowded	5
No particular reason	3
Miscellaneous	28

Table 7 On your major grocery shopping trips, how often do you buy advertised special offers?

	%
Frequently	35
Occasionally	15
Seldom	10
Never	38
No response	2

Table 8 Which of the following are your best source of special offers? Which second and which third?

	Source		
	First	Second	Third
Newspapers	40%	10%	21%
Store leaflets	25%	24%	15%
Leaflet drops	15%	31%	19%

Table 9 Please look at these advertisements and tell me the reference number of the one you like best

	%
Safeway	20
Fine Fare	16
Asda	14
Gateway	13
Kwiksave	10
Tesco	9
Sainsbury	8
Co-op	6
Robinsons	2
Aldi	1
No response	1

Table 10 Why do you like the advertisement you picked?

	%
Special offers are easy to find	42
Eye catching	38
Easy to read/large print	27
Easy to find specific brands	19
More bargains	17
Good variety of items	15
Other replies, none more than 8 per cent	45
No response	3

REPORT ON SHOPPING HABITS AND SUPERMARKET ADVERTISING

Report Commissioned By:	Managing Director, Robinsons Grocery Chain
Report Written By:	Any Candidate
Date:	12 September 200X

1. TERMS OF REFERENCE

This report is an analysis of the information resulting from a survey on shopping habits and supermarket advertising conducted by 'Food Retailer' magazine.

2. METHODOLOGY

A total of 1750, mainly female, shoppers selected at random from the electoral register, were interviewed in the north of England. The average age of the respondents was 40, and 78 per cent of those interviewed had children.

3. FINDINGS

3.1 Shopping habits

The survey showed that most people (60 per cent) do a weekly shop, with 17 per cent shopping twice a week and 11 per cent only shopping once every two weeks. The most popular day for shopping was Friday (40 per cent), with 31 per cent doing grocery shopping on Saturday and 24 per cent on Thursday. The least popular day was Tuesday with only 4 per cent of respondents saying they shopped on that day.

The main reasons for shoppers choosing a particular day to do their shopping was because it was the most convenient time (45 per cent) while 30 per cent said that it was because it fitted in with when they were paid and 26 per cent because it was a good day for special offers.

3.2 Store preferences

The stores that respondents shopped at most often was Sainsbury (11.2 per cent) and Tesco (10.4 per cent). Robinsons and Fine Fare were sixth in the list with 4.5 per cent of shoppers prefering to shop at these two stores, but 6.9 per cent of respondents shopped most often at the Co-op, 5.7 per cent at Asda and 4.7 per cent at Safeway.

Gateway, Spar and Kwiksave each attracted about 3–4 per cent of shoppers but just over 40 per cent of respondents cited 'other' smaller stores and shops to do their grocery shopping.

The most popular reasons for shopping most often at a particular store are convenient location (42 per cent), special offers/low prices (38 per cent), good meat (25 per cent), stock all brands (22 per cent) and friendly assistants (20 per cent).

The most popular reasons for not shopping at other stores were high prices (45 per cent), travel distance (27 per cent) and slow check-outs (22 per cent).

3.3 Advertising

Items that are advertised as special offers are frequently purchased by 35 per cent of shoppers although a similar number (38 per cent) never bought them.

Most respondents obtained special offer coupons from newspapers (40 per cent), 25 per cent used store leaflets while only 15 per cent used leaflet drops.

Most respondents preferred Safeway's advertising (20 per cent), with 16 per cent preferring Fine Fare's and 14 per cent preferred Asda's. However, only 2 per cent preferred Robinsons' advertising.

The reasons cited most for liking advertisements were that 'special offers are easy to find' (42 per cent), or that the advertisements were 'eye catching' (38 per cent), 'had large print' (27 per cent) or were 'easy to find specific brands' (17 per cent) or featured 'a variety of items' (15 per cent).

4. CONCLUSION AND RECOMMENDATIONS

The survey presents Robinsons with some interesting findings. From the shoppers surveyed Robinsons came sixth out of the top ten named stores for grocery shopping. However, 40 per cent of respondents shop most at stores other than the top ten, which indicates that many people are shopping at smaller stores.

This probably links in with the most popular reasons for store choice, which are convenient location and special offers/pricing.

This indicates that Robinsons should further investigate the convenience of its stores to where people live (which may mean looking at 'free' bus rides if stores are not convenient for transport or looking at where stores are located in relation to housing estates).

In addition, Robinsons should compare its prices with those of its main competitors and, if necessary, alter its pricing strategy in order to attract more shoppers.

One reason cited for not using stores was 'slow check-outs' and Robinsons could check the average time check-out staff take to deal with customers and the amount of time shoppers spend queueing to ensure that these factors do not put off potential customers from shopping at Robinsons.

The survey also showed that Friday and Saturday were the most popular shopping days and Robinsons should ensure more staff are on duty on these days.

One important feature of the survey related to advertising. Robinsons' advertising was one of the least preferred from the top ten stores named in the survey. Therefore, advertising needs to be reviewed with a view to making special offers and specific brands more obvious, using large print and making more visual impact on customers.

Media trends showed that newspapers should be the main medium used for special offer coupons advertising.

Why use visual information?

Visual presentations including pictures, diagrams, icons, logos, charts and graphs can be quickly assimilated and can make information much easier to comprehend. People are adept at speed-reading visual messages and find it easier to interpret figures shown pictorially.

You can use graphics to explain relationships and actions that would be difficult to convey concisely in words. For example, you could use a pie chart to show market share more effectively than a list of percentages or you could use a bar chart to show rising sales figures over a five-year period rather than explaining the year-on-year increases.

You can use visual messages to create impact and attract the attention of an audience. If you present information visually it is also more likely to be retained in your target audience's memory.

You can choose from a variety of ways to display data visually:

o Tables can be used for recording and displaying a wide range of numerical data
o Bar charts help to compare changes in relative quantity
o Line graphs help to show trends and moving averages over time, so are useful for planning and forecasting
o Pie charts help you see proportions of a whole
o Pictograms show pictorial symbols of statistics to simplify messages
o Organograms show reporting relationships between people in organizations
o Gantt charts help with project planning.

How to present visual information

Nowadays it is much easier to generate graphs and charts with a professional appearance on a computer using a spreadsheet or database software. (See Figures 8.1 for examples of how computers can produce three dimensional and other visual techniques to represent data.)

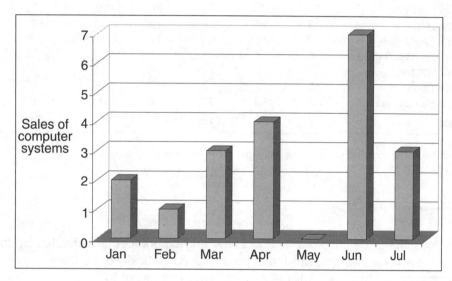

Figure 8.1

However, you should be aware of how each of the main display options can be used and should be able to produce them without the aid of a computer.

As a general rule it is best to keep charts and graphs simple. Visually it is better if the chart takes up the full axis space available. Use of colour or a three-dimensional aspect can create impact. All graphs and charts should have a title indicating the content – for example, 'marketing spend for product x' – and sometimes this is used to indicate the values being shown, for instance, whether it is £000 or %. There should be two axes on each graph, a horizontal axis (the x-axis) and a vertical axis (the y-axis). It is best to orient the data so that values on the horizontal axis are those where there has been a choice, such as, when to measure or where to measure (this is known as the independent variable). Values on the vertical will depend upon the corresponding position on the horizontal axis (they are therefore known as the dependent variable). For example, when showing the change in sales revenue over the course of a year, the independent variable is time since we can choose when to measure sales revenue. The dependent variable is sales revenue since it will change according to the time at which it was measured.

The key or the legend relates the shading or pattern used on a chart to what it represents. In addition to or in place of a legend, labels can be used to mark what each bar, segment or line represents. All bars and charts should display the source of information. It is also advisable to cross reference all graphs and charts within the text, such as 'see figure x' or 'see attached appendix y'.

Tables

Tables can be useful for presentation purposes to sort complex data. However, the information presented in this way can often be used as the basis for further analysis because while the information is in this format it is often difficult to read or follow trends.

Salesperson	Product line sales turnover (£000s) 2000–2001					Total (£)
	A	B	C	D	E	
Helen Jenkins	13	15	8	12	10	58
Jane Atkinson	8	10	9	6	5	38
Andrew Salter	16	12	10	12	14	64
Luigi Romero	23	26	13	28	22	112
Karen Mann	33	34	24	22	30	143
Sunil Singh	12	16	11	17	15	71
George Vassiliades	4	7	3	8	11	33
Alan Bennet	11	12	12	12	11	58
Tony Taylor	15	7	7	9	8	46
Christine James	22	13	21	10	15	81
Total	157	152	118	136	141	704

Figure 8.2 A table showing product line sales per representative

Bar charts

Column/bar charts demonstrate relationships and differences in variables by the respective heights of the columns/bars, which can be displayed vertically or horizontally, with the data on or near the bars. They are particularly useful when you want to:

1. Compare the size of several variables in one presentation
2. Demonstrate important differences between the variables
3. Demonstrate changes over a period of time
4. Demonstrate the composition of variables.

There are three types of column/bar chart that can be presented:

1. Simple column/bar charts
2. Multiple column/bar charts
3. Component (stacked) column/bar charts.

Guidelines for producing simple column/bar charts

Simple column/bar charts demonstrate the value of one piece of data by the respective length of the column/bar(s) on the chart. Where the horizontal axis cannot have values midway between each measurement (bar), such as between two brands or between two countries, then a bar chart should be used. Where the horizontal axis has values which can gradually change, then a line graph is best, since it shows the possible points midway between each measurement.

1. The chart must be titled and each axis of the graph must be labelled
2. There must be a scale to indicate values on each axis (see Figure 8.3 where market share percentages are shown on the y-axis)
3. The vertical axis must always start at 0, so that the relative values can be accurately demonstrated, or indicate with a staggered line that the data does not begin at 0
4. If possible, the data should be presented in some order of value, i.e. lowest to highest or vice versa; this is usually not possible if time comparisons are made
5. Use spaces between columns/bars for ease of interpretation
6. Use shading to highlight the columns/bars, making them easier to view. Figure 8.4 demonstrates how to draw a simple column/bar chart based on the data below.

1995	1996	1997	1998	1999	2000	2001
0.4%	0.7%	1.9%	2.6%	3.0%	3.0%	2.8%

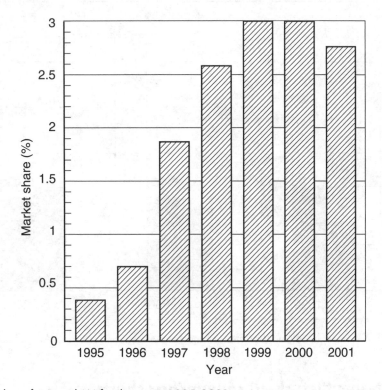

Figure 8.3 Market share for Brand 'A' for the years 1995–2001

Multiple column/bar charts

Multiple column/bar charts use several columns/bars for each variable, each column/bar demonstrating a particular aspect of the overall data.

Guidelines for producing multiple column/bar charts

1. Two or more columns/bars are used to present aspects/divisions of the data
2. Shading must be used to distinguish the columns/bars representing different data
3. Use spaces appropriately to draw attention to similarities, differences or trends, either in the columns/bars separately or groups of data
4. Columns/bars can be drawn horizontally or vertically.

Table 8.1

	1999 (000s)	2000 (000s)	2001 (000s)
B1	150	180	225
B2	230	245	205
B3	340	560	480

The multiple column bar chart example shown in Figure 8.4 has been based on the information in Table 8.1.

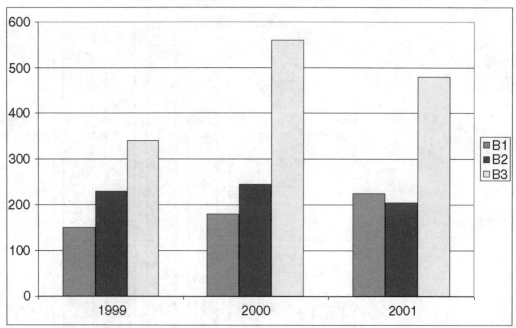

Market competition for Product B

Figure 8.4 A multiple column/bar chart of market competition for Brand A

Component (stacked) column/bar charts

Component (stacked) column/bar charts can be segmented or broken lengthwise to show the relative size of components of an overall total. An example is presented in Figure 8.5.

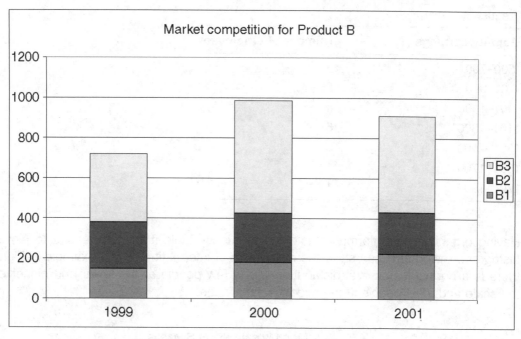

Figure 8.5 A component bar chart

Guidelines for producing component column/bar charts

1. The components can be ordered in any way on the column/bar, but must remain consistent if more than one column/bar is demonstrated
2. The relative values should be kept in order, with either the highest or lowest at the top, and then presented in ascending or descending order
3. Use shading and/or a key if the components cannot be labelled directly.

Histograms

Histograms should not be confused with bar charts. Bar charts are used for discrete or non-continuous data and so are best drawn using a separate bar for each item that is being represented. Histograms are used to display continuous data such as earnings, mileage, examination marks, heights of people, etc. and as such there is usually no gap between the bars to indicate the continuous nature of the data.

If you were to show the monthly salaries of the marketing staff at Swizzles (listed below), in a histogram, you would first group the information together to produce a frequency table.

Monthly salaries of marketing staff at Swizzles Limited: £1150, £690, £1270, £1450, £1350, £880, £750, £970, £1080, £1290, £1600, £1700, £680, £1090, £950, £1400, £550, £1180, £1250.

From this you can see that the there are three staff whose monthly salaries are in the £500–£700 category.

Frequency Table

Monthly earnings (£)	Number of employees
500–700	3
701–900	2
901–1100	4
1101–1300	5
1301–1500	3
1501–1700	1
1701–1900	1

Having organized the information into the frequency table it is much easier to plot it on a histogram. Histograms can show the distribution of information. In the example in Figure 8.6, there is a normal 'bell curve' distribution with a few people at the lower and higher ends of the scale and most people in the middle salary range.

Monthly salaries at Swizells

Figure 8.6 Monthly salaries at Swizells

Pie charts

Pie charts are circular diagrams that are particularly useful for showing the composition of all the data, with the segments demonstrating the relative values of the data. They are used to show the relative size of different items making up a total, and are useful to show proportions of a whole. Ideally there should be no more than eight sections with the largest segment usually shown running clockwise from the top of the pie. Each segment should be labelled, sometimes including a value and a percentage share. The overall total is usually stated.

Guidelines for producing pie charts

1. Pie charts should be drawn accurately with a compass to represent the 360° of a circle and divided up into segments
2. The component parts must represent 100 per cent
3. To draw the segment sizes accurately, use a protractor by putting the base line across the middle of the circle and marking off degrees to represent percentages (which must be worked out, based on numerical values). For example, 180° represents 50 per cent, 90° represents 25 per cent, etc.
4. Keep the maximum number of segments to seven, otherwise the chart will look too congested and more difficult to interpret
5. Place the most important (largest) segment at the 12 o'clock position and the others relative to it in some logical order
6. Use shading to draw attention to salient features, usually largest and/or smallest segments
7. Label all the segments and show their relative values either on the segments or beside the chart. A key will be necessary for this.

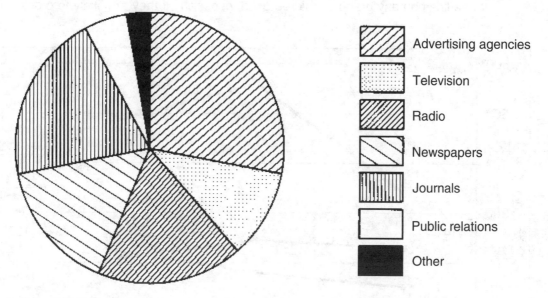

Figure 8.7 A pie chart

 Activity 8.2

Draw a pie chart based on Table 2 in the *'Food Retailer'* survey featured in Activity 8.1.

Line graphs

Line graphs are a series of points joined together to form a straight or curved line and are usually used to reflect a trend over a period of time or the interaction of two variables. In many cases, several lines will be used to show comparisons between the data.

Guidelines for producing line graphs

1. The horizontal axis should show the time period (years, months, hours, etc.)
2. The vertical axis should show the amount or value being measured
3. Both scales should begin at 0 and increase in equal amounts, or indicate with a staggered line that the data does not begin at 0
4. Both negative and positive values can be shown on line graphs
5. Use different colours for more than one line on the same graph, to distinguish between them
6. Use solid lines or broken lines to distinguish between different data or to draw attention to significant features of the data
7. In order to avoid clutter and to make observation of the chart easier, a maximum of three lines on any graph should be used, especially if they are likely to cross over.

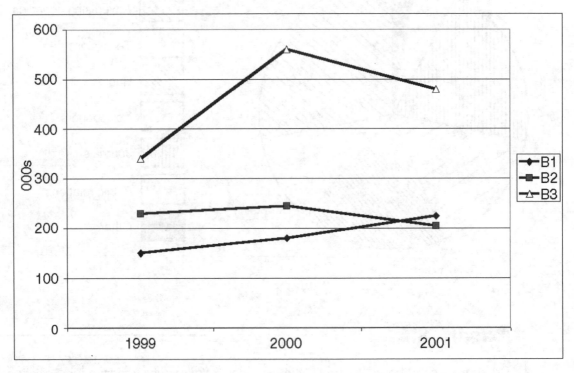

Figure 8.8 A simple line graph

Gantt charts

Gantt charts are a type of column/bar chart which show dimensions of a variable over a period of time and can be used to measure a number of different aspects of business activity in terms of actual, planned and cumulative. They are often found in marketing plans to show how the plan will be 'phased in' over a period of time.

Figure 8.9 Gantt chart. Rolling national launch of Brand Q in different regional cities in the UK from January to September 200X

Pictograms

Pictograms are charts in which the data is represented by a line of symbols or pictures. They are usually used for presenting information in a novel format and are often used in the transmission of simple messages. They can give impact to data as it can be represented by a striking image or picture. For instance numbers of employees or customers can be represented by matchstick people; aeroplane sales can be shown as drawings of aeroplanes.

An increase in quantity can be shown by more images (where the image is given a value) or the size of the image might increase to represent the quantity change. However, the problems with doing this are that quantities can be misrepresented because the scaling is unclear.

In addition, although pictograms can make a visual impact, certain audiences could perceive them as frivolous or patronizing.

Guidelines for producing pictograms

1. Use a symbol which will be clearly representative of the subject matter, eye-catching and appealing
2. The number of pictures or symbols must reflect the values they represent
3. Use a key to indicate the value of one picture or symbol
4. Keep the size of the pictures and graph consistent with the overall presentation.

Figure 8.10 Examples of pictograms

Flow charts

Flow charts are useful for demonstrating conceptual relationships, processes, and procedures and business activities, where numerical values are not important. The relationships between various parts of the activity being demonstrated are shown in sequence from beginning to end and geometric shapes are used to distinguish between various aspects.

Figure 8.11 A flow chart for the stages involved in the introduction of a new product

Organization charts

Organization charts are frequently used in business organizations to show the hierarchical positions and relationships of employees, which also represent the main formal channels of communication.

Figure 8.12 An organization chart for the Marketing Department of Swizzles Financial Services

Problems with distorting information

You should avoid using value-loaded expressions to alter how a statistic sounds as this could distort the information. For example, 47 per cent sounds different when described as 'nearly half the population', which sounds different again from 'barely half' or 'not even half those questioned'. Similarly you should remember that if 'nearly one in ten of the population has a problem with x, y or z' it means that over 90 per cent of people don't have that problem.

Graphs and charts can be very effective communication media, but it is easy to confuse an audience or be confused yourself if the wrong medium is used to communicate data or if it is constructed incorrectly.

Be aware that you can distort the information you are presenting if the axis on graphs and charts does not start from zero. Trends in the top part of a chart will be more exaggerated if you see the whole picture with zero at the bottom left-hand corner.

Similarly, if you use a set of line charts but use a different scale on each of them you could distort the information. For example if you expanded or compressed the *y* axis (vertical axis) you could make a curve showing sales steeper or flatter which could affect the way that sales performance is perceived. Spreading out or compressing the distance between values on the *x*-axis (horizontal axis) could cause the same effect.

Computer packages offer you the facility of producing graphs and charts that have a three-dimensional appearance. However, sometimes the cosmetic benefits of blocking out areas of graphs and charts can be outweighed by the problems of readability. The problem is that it is difficult to see the how the 3-D lines and bars line up against the relevant scale and so data values are difficult to determine.

Summary

In this unit you have studied:

o   Why data is relevant to marketing

o   How to interpret and summarize data

o   Why visual data is an effective communication tool

o   How to present a range of visual data, including charts, graphs and diagrams

o   How to avoid distorting data.

Further study and examination preparation

Attempt Question 1(a) and (b) as well as Question 3(a) from the June 2000 examination paper and do Question 1(b) and (c) from the December 2000 paper. Go to www.cimeduhub.com to access Specimen Answers and Senior Examiner's advice for these exam questions.

Exam hint

Candidates studying for the examination should be aware that this unit is particularly relevant to the compulsory Part A question. Ensure that you can interpret written and/or visual data in order undertake a number of tasks, such as, writing a report (see unit 'The communication process' for information about report writing) and producing graphs and charts. Ensure that you can analyse, interpret, summarize and present information in a concise and accurate manner.

unit 9
written communication formats

Learning objectives

In this unit you will:

○ Examine the variety of written communication formats

○ Look at when and why you would use a particular written communication format

○ Develop your writing skills for each of the formats included here.

By the end of this unit you should be able to:

○ Use the correct layout and presentation format for different types of written communication

○ Communicate effectively using each of the formats included here.

Study Guide

This unit covers 4.7 and 4.8 of the syllabus. It provides you with the knowledge and understanding necessary to enable you to use a variety of written formats to communicate with internal and external customers. These formats are letters, memos, e-mails, notices, reports and articles. It will take you three hours to read through this unit and a further three hours to work through the activities.

Study tip

Spend some time evaluating the written communications that you are exposed to in your personal and working life. Select a good and bad example of each of the following:

- o Letters
- o Memos
- o Notices
- o Reports
- o E-mails.

For each example note down why it is effective or not.

Why study communication formats?

Written communication is still important in marketing even in these days of sophisticated information communications technology.

You may use your writing skills in letters, memos, e-mails and reports regularly, in which case you may wish to proceed directly to the activities and past examination questions to check how well prepared you are to be tested in this area. On the other hand, you may find that, because of your role or the type of organization you work in, all letters and memos are produced by someone else (such as a secretary). Or it may be that you are not yet in a position that requires you to use all the communication formats tested in the exam (such as reports). Whatever the case, you should be aware of how to use the various communication formats, and you may need to spend some time looking at how you could develop your writing skills.

If you work in an organization where there is a 'house style' for reports and letters, then this style can be used in the examination situation, but if this is not the case, then you may find you can use and adapt the templates and examples provided in this unit.

Written communication skills in marketing

For any situation, whether you are writing a letter, memo or report, the following structure should be adopted:

- o *The beginning* Where you get to the point of why you are writing, whatever you are writing
- o *The middle* Where you communicate your message
- o *The end* If appropriate, where you summarize the main points (especially for reports) or where you state any action required (more for memos and letters).

The PASS (purpose, audience, structure, style) mnemonic can prove to be a useful guide when you are writing (see Unit 6 for more details) or be a useful way to cross-check when you review your writing.

In addition, the AIDA principle (see Unit 3) is relevant to most written communications:

Table 9.1

A	Gain **a**ttention of the recipients by putting the essence of your message at the beginning.
I	Stimulate **i**nterest and create **d**esire by writing positively, for example referring to benefits
D	of writing from the perspective of the audience and/or taking a personal approach when appropriate (using the word 'you' but not in reports).
A	Generate **a**ction by motivating the recipient to undertake the desired course of action, for example, 'please confirm/reply by' or just getting the reader to read your message.

Most business documents should be clear and concise. To keep letters, memos and reports brief it is best to keep to short sentences, simple expressions (avoid analogies) and words that people can understand. In other words, try not to use words that your audience may be unfamiliar with and avoid jargon. All abbreviations should be explained by giving their meaning in full the first time they are used.

Start new paragraphs when you move on to new ideas. Arrange your thoughts in a logical sequence so that ideas and information flow from one paragraph to another in a clear and easy-to-understand way.

Use terms that are unambiguous. For instance, the words 'quickly', 'as soon as possible' and 'large' could be interpreted in different ways by different people. Generally it is better to be specific, giving an amount or a date instead of using words that could be misinterpreted.

For letters, in particular, you should avoid the kind of official and cliché-sounding terms that can lead to readers not understanding exactly what you are trying to say. For instance, instead of 'Re your correspondence dated'. You could say, 'Thank you for your letter of ', And the phrase 'The contract should be submitted to the undersigned upon completion' could be more simply written as 'Please return the contract when you have completed it.'

In general, you should avoid passive phrases, such as 'should be sent to' and use the active form, 'please send to'.

You should try to avoid negative terms when writing to customers. For example, 'I am unable to make a booking until you pay a 25 per cent deposit' could be phrased in a positive way as 'When you pay a 25 per cent deposit, your booking will be completed and confirmation sent to you within three days.'

You will get a better response to the letters and memos you send if you use a courteous 'please', 'thank you' or 'I would be grateful if you could' instead of using a brusque or directive tone.

If you are writing a memo which does not require a specific action, then you should include the phrase 'for information only'.

If you are writing a report, you should avoid sexual bias in your writing. By using 'he' or the masculine form of a noun, you could cause offence. Either use non-gender specific terms such as 'staff ', 'employees', 'individuals' or 'people', or change the sentence round. For example, the sentence, 'The number of air stewardesses will have to be increased on each flight' could be changed to 'The number of air crew will have to be increased on each flight.'

When to use letters

Whatever type of organization that you work in, if you are in an office, you are likely to write and receive letters. However, if you work in marketing then communication is likely to be a vital part of your job and therefore letter writing will be too.

Although letter writing is not the quickest way to communicate there are many different types of letters and occasions when letters are the suitable format for communication.

Letters provide a permanent record of a message, which could be useful if you are confirming details of an exhibition stand booking or enquiring about late payment and need proof at a later date that a letter has indeed been sent.

Letters are also quite formal, which means they are an excellent way of sending important information. For example, you would want to send a formal letter if you were informing someone that they were successful in a job interview, if you were giving someone notice about a disciplinary matter or if you needed to send a covering letter with a cheque payment.

Letters are suitable for long, complex messages that can be read and re-read over a period of time. Consequently they are often used for direct marketing purposes (mailshots) where the 'offer' has a number of benefits that need to be read in detail. They are often used where the product is quite complex as they can be read again when the person has had more time to think about the offer.

Letters are suitable for communicating personal information directly to the individual concerned. The use of computers in even the smallest firms means that professionally presented letters can be produced easily by most staff, not just trained secretaries.

The use of mail-merge facilities means that standard letters can be produced, saving time and money. This means an organization can decide to communicate with some or even all of its customers by linking letter production to an updated customer database.

And if a letter is necessary and speed is important, then it could be sent by facsimile machine or as an e-mail attachment.

Letters are generally sent to external customers although in very formal situations (such as confirmation of terms and conditions, requests for leave or with disciplinary matters) letters may be sent internally within an organization.

The layout of a business letter

Undoubtedly you would already have been involved in writing business letters as millions are composed, produced and delivered daily. Every organization has its own style (which is important in reflecting image and efficiency) but there are a set of basic rules of layout that all will follow:

1. A blocked layout with all entries starting from the left-hand margin or an indented style where the main body of the letter is set to the left-hand margin and all other parts are centred; either method may be used but should be consistent throughout the organization or department (Figure 9.1)

2. Business letters are made up of the following parts:

- ○ *Letterhead and/or logo* Communicates the corporate image through its graphic style and usually also contains address, telephone, telex, fax and e-mail details
- ○ *Letter references* Initials of the typist and author
- ○ *Date* Usually the month is placed first, fully written (not numerals), followed by the day
- ○ Recipient's title, name and address
- ○ *Salutation* For example, Dear Sir, Dear Madam or Dear Mrs Jones
- ○ *Subject heading* This is usually indented and underlined, for example, Conference on Marketing Communication, 25 September 20XX, Queen Elizabeth's Hall, London
- ○ *Body of the letter* Short paragraphs centred on the page
- ○ *Complimentary close* 'Yours sincerely' for named recipients, (i.e. Dear Mr Brown); 'Yours faithfully' for formally addressed recipients (i.e. Dear Sir(s), Dear Madam)
- ○ *Signature* Usually in the sender's own handwriting
- ○ Position/title of sender
- ○ References to enclosure and copies.

Figure 9.1 Layouts for business letters: (a) blocked; (b) semi-blocked

```
┌─────────────────────────────────────────────────────┐
│                      LETTERHEAD                       │
│                                                       │
│   Letter references                                   │
│   Date                                                │
│                                                       │
│   Inside address of recipient                         │
│                                                       │
│                                                       │
│   Attention leader                                    │
│                                                       │
│   Salutation                                          │
│                                                       │
│   Subject heading                                     │
│           Body                                        │
│   Complimentary close                                 │
│                                                       │
│                                                       │
│                                                       │
│   Signature                                           │
│   Name                                                │
│   Position                                            │
│                                                       │
│   Enclosure reference                                 │
│                                                       │
└─────────────────────────────────────────────────────┘
```

Figure 9.2 A template for a business letter

Types of letters

Letters in marketing can be about any topic. Here are some examples of different types of letters:

- o Letters giving information to customers
- o Letters confirming negotiations or a booking
- o Sales letters
- o Letters requesting information
- o Letters requesting a meeting or an appointment
- o Complaint letters
- o Letters of adjustment
- o Letters requesting payment
- o Covering letters to go with payment, maps or leaflets
- o Letters querying an invoice.

Writing customer letters

These can deal with any topic and you have to be clear about the message you are trying to convey as well as what you want the customer to do.

Midshire Bank Plc

High street
Assington
Berkshire AS1 6EL

Mr Joe Davies
17 Goldthorpe Way
Assbury
Berkshire AS2 4WQ

12 April 200X

Dear Mr Davies

At Midshire Bank we try to provide banking facilities of the highest quality in order to accurately meet our customer's needs. To do this it is essential that we listen to what our customers have to say. We would like you to help us by giving us your opinion of Midshire Bank's services.

We are asking an independent market research company. TMI Limited to interview a number of customers over the next few weeks. TMI Limited is a reputable company and your individual responses will be completely confidential to them, according to the Market Research Society's Code of Conduct.

They will be conducting the interviews by telephone and so an interviewer may telephone you at some point over the next few weeks.

Because TMI Limited will choose who to overview, you might not be contacted in this instance. If you are, we would value your contribution and hope you will be able to help us if asked.

Yours sincerely

CGowers

Charles Gowers
Branch Manager

Figure 9.3 A sample customer letter

Writing order letters

Letters are rarely used for placing orders because pre-printed order forms are usually more convenient and efficient. However, if you need to write an order letter, state your needs clearly by presenting the information in column form, with double-spacing and totalling the balance of prices at the end, explaining to which account the balance should be charged. State the delivery address (it may be different from the address on the letterhead) and the mode of transport which should be used.

MAKE-IT BUILDING SUPPLIERS
Churchyard Grove
Pickwick
Lancashire LUI 5TF
Tel: 0123 668791

Our ref: HBJ/abc

October 1st 20XX

The Timber Merchants Ltd
Station Road
Ripon
Yorkshire YU8 TR3

For the attention of Deborah Jones

Dear Ms Jones,

Account Number: 5690   Special order under invoice 123

Further to our last order, would you supply the following additional items:

1   20 metres of extra hard-wearing
    timber for fencing.   £5.95 per metre excl. VAT = £119

2   5 litres of creosote liquid in
    natural colour.   £2.75 per litres excl. VAT = £ 13.75

3   24 litres of indoor wood varnish
    in antique pine.   £1.44 per litres excl. VAT = £ 34.56

                                    Balance   £167.31
                                    VAT on items   £ 29.28

                                    Total balance   £196.59

The balance should be started on the above invoice and charged to our existing account. I would appreciate delivery by November 15th, latest.

Yours sincerely,

Harold Jenkins
Purchasing Manager

Figure 9.4 An order letter

Letters of enquiry or request

These can deal with a variety of questions, such as asking readers to supply certain information or make a presentation or inviting them to attend a function. Such letters almost always require a reply and some action to be taken, therefore they should be sent out in advance of the action date and be well-written and tactful.

The opening paragraph should state the nature of the enquiry or request clearly and simply, with a personal tone that will make the reader want to respond.

If further explanation or justification is needed, explain the importance of the information required and the situation which prompted the inquiry or request and, if appropriate, the benefits to the reader. Next, specify the desired action in a positive manner.

Close the letter with a courteous statement and explain the type of action needed, the deadline by which a reply should be made and assure the reader that the information will be treated as confidential (if appropriate).

ULTIMATE COMPUTER COMPANY Ltd
3 The Gateway
Hounslow
Middlesex TW15 6TU
Tel: 0181 967 6345

TRJ/abc
October 1st 20XX

Mr Andrew Collins
Marketing Communications Consultants
'The Nook'
Twinkle Lane
Beaconsfield
BUCKS DU18 74R

Dear Mr Collins

Ref: 'Computers of the World' Exhibition, London, 20XX
I had the pleasure of using your professional services in helping us to prepare and present at the above last year.
We are now in the process of planning to exhibit our new product range again this year and would like to know whether you would offer us your services. I am pleased to enclose our latest catalogue.
Please contact me at the end of next week to arrange for a meeting at our offices.
I look forward to hearing from you.

Yours sincerely,

Timothy R. Jones
Marketing Manager

Enc. Catalogue of product range X.

Figure 9.5 A letter of enquiry

Activity 9.1

Draft a letter asking current and lapsed health club members to renew their subscription. Use the communication to clean your database and update names and addresses.

Writing sales or persuasive letters

(Also see the section on Direct Marketing in Unit 4)

You could use the AIDA formula:

Grab the reader's **attention** by putting the focus on the reader and their situation.

- o Know who you are writing to. One way to grab the reader's attention is to use their name and to personalize the letter by using 'you', 'your' and 'yours'
- o Ensure you know what need your 'offer' is fulfilling. You must write from the reader's viewpoint in relation to their needs and wants
- o Know all the benefits, particularly the most important one
- o Attract the reader's attention with a headline, picture and colour.

Create **interest** in your product or service by stating how the reader may benefit.

- o Convert features into advantages and benefits for the reader. Keep sentences short and simple
- o Use sub-headings, white space, double spacing, underlining, italics, emboldening, and graphics to keep the reader's eye moving
- o Use the word 'you' often
- o Use facts.

Stimulate **desire** by using persuasive language where possible.

- o Make the reader desire your product/service by telling them how it will improve their life
- o Make it sound easy to obtain
- o Repeat your offer/best benefit using new wording
- o Be credible
- o Use the present tense as if the reader already owns the product/service
- o Use testimonials with signatures and pictures of people.

Engender **action** by explaining what the reader needs to do next.

- o Put a close date on your offer
- o Offer a bonus for quick reply
- o Use reply paid envelope or free-phone number
- o Make it easy to reply, e.g. using a coupon or order form which is easy to complete and cut out
- o Show the telephone number prominently.

Figure 9.6 A sales letter

Writing complaint letters

In marketing, complaint letters are likely to deal with faulty, mishandled or lost merchandise and other types of customer complaint.

If you are writing a letter of complaint, your motive for communicating is to have the claim sorted out and therefore written documentation is better than verbal communication as there is evidence of action you have taken.

In writing a complaint letter, you should include the following:

1. Opening paragraph with a clear statement of the problem
2. Further information that will verify the claim or adjustment needed
3. Closing statement with a polite, non-threatening request for action, emphasizing that the business relationship need not be affected if the matter is resolved satisfactorily.

BEAUTY POTIONS LTD
2–6 Staines Road
Windsor
Berkshire BK7 9LE
Tel: 01753 576423

JK/abc
October 1st 20XX

Variety Fragrances
10 Harrow Road
Wembley
Middlesex 8TU 65R

For the attention of Mr Gardiner

Dear Mr Gardiner,

On September 5th 20XX, we received your order 1112, together with the invoice, 2224.

Your will note that the first item on the invoice is listed as 50. Fragrance 'Irresistible', but unfortunately we received 50. Fragrance 'Uncontrollable'. A copy of the invoice is attached.

Please be kind enough to collect the wrong items and have them replaced by 50. Fragrance 'Irresistible' at the same time.

I look forward to receiving the correct order by November 1st 20XX.

Sincerely,

Joanna Kemp
Sales and Purchasing Manager

Enc. copy of invoice 2224

Figure 9.7 A letter of complaint

Answering complaint letters (letters of adjustment)

If you are replying to a complaint letter you should not delay your response, even if all you do is confirm receipt of the letter and explain that you need to investigate the matter, if it is a serious complaint. You should show empathy and concern for the customer and if you can make an adjustment, you should apologize and do so.

If the matter is not a legitimate complaint then you should explain your reasons why there will be no compensation or adjustment. In this situation, the following layout should be used:

1. An opening statement with reference to the claim or adjustment but with a notable point on which both parties might agree
2. An explanation which is tactful and maintains the goodwill of the organization, whilst ensuring that the claimant accepts (some) responsibility for the nature of the claim
3. The refusal, possibly with the suggestion of an alternative course of action
4. A pleasant close.

Activity 9.2

You are the manger of a restaurant and receive a letter from a customer complaining about the quality of service and the rudeness of one member of staff. You have investigated the complaint and have found it to be genuine. Write a letter in reply to the complaint.

Writing letters of credit

In most organizations today, the process of buying and selling goods and services is facilitated by credit. The credit manager has responsibility for accepting or rejecting an application for credit, which is based on an assessment regarding the person or organization's financial viability and outstanding debts, in relation to the type and value of credit required.

Approving credit

1. A pleasant opening paragraph which grants the credit request
2. Details of the terms and conditions under which credit is granted, addressing any specific points that may not be in line with company policy, but which have been raised
3. A courteous close.

Refusing credit

1. An opening statement appreciating the request for credit. Make the refusal, but with a notable point that both parties may agree
2. Details for the refusal in positive terms which are specific to the reader, whilst maintaining a tactful tone to ensure goodwill
3. A courteous close, with a sales pitch in relation to the correspondence, if appropriate.

CATERING WHOLESALERS LTD
35 Redruth Avenue
Tunbridge
Kent TN15 UCI
Tel: 01932 57311

HB/abc

October I st 20XX

Mr R.Anderson
The Manager
'The Restaurant'
76 Sevenoaks Road
Sevenoaks
KENT

Dear Mr Anderson,

Thank you very much for your recent application for credit. I am pleased to inform you that this has been approved.

Our terms and conditions are as follows:

1   A credit limit of £2000 is available for your establishment.
2   Invoices must be settled within 15 days of the date of issue, after which an interest charge of 5% will be levied on outstanding balances.

Yours sincerely,

Harry Bains
Credit Manager

Figure 9.8 A letter approving credit

Writing letters of recommendation

Letters of recommendation convey information about people, their characteristics and suitability for the position. Figure 9.9 gives an example of a letter of recommendation. These are usually confidential and must contain the following:

1.   The name of the person
2.   The position that the candidate is seeking
3.   The nature of the relationship between you and the candidate
4.   Relevant details to the position being sought by the candidate
5.   Evaluation of the candidate by the correspondent.

If you feel unable to provide a letter of recommendation, be brief and factual in your reasons.

FINANCE and INSURANCE Co
The Causeway
Newcastle upon Tyne NN4 65T
Tel: 0191 35202

SB/abc

October 1st 20XX

The Membership Secretary
Chartered Institute of Marketing
Moor Hall
Cookham
Berks

Dear Sir/Madam,

Re: Caroline Taylor

I am pleased to support Ms Taylor's application for membership of the Chartered Institute of Marketing.

Ms Taylor has been in our employment for 6 years working in the area of Direct Marketing.

I understand that she has passed all her CIM examinations and will be pleased to receive further benefit as a member of the CIM.

Yours faithfully,

Sheila Brown
Marketing Director

Figure 9.9 Letter of recommendation

Memoranda

Memoranda (or memos) are widely and routinely used by organizations, mainly for internal correspondence to convey short specific information. They could be written for any of the following reasons:

- To arrange a schedule of meetings
- To give the results of research
- To book a meeting room
- To organize training
- To organize attendance at an exhibition
- To ask for staff cover.

Of course, this list is not comprehensive as the reasons for sending a memo are almost unlimited. What can be stated is that memos can be stored for future reference and follow composition principles similar to that for writing business letters.

Memo paper is often pre-printed on A4 or A5, in the following format:

MEMO To: From: Date: Subject:

The sender and recipient of the memo are usually addressed by job title (e.g. sales manager), but their full name may also be included. It may be necessary to circulate the memo to other interested parties, and this should be indicated on the memo.

The subject title should be clear and concise and tell the recipient exactly what the memo is about.

The body of the memorandum should be in short paragraphs, with summary headings if appropriate.

MEMO
Medical Software Ltd

To: Carole Francis (Sales and Marketing Director)
From: Clare White (Marketing Manager)
Copy to: Hannah Craven (secretary)
Subject: Software 20XX Exhibition, Amsterdam, December I st – 3rd
Date: October Ist 20XX

We have 8 weeks before the exhibition takes place and need to finalize the details of the follow-up campaign, particularly the role of our sales force.

Further to our meeting last week, we also need to discuss the sales promotion initiatives to push our products following the exhibition.

Please confirm that a meeting on October 5th at 3 pm in my office will be convenient.

Figure 9.10 A memo

E-mail

E-mail is a quick and simple way to communicate internally and with external contacts who are connected to the Internet. There are no rules about layout and the medium is usually used to send short messages though longer documents, such as letters and reports, are attached by selecting the Insert, File Attachment option.

The best way to experiment with e-mail is to send and receive some and you will soon become adept at recognizing when e-mail is appropriate and when it is better to telephone someone, write a formal letter or send a memorandum.

As a rule of thumb, if you need an urgent reply, the telephone is the best way to actually check details with a colleague or an external contact. This is because you will know if you have got through to the person or not by telephone whereas you cannot be sure that your e-mail message has been read, which can lead to uncertainty when you want an instant response.

For more formal communications it is better to send a letter to external customers or a memorandum to colleagues.

Figure 9.11 An example of an e-mail message

How to write effective e-mail

Some people do not use normal punctuation, such as capital letters and full stops, but this can lead to confusing messages and is best avoided.

Because of the speed, e-mail is like a cross between a telephone conversation and a letter. Consequently, it is often too easy to send an e-mail which is like an unstructured written conversation.

Before you send a message you should consider what you expect to happen as a result of sending your message. If it is purely to provide information or an update you should say so. If you require a certain action then you should make sure your message is focused on achieving it.

It is better to avoid sending a message that attempts to fulfil many different purposes at once as you risk causing confusion.

You should ensure that you are sending your message to the right recipients and if appropriate you can use the Bcc (blind carbon copy) line to send the message to other recipients without others knowing.

If you expect anyone on the Cc list to take specific action as a result of receiving your message, then you should make it clear in the message. Otherwise recipients in the Cc list might assume that the message is 'for information only'.

Your message will be one of many that a recipient might receive in a day. Therefore your subject line should be concise but give an indication of the context of the message.

There is no set rule about using a salutation, such as Dear John or Dear Sir. If you are unsure of what to do, it is better to err on the side of caution and include a greeting as the absence of one could make you appear rude. Generally though, e-mails do not require formal greetings in the way that letters do. Similarly you do not need to use a formal close such as 'Yours sincerely' or 'Yours faithfully' unless you have opted for a formal greeting. Most people sign off with a closing term such as 'regards' followed by their first and last name if they do not know the person even though it is usually clear who is the sender of an e-mail message. If you do include a formal greeting you may want to include your job title and company website details.

Although you do not really need to think about layout in conjunction with an e-mail, it is better to avoid sending e-mails that are one long block of text. They are much easier to read if you use spaces between paragraphs.

If you are sending attachments you should say so in the main body of the e-mail. If you are worried about other people being able to access the document you can password protect the document so that it can only be opened using the password. You could then contact the recipient by another method and provide them with the password so then they can open the document.

As running costs are often related to the time on-line, problems could occur with being too brief. It is much better to work off-line and send a message that you have planned out and considered rather than rushing off a message and sending it without adequate forethought.

A good e-mail message should:

- o Have a definite purpose
- o Be properly addressed
- o Be well structured
- o Be written clearly
- o Use attachments wisely
- o Be protected appropriately.

Activity 9.3

S & G Construction Group has relocated its head office to Hong Kong and has been forced to undertake a restructuring exercise, which has resulted in the company reducing its international sales operation. As Sales Director, you will move to Hong Kong. Offices in Nairobi, Singapore, Dar-es-Salaam, New York and London will be retained.

Write a memo to the sales managers at each of the offices advising them of the importance of keeping open the lines of communication with their colleagues in each of the sales regions. Outline the disadvantages of relying on writing letters and explain the advantages of using existing IT and telecommunications facilities such as e-mail, fax and voice mail.

Notices

Notices can play an important role in disseminating information to a large number of people who share a common interest. Effective notices should follow these rules:

1. The size of the paper should correspond to the amount of information to be conveyed and its effect when displayed on the noticeboard and possibly viewed from several feet away.
2. The AIDA principle can again be used with a large, bold heading to capture attention, detail which holds the reader's interest and creates desire, and clear instructions as to the action which should be taken
3. The message should be simple and concise.

SAFETY FIRST!

A Special First-Aid Course designed to give you basic introduction will be available free to all employees on the following dates.

October 1st 5–6 pm
November 1st 5–6 pm
December 1st 5–6 pm

The number of places is limited to 20 per class so early booking is advisable.

Contact: Jane Slater, ext. 123

Figure 9.12 A notice

Reports

Reports can be used internally and externally in a range of contexts either to give information or to make proposals with justifications.

Progress reports may be of a routine nature to provide an update on a particular job or project. Special one-off reports can be requested or prepared voluntarily to interpret data, inform and/or influence recipients – for example, to analyse market research data, give information about sales trends or to propose a change of company policy.

Reports are used for a variety of purposes and can be short (such as progress reports) or long (such as investigative reports or the annual report), formal or informal, routine, occasional or specially commissioned. Before any report can be prepared, decisions about the exact nature and purpose of the report, the recipient, distribution and likely reaction all need to be addressed because these factors will determine the structure, length and style (i.e. the degree of formality) of the report.

In marketing, a formal report could be written on the current state of the market in a particular sector, or a short memorandum report could provide a range of quotes from printers for a new catalogue. Somewhere between these two extremes, an informal report could be written, proposing the use of videoconferencing in a firm, for example, or outlining sponsorship opportunities or reporting back from training or the success of an exhibition stand.

How to write reports

A report should not be written in a personal style highlighting the report writer's personal view if it has been commissioned to uncover facts and/or highlight the views of several people. A report should therefore be factual and written in an unbiased style. If necessary, it should show a range of opinions and conclude with the majority or most accurate viewpoint.

The report will sound more objective and professional if impersonal sentence constructions are used, such as:

- o 'It was found that'
- o 'It was evident that'
- o 'The statistics revealed that'
- o 'The investigations showed that'
- o 'It seems that '
- o 'It appears that'.

Your report will be more balanced and objective if you avoid emotional sounding phrases, such as 'a desperate situation' or 'This must be done at all costs'.

How to structure a report

The guidance given in the first part of the unit also applies to reports – they should have a beginning, a middle and an end. However, you can also organize the material schematically, using a system of numbers and/or letters. This approach not only makes the material easier to read and follow but is also useful for referencing purposes.

Using a combination of numbers and letters, your report could appear as follows:

1. Terms of reference
2. Procedure
3. Findings

    a.   Main point

        i.   Sub-point.

Or you could use a decimal numbering system:

1. Main heading

    1.1   Sub-section

    1.2   Same sub-section but dealing with another area

        1.2.1   Subordinate point.

In addition to using a numbering system to organize a report's contents, you could use different types of headings. These are used with the three main different types of reports: formal reports, informal reports and memorandum reports.

Formal reports

Formal reports are designed to achieve a number of goals but mainly to provide information and arguments based on investigating a problem or opportunity.

For a formal report, it is usual to have the following headings/sections and structure:

- Report title (this should be brief, specific and informative)
- Recipient's name
- Author's name
- Date
- Contents table (including headings and page numbers) if the report size warrants this
- Terms of reference (which should outline the scope of the report and the reason why it is being written)
- Procedure or research method/methodology (should identify how the information in the report was obtained)
- Findings (relevant facts and findings in order of importance, chronological order or just grouped together in relevant categories)
- Conclusion (should summarize the main findings and should not introduce new findings)
- Recommendations (not always required and used only if there are solutions to a problem which has been identified and if these solutions have emerged from a detailed analysis in the report)
- Appendices (where there is a large amount of factual data, tables and diagrams that could interrupt the flow of the document and cause confusion.) Appendices appear at the end of the report and their presence should be highlighted in the report. Each appendix should be numbered.

REPORT

TO: Denise Wood, Marketing Manager

FROM: Amy Mills, Marketing Assistant

DATE: 6 December 200X

GO EASY – THE CASE FOR A WEBSITE & ON-LINE BOOKING SERVICE

1. Introduction

The aim of this report is to identify reasons why our company, Go Easy, should invest in a web site and on-line booking service. This will be demonstrated by looking at the current state of the Internet market, predicted trends and competitor Internet activity.

2. Findings

a. The On-line Market

Recent studies by Business Research (December 2000) have looked at the US and UK on-line markets. Their information shows that in the US a third of all households with the Internet have shopped on-line in the past six months. Similarly, the figures for the UK are high, with 22% of internet users making a purchase on-line within the past three months.

Their data indicates that in the UK, travel is the third most popular on-line purchase after PC's and books, with 15% of on-line expenditure being spent on travel.

In the US, expenditure for on-line travel is set to grow from 0.5$ billion to over 7$ billion.

b. Competitor Activity

easyJet, one of our competitors, has made significant headway in this area since launching their web site and booking service in October of last year.

A recent report by 'Promotions and Incentives' magazines shows that 4% of all their bookings are currently made on-line. easyJet's aims to increase this to 30%, equating to £60 million worth of revenue.

easyJet have linked up with the *Times* to offer discounted flights to customers who book on-line.

c. Benefits of on-line booking

The information given in the Promotion and Incentives report shows that easyJet can handle up to 200 bookings at a time over the Internet, but only 90 at a time by telephone. Thus Internet booking gives a more efficient service to their customers.

Benefits to easyJet itself are they do not have to pay 80p commission to the telephonists, who would normally handle the incoming calls.

3. Conclusions

On-line sales are continually growing, with huge numbers of individuals potentially purchasing from the travel sector. Go Easy flights should have access to this market.

Our competition are establishing a firm foothold in this valuable market, using huge promotion and above-the-line advertising activity to do so.

On-line purchasing has advantages for both the consumer and the company.

4. Recommendations

In order not to miss out on the ever-growing on-line market, Go Easy must introduce a web site with a suitable and efficient on-line purchasing capability.

Figure 9.13 An example of a formal report

Informal reports

For an *informal* report it is usual to use the following headings:

- Introduction
- Findings
- Conclusion.

or

- Purpose and scope of report
- Background information
- Findings
- Conclusions and recommendations.

PRINTMAN PRINTING COMPANY

Report on Office Telecommunications Facilities

To: Mark Scrivens, Managing Director

From: Jo Goodwin, Sales and Marketing Manager

Date: 2 December 200X

Introduction

As a small printing company trying to succeed in a competitive market, we need to be able to use various office equipment to improve our efficiency and effectiveness when communicating with customers and internally. This report sets out to identify where we could upgrade our current systems and equipment to improve how sales representatives and account managers operate.

Findings

Voice Mail

During busy periods customers often have problems getting through to the switchboard with our current telephone system. With a voice mail system connected to a computer, customers could use an interactive menu system which would mean they could ring up and choose to be connected to any one of a number of our account managers without having to go through the switchboard. Customers could also leave messages when a person is not at their desk, which saves colleagues spending time taking down messages.

Networked Laptop Computers

Laptop computers could be used by our account managers and sales team while they are out visiting clients. It means they could access information here at the office and give clients quotes on print jobs immediately. In addition they could show clients examples of relevant jobs we have done on their laptops rather than carrying round a large portfolio or briefcase of printed materials. Also when it is not worth staff coming back to the office because their last client visit was near to their home, it makes sense to give them the means to finish off work, such as, quotes, reports and design briefs, in their own time at home.

An Extranet

As we have now got a computer system with Internet access, it would be good to upgrade the system to incorporate an extranet so that customers can access their accounts and check the progress on their various print jobs with us. This would reduce the number of 'checking' calls that account managers deal with and free them up to develop new business and cross-sell our services to clients more effectively.

Conclusions

These are the three main systems and pieces of equipment that we could use at the moment to improve how we operate in sales and marketing. If these proposals are of interest, then it would be a simple task to collate various information about different systems and do a price check against different products in the market.

Figure 9.14 An example of an informal report

Memorandum report

For memorandum reports, it is usual to use a memo format and to group relevant information together under different headings and categories.

Memorandum

To: Bob, Bloggs, Sales Manager

From: Marcia Merchant, Sales and Marketing Assistant

Subject: Report on Negotiation Skills Course

This memorandum report outlines the value and effectiveness of the recent Negotiation Skills course attended on 4 December 200X run by Total Training at the Willow Bank Hotel.

Course Details

It was a one-day course and cost £150 per delegate. Delegates who attended were from a variety of sectors but all were working in sales and marketing jobs.

Course Content

The course was delivered with a mixture of input, case studies and interaction with the audience. The course was well organized and the trainer was well organized and interesting.

Topics covered included preparing for negotiations, building rapport, trading concessions, maintaining advantage and controlling interpersonal behaviour.

The course was delivered from a 'buying and selling' perspective and provided comprehensive coverage of theory, practical and suggestions and skills testing.

Conclusion

The course runs again early next year and I recommend that others in the department attend it.

Figure 9.15 An example of a memorandum report

Articles

If you work in the marketing department of a firm that produces a staff newsletter with the aim of improving internal communication, you could occasionally be asked to contribute – or you might even be responsible for all aspects of it, such as writing, designing and arranging the printing. However, you might never be asked to write an article or an advertorial (like a press release but in the form of a newspaper or magazine article) because it is not part of your job. Nevertheless an article is a communication format that is occasionally tested on the examination paper.

The way to approach writing an article is to use the writing skills you have honed when you have written letters and reports and to combine that with your skill in producing press releases. When you are writing an article for an advertorial or for a company newsletter, you must try to adopt an independent, unbiased tone – in other words, the 'sell' should be very subtle.

Figure 9.16 is an example of an advertorial article, written by a partner in a small labelling and sign company for a newspaper, about why logos, letterhead design and graphical symbols are important for companies' internal and external communications.

Design Works

Labelling and Signage Designs know that good design is essential for firms that need to communicate with their staff, customers and suppliers.

Essential safety notices in the workplace need to stand out so people take notice of them – in a way that words alone cannot manage. Graphical symbols can show hazards and directional symbols can indicate specific areas, e.g. toilets, disabled access, fire exits, litter bins, etc. At Labelling and Signage Designs these can be tailor-made for any individual work environment. Just visualise the 'Keep Britain Tidy' logo or the Olympic Games symbol or even a 'No smoking' symbol to understand the power of images in communicating with people.

To communicate instantly with members of the public who are unfamiliar with an area or environment, it is important to use signs which indicate where dressing rooms, pay points and exit doors are located.

However, all imagery in the corporate environment should be consistent with the image and identity the company wants to communicate to its staff and public.

Consequently, handwritten, poorly designed signs and images would portray an amateur, uncaring and unprofessional image. A professional signage company knows how important the right typeface, shape and colour is to presenting the correct image and conveying the message effectively.

Corporate Identify

The Corporate image that is communicated in a company's logo is seen on its letterheads, business cards, lorries, shop or office front, sales promotion literature and packaging or carrier bags, depending on the firm's type of business.

The designers at Labelling and Signage can use graphical symbols, visual communication and typefaces to give a company an appropriate image. A particular typeface can convey a certain personality or culture, e.g. formality, long-established or modern and technical. A logo which stands out can create recognition and differentiate the firm from its competitors. The right logo can link the various products and services of one organization into a single, consistent identity. Think about the distinctive type style of the Coca-Cola logo, the use of the black horse symbol that distinguishes Lloyds Bank; Kodak's outstanding black and yellow packaging certainly makes its products stand out. These well-known logos and symbols actually provide customers with reassurance that they are dealing with the best.

The logo can even indicate a firm's field of activity: an international worldwide firm might even include a globe; a people-oriented firm might show linked hands.

It is difficult with a new firm, or a company with a new product, to find a name that has not been used before. But the right acronym such as Esso or Persil could mean a product is easy to pronounce and has a distinctive name. In a similar vein, the right slogan can help customers remember a firm or its products.

Figure 9.16 An advertorial

Summary

In this unit you have studied:

o   Why you need to be familiar with a range of communication formats

o   How various communication formats are structured

o   How and when to write effective letters, memos, notices, e-mails, reports and articles.

Further study and examination preparation

Attempt Questions 4 and 7 from the June 2000 paper and Question 6(c) from the December 2000 paper. Go to www.cimeduhub.com to access Specimen Answers and Senior Examiner's advice for these exam questions.

Exam hint

You need to be familiar with all the communication formats used in this unit as they will be tested throughout the examination paper. You will find that most questions in fact require candidates to write their answer in the format of a letter, report, memo or e-mail. Also Question 1 usually includes a report which is often awarded a possible 20 marks and so this is obviously an important area for you to study.

unit 10
customer service and customer care

In this unit you will:

o Examine the changing context of customer needs

o Appreciate the role of communications in implementing customer care

o See how customer communications help build customer relationships

o Learn how to plan and establish a customer care programme

o Look at why customer care systems sometimes fail

o See how Information and Communication Technologies can be used in customer service.

By the end of this unit you should be able to:

o Use communication skills to establish good customer care

o Handle customer complaints effectively

o Identify how customer care could be improved in a given situation

o Devise appropriate customer communications as part of a customer care programme.

Study Guide

This unit develops the customer theme from Cross-reference: Unit 1 and focuses on how customer communications are a vital part of good customer care and customer service.

The unit covers indicative content areas 1.3–1.5 and 5.1–5.6 of the syllabus. This unit also links to the Marketing Fundamentals syllabus, in particular with indicative content 1.1.1. and 1.4.2.

Both syllabuses deal with the issues around adding quality to product/service delivery in order to close the gap between customer expectations and their experience, and the importance of creating a dialogue with customers to promote a long-term relationship. However, the emphasis in the Customer Communications syllabus is on the practical aspects of improving interaction with customers. Consequently this unit deals with how customer service can be improved to meet customer expectations by improving customer interaction and communication with customers.

There is further reading on the areas covered in this unit in Unit 1 and Unit 9 of the *Marketing Fundamentals* coursebook.

You should take two hours to read the unit and a further two hours to complete the activities. At the end of this unit you are also directed to relevant examination questions at the end of the book.

Study tip

At the end of this unit you could check whether your place of work has specific policies or procedures for dealing with quality or customer care issues. Consider how these are implemented.

In addition, you could undertake an audit of the various ways that customers are communicated with and check whether they comply with stated customer care standards.

For example, if you work in a doctor's surgery you could look at the following:

- How easy it is for patients to communicate with the surgery
- How patients' telephone queries and complaints are dealt with
- What is the attitude of staff to patients when they deal with them face to face or on the telephone?
- How could the appearance and content of any documentation be improved, for example, appointment cards, patients' booklets or notices that are displayed in the surgery?
- How could any of the 'behind-the-scenes' processes be improved to make things easier for patients?

Relations with customers

Customer care, customer service, customer satisfaction. Are these merely buzzwords that organizations pay lip service to, or have we really entered a new age of customer focus? Customer focus, or putting the customer at the centre of the organization's operations, has always been central to marketing philosophy, but for a time it seemed that many firms in various industry sectors had forgotten the customer in their bid to maximize profits and minimize costs. However, the desire to meet the growing demands of customers and the need to keep up with more innovative customer-focused competition has forced many firms to re-examine how their customers are really treated. And even firms operating in markets that traditionally compete on price have been faced with the fact that it needs only one competitor to break rank and raise customer expectations for all to be faced with a compelling need to jump on the customer-care bandwagon.

The changing context of customer needs

Consumers wherever they come from, are far more likely to complain nowadays. This is simply due to the fact that in general terms, consumers are travelled more widely and more educated than ever before. Many consumers have developed sophisticated tastes and have higher expectations having seen the superior service standards in the USA and the innovative approaches to quality control that originated in the Far East.

As a consequence, images of deferential consumers from the Far East or of stiff upper-lipped British consumers are fast becoming old-fashioned stereotypes that do not apply to the modern, global society we inhabit. The trend is for more consumers to be more demanding than ever before.

In a Henley Centre research survey (in *Marketing*, November 1998), 56 per cent of people said they complained in person about poor services or faulty goods over the past year, a massive leap from 39 per cent in the previous year. The Henley Centre survey showed that consumers are more assertive and willing to take action against companies. This may range from complaining about faulty goods or inadequate service, or warning friends and family away from a company, to stopping purchasing from a company because it is viewed as unhealthy, unethical or environmentally unsound.

Furthermore, in 2001, a Henley Centre research survey of the insurance sector (Insurance Day, 2001) found that, despite the investment in customer relations by insurance businesses, customers are generally cynical about whether companies really listen to them. The facts support this: 20 per cent of general insurance consumers who have complained to their provider, only 5 per cent felt they had been dealt with satisfactorily. Worse still, out of 5 per cent of pension customers who complained, no-one was happy with the response.

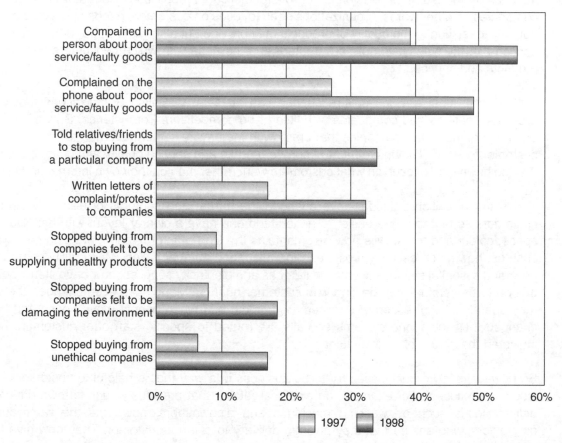

Figure 10.1 The rise of the assertive customer. Reproduced with kind permission from *Marketing* magazine

However, things are changing slowly and organizations have begun to realize that they operate in a more competitive and litigious environment where they must respond to consumer demands. Most organizations also realize that it is far easier and cheaper to retain current customers than it is to cultivate new ones. Moreover, research shows that dissatisfied customers tend to spread the news of their bad experiences very quickly – something that affects not only an organization's image but also the bottom line in the long run.

Interactivity – the case of Federal Express

'FedEx' is a package delivery multinational which delivers millions of packages every day. Since 1994 it has run a service online in which customers have a direct window into FedEx's package-tracking database. 12,000 customers per day click through web pages to pinpoint their parcels. That, customers feel, adds to the service and saves FedEx millions of dollars in customer service cost savings.

Source: A. Tapp, *Principles of Direct and Database Marketing*, 2nd Edition, 2000.

Customer focus

The consumers trend to being less tolerant and more demanding transcends industry sectors. Consumers are less willing to accept shoddy workmanship from builders, lame excuses about unsatisfactory hotels from holiday companies, poor service from shop assistants, overbearing attitudes from health professionals or overcomplicated application forms from mortgage companies. In other words, organizations need to focus on customers needs and expectations, not only in relation to the quality of products they provide but also with regard to their quality of service (i.e. the way customers are treated) and the ease with which consumers can access products and services.

Perhaps the most obvious culture change can be seen in British organizations that were previously nationalized companies with little or no competition. For instance, British Telecom and most of the utility companies that are now in the private sector have had to become more customer focused. They have had to improve product and service quality and change the way they do business, to focus on what customers want rather than on their own internal processes.

For example, British Telecom have changed the format and contents of bills they send to customers so that they are easier to understand and have a clearer layout with better use of space, colour and fonts. Bills now also contains the kind of information that customers want, such as, how much each call costs and the telephone number called. Many utility companies providing essential services such as water, gas and electricity supplies, now have staff who are trained to be helpful when dealing with customer queries. Many have even changed the way they operate so that essential services are not 'cut off' when people move house and have changed their telephone systems so calls are routed to specific staff after customers have indicated the nature of their enquiry.

So nowadays more businesses try to do business in a way that is helpful to customers or is 'customer focused'. For example, an electrical retailer that previously used its own drivers to deliver goods such as washing machines and dishwashers, now puts the work out to contractors, who ensure that they arrange delivery to suit the customer. They now give time slots within which the delivery will take place, so customers do not have to take a whole day off work to wait for a delivery.

One-to-one marketing: a DIY company

Let's say you run a chain of DIY 'out of town' warehouse stores. You have two ways of running the company. Traditional thinking would push you to competing on market-share terms with your rivals, trying to get as many customers in as possible to buy your products. You may advertise in local press or radio. To boost sales you run incentives and broadcast these, hoping to pinch some of your competitor's customers.

Your alternative is one-to-one marketing. A customer comes in and buys some tomato seeds. He mentions that he is starting up a greenhouse in his garden. You note this onto a database with that customer's name and address, which you asked him for at the till. When a new book, *A Guide to Greenhouse Gardening* comes out, you write to him, telling him about the book and offering it to him with a couple of packets of seeds thrown in. If he wants it, you suggest, phone in and you will send it to him. Next time he pops in you learn more about what he is doing with his garden, and again you note it.

What you are doing is learning with the customer what they want of you. You are offering them value by giving them relevant, timely information. You are making it easy for them to do business with you. You have tailored your product and your communication to that individual, in an attempt to grow your business from that one customer.

Source: A. Tapp, *Principles of Direct and Database Marketing*, 2nd Edition, 2000.

Consumerism

The pressure on organizations from consumers to be more customer focused has seen a rise in consumerism. The impact of consumerism can be seen in a more customer focused National Health Service (NHS) in Britain. This has come about after a long period of intense criticism about levels of hospital care. The NHS has produced a 'customer charter' that lists the minimum service levels that patients can expect in an attempt to show its focus on patients' rights and expectations.

Rights and Standards throughout the NHS

Access to services

You have the *right* to:

 receive health care on the basis of your clinical need, not on your ability to pay, your lifestyle or any other factor;
 be registered with a GP and be able to change your GP easily and quickly if you want to;
 get emergency medical treatment at any time through your GP, the emergency ambulance service and hospital accident and emergency departments; and
 be referred to a consultant acceptable to you, when your GP thinks it is necessary, and to be referred for a second opinion if you and your GP agree this is desirable.

Figure 10.2 Example of a customer charter (Taken from The NHS Patient's Charter and is reproduced with the kind permission of the Department of Health.)

More organizations are using customer communications, such as newsletters, leaflets and even advertising, to respond to pressure groups that complain about products, prices, packaging, advertising or ways of doing business. For example, Shell paid for a high-profile newspaper advertising campaign defending its right to produce petroleum in Nigeria. Similarly McDonalds produced leaflets to explain that by sourcing its beef in North America the company did not damage South American rainforests.

Some firms have seized upon 'complaints' and turned them into opportunities to provide products and services that are more in tune with the market and have used their customer communications effectively to promote the product/service strengths via packaging, advertising or public relations. An example of this is the number of different organizations that have made 'green' claims in recent years.

However, it is important that if a firm gives in to public pressure, it should use its communications with customers to get the best publicity from the situation.

Case history

The Bank of Scotland's customer communications

An example where this did not happen was when the Bank of Scotland outraged many sections of its customer base when it announced a deal with a US television evangelist. In the face of angry customers it scrapped the plan to provide a telephone bank service for millions of his US followers, after he made outspoken attacks on gays, feminists, Muslims, Hindus and effectively insulted the whole of Scotland.

Initially the bank stood its ground even as many customers closed accounts, local authorities, charities and trade unions threatened to take their trade elsewhere and protesters handcuffed themselves to its headquarters.

Then, after senior management realized their blunder, they authorized an extensive media campaign of damage limitation.

However, during the campaign at an annual shareholders' meeting, the Bank's Governor appeared to only begrudgingly apologize for the fiasco, apparently seeming not to regret what the bank had done but appearing more to regret that people did not like what it had done. Thus an extensive media campaign to apologize and acknowledge public pressure was wasted because the people at the top of the company lacked a customer focus in communicating with an important group of stakeholders.

 ## Activity 10.1

Consider an issue of public concern that might affect a firm of your choice. Explain how stakeholders might communicate their objections about the issue to the firm. Suggest how the firm might react and what it could do to ensure that customer relations were not damaged.

Ethical marketing

Ethical businesses are those where staff recognize that they have a social responsibility, i.e. that they cannot conduct their business without due regard to broader social concerns. They may go one stage further than obeying the law or may even set themselves a voluntary code of practice where no law exists.

In the UK, strict employment law protects workers from exploitation but there is no law that prevents firms from sourcing supplies from countries where workers are exploited. An ethical business might respond to consumer pressure as part of its customer focus and only contract with suppliers that do not exploit their workers.

Case history

Lands' End

Lands' End supplies casual clothing by mail order. They use their catalogue to communicate with customers about their customer focus. They feature endorsements from satisfied customers, for example:

When I tore my trousers on a railway carriage door I asked if you could repair them. Instead you replaced them immediately. You really do push the boundary of customer service further than anyone could reasonably expect.

They also feature a statement about their business ethics:

We contract only with suppliers who produce products of high quality and value, who ensure their employees are of legal age, work under safe and healthy conditions, are paid fairly and are not discriminated against.

They also provide a free copy of their Standards of Business Conduct via a free-phone number.

Quality and customer care

Customer care and its close relation, quality, are not new ideas, only old ones that have been brushed down and spruced up. They help to remind organizations that they should not rest on their laurels in an increasingly competitive and unforgiving world.

Customer care and quality are linked in that both are concerned with getting things right first time. Quality management is usually associated more with production issues whilst customer care is more concerned with the organization's relationship with its customers and customer service issues.

Quality management is basically concerned with: establishing standards for a product or service; establishing procedures, production methods and service criteria to ensure that standards are met; the monitoring of actual quality; and taking action when quality falls below standard.

With customer care, the aim is to close the gap between customers' expectations and their experience. This is often achieved by finding out what the customer thinks and what they want in terms of product/service quality, packaging, delivery and after-sales service.

For some large service-delivery organizations, such as banks, it has been a case of realizing that customers need to be treated as people who matter and they have had to concentrate on delivering a personal service that makes people feel welcome.

For Lloyds Bank in Britain, in the early 1990s, it was a case of laying down a service challenge to staff that set out a number of minimum standards. These included:

- o Not letting the telephone ring more than four times before it is answered
- o The person answering should introduce themselves by name
- o Queues at tills should not have more than five people in them
- o Establishing various levels of product knowledge that staff should have.

Some organizations have considered the total product concept and have looked to add value. An example of this is the toy car manufacturer that packs the product in a box which folds into a toy garage.

Other organizations have gone further and have gone through a process of business process re-engineering. In these cases firms have looked at the whole transaction process a customer goes through from the customer's point of view in order to simplify it and make it easier. In the insurance industry this has revolutionized the way some firms operate so that services are no longer sold through intermediaries but delivered direct and therefore more cheaply to the consumer.

Delighting the customer

Some companies have gone to great lengths to get the detail right. For example, when Nissan dealerships take a car in for a service they provide a replacement courtesy car, check the car over and undertake repairs, clean it and leave a free air freshener inside. A few days later they telephone the customer to find out if there are any problems and to check whether the customer is happy with their treatment.

However, the most innovative companies have gone even further to exceed customer expectations. In many cases these organizations consider that most jobs have two parts – the mechanics of what needs to be done, and the people part. Maws, manufacturers of baby feeding products, established a customer care line to answer new mothers' queries. When one anxious mother called the number to ask about stockists for a product to soothe a crying baby, a highly trained member of staff manning the care line not only provided clear information about stockists and how the product should be used but also felt empowered to send out a complimentary pack of the product. Good business practice indeed, because these relatively inexpensive items have to be replaced every six weeks – and, of course, by exceeding customer expectations they won a loyal customer who is also prepared to sing the company's praises to other potential customers.

Customer delight will ratchet up standards – it is not a static relationship. If the customer is delighted by something for the first time, they eventually get used to the extra service. For example, delivering a fresh bowl of fruit to a hotel room as part of the service soon becomes expected and customer expectations rise even further.

Activity 10.2

Think of an incident when you have been delighted by the service you have received. It could have been when you have been doing your weekly shop at the local supermarket, or buying items at a chemist, or when you were making an enquiry at the bank, or when you were travelling on business. Explain how you were delighted and estimate the cost of the service improvement in relation to the cost of attracting a new customer.

Relationship marketing

The main idea behind relationship marketing is to build strong relationships with customers in order to retain them instead of concentrating efforts on recruiting new ones.

There are several factors which influence customer retention:

- o High-quality products to encourage repeat purchase
- o Customers need to feel valued to be loyal, and this can be created by only excellent customer service
- o Taking long-term marketing decisions, for example continuous improvement or innovation to keep ahead of customer needs
- o Frequent customer contact to establish customer profiles in order to ensure accurate customer targeting of goods, services and information.

Consequently relationship marketing is closely aligned with both customer care principles and the basic tenets of consumerism. From a customer communications perspective, the most important factor in relationship marketing is the creation of a dialogue between the organization and the consumer. This results in the consumers getting what they want and at the same time becoming a loyal customer who recommends others to the firm.

A good illustration of relationship marketing is the way supermarkets have established loyalty cards to encourage customers to collect reward points when they shop at stores. The advantage to customers is that after collecting so many reward points these are converted into money-off coupons. The advantage to the store is that when customers register for a loyalty card they provide the store with valuable customer information. This information is used to build up profiles of customers who use a particular store in a particular area. This can help individual stores to stock the products wanted by their particular clientele. So, for example, a store in a location with a large Jewish community would know to stock a range of kosher products.

Each time a customer uses the card to collect points from shopping, the customer's purchase history is added to. The value of this information is that past purchase history is the best indicator of future purchase behaviour. This helps stores with many marketing decisions, including, for example, planning appropriate targeted customer communications such as direct marketing and advertising campaigns.

Case history

Relationship marketing in the hospitality trade

Every few months the Isle of Eriska Hotel, near Oban, Scotland, sends out a newsletter to former guests updating them on what has been happening in the hotel, any special offers available to them and news of the owners' pets. Although details are obviously derived from a database the former guests are still made to feel special. The personal letter of the proprietor essentially thanks them for staying at the hotel and invites them to visit again.

Thus the basic components of relationship marketing are implemented: knowing the customer, listening to the customer, competing for the customer and finally, thanking the customer.

This simple example was given by Gordon, R. (1994), The personal touch, *Caterer and Hotelkeeper*, 9 June, p. 26. It is typical of the personalized service that an individually owned hotel owner can offer its guests. But what of the larger organization with hotels distributed throughout the world?

Dev, C. S. and Ellis, B. D. (1991), Guest histories: an untapped service resource, *Cornell HRA Quarterly*, August, pp. 29–37, use the example of a business traveller arriving at the airport, being met by the hotel courtesy vehicle and supplied with his favourite soft drink.

On arriving at the hotel he is greeted by name at the front desk, has been pre-registered and all details completed including method of payment. His room has been customized, from his preferred daily newspaper to a selection of the brands of drinks and snacks he consumed on his last stay. Tickets are booked for a theatre production he wanted to see that night. Excellent customer service or invasion of privacy?

This example was only hypothetical but served to illustrate the power of the guest history system if used to its full potential.

Source of both examples: F. Buttle, *Relationship Marketing Theory and Practice*, 1996, Paul Chapman Publishing Ltd

Customer loyalty and retention

The growing realization that keeping the customers you have is as important as customer acquisition has come about because of the costs involved in attracting new customers. This realization has evolved into understanding a customer's *lifetime value*. By doing this, you can be selective about who you try to keep as well as who you want to attract.

Smith (*Meeting Customer Needs*, Butterworth-Heinemann, 1997) believes that customer retention affects the bottom line and quotes the following facts:

o A 5 per cent increase in customer retention could create a 125 per cent increase in profits
o A 10 per cent increase in retailer retention can translate to a 20 per cent increase in sales
o Extending customer lifecycles by 3 years could treble profits per customer.

For example, a client who occasionally uses the services of an advertising agency to produce its low-cost press advertising but places all its high-value promotional literature and exhibition design work with a design consultancy is not a particularly valuable client to the advertising agency. However, the client that stays with the advertising agency and as it grows gives more work each year to the agency could be said to have a high 'customer lifetime value'.

The idea of 'cherry picking' valuable clients and directing more resources to these key clients has been used by many types of organizations. Financial services companies have used the idea well to target graduates with cheap loans and free bank accounts in the hope that these customers will buy a range of financial products over the years of their customer life, for example, personal loans, life assurance, mortgage and pensions. Obviously, by analysing customers and trends, organizations can target appropriate communications depending on the customer's lifetime value.

In business-to-business marketing situations, some organizations have structured their departments and staff, so that individual staff can be responsible for certain key accounts or clients. By having a single point of contact organizations find they can look after clients in a 'seamless' way.

One company that builds masts as part of the physical infrastructure for telecommunications companies does not have a large number of different clients, but its 'key' clients spend massive amounts of money. Consequently, 'key account managers' have been appointed to work closely with the staff from the client firms. They provide expertise and technical support beyond the physical product that they provide. Building this kind of client relationship almost builds in client dependency and enhances the relationship. Very generous credit facilities and reciprocal buying practices have been established so that clients do not want to put their business elsewhere.

Client communications are such that account managers regularly 'network' with clients to ensure that they are happy with the way contracts are proceeding and close relationships are built up. Regular telephone contact and progress reviews mean that any problems are resolved before they become serious issues. A high level of face to face, telephone and electronic contact means that account managers understand their client's business so that they can anticipate further contracts and cross-sell other construction and site management services to clients.

Case history

Banks and retaining customers

Most students have a bank account. When it is opened, several incentives are offered, and during the time as a student costly facilities such as free overdrafts are allowed. Research by a student at Coventry University suggests that it takes between five and nine years for the bank to recover the cost of this type of account. However, many students are not very loyal to their original bank, with up to 40 per cent switching to another in the three years following graduation.

Unless the banks take action to build strong relationships with students this situation will continue. The result will be heavy losses on student accounts and this is obviously very bad business for those banks who cannot retain customers.

Source: D. Adcock, R. Bradfield, A. Halbourg and C. Ross, *Marketing Principles and Practice*, 4th Edition, 2001, Pearson Education Ltd

Activity 10.3

Consider a loyalty scheme that you are familiar with and describe how it works to the advantage of the customer and the organization.

Managing the customer relationship

Customer relations should not concentrate on handling complaints, i.e. putting wrong things right, it should be about quality issues and customer service improvements.

According to Bee, F & R (*Customer Care,* Chartered Institute of Personnel and Development, 1999), 'Customer care is not just a set of tasks, a list of do's and don'ts: it is a way of life.' They hold that customer care is important because:

o Satisfied customers take up less time
o Satisfied customers cause less stress and bring job satisfaction
o Satisfied customers tell other people which enhances your organization's reputation
o Your customers are your business – without them there is no business.

Steps involved in establishing quality

o Establish standards of quality for a product or service
o Establish procedures to ensure that quality standards are met
o Monitor quality
o Take control action when quality falls below standard.

Steps involved in improving customer service

o Measure standards by finding out levels of customer satisfaction
o Analyse the feedback
o Act upon the information and develop what people want, for example, customer-friendly systems or getting the detail right
o Train staff to ensure competence
o Review processes and procedures to ensure they are customer-focused
o Consider how much further you could go in terms of exceeding customer expectation.

 Activity 10.4

In the following situations consider what the minimum need is and suggest what additional 'customer service' needs should be met, particularly in relation to how the organization communicates with customers:

1. Where a customer goes to a garage for petrol
2. Where a customer travels on a train.

What do customers want?

Customers certainly do not like any of the following:

- o Rude staff
- o Insensitivity and apathy to customer requests
- o Delayed service
- o Difficulties in getting through to a company (often unanswered telephones)
- o Poor billing or letters that are inaccurate or do not make sense
- o Misinformation, i.e. different information from different staff.

All of these create an unprofessional impression. Research shows that when a customer has a negative experience with an organization, the customer will tell on average about eleven people, and nine out of ten people do not complain but take their business elsewhere.

In analysing customer feedback it appears that most feedback and complaints are not about actual products but seemingly peripheral issues, such as late delivery, the way the product does not pour easily from the carton, the way the customer was spoken to or given the wrong information. There are four key characteristics of good customer service.

A positive/proactive attitude

Customers do not want to be faced with apathetic staff who have to be asked the right question before they will be helpful and suggest a solution to a customer problem. They want staff who take responsibility for making things go smoothly and keep customers informed – customers do not want to chase staff to find out things.

Customer-friendly systems

Customers need payment to be made easy, user-friendly application forms and store layouts or computer programmes to be designed with the user in mind. The organization's systems should be set up so there is a degree of flexiblility, for instance, if a customer wants to change an order or cannot answer all the questions of an application form.

Knowledgeable/courteous staff

Customers want to be dealt with by trained staff who have a satisfactory level of technical knowledge. They also want friendly and courteous staff to deal with, who do what they say and genuinely seem to care.

Product/service reliability

Products that work consistently. Services that turn up on time – every time.

Rules of good customer service

- o Getting it right first time
- o Listening to customers to find out what they actually want
- o Communicating clearly and positively with customers
- o Making it easy for staff to help customers
- o Employing staff who are genuinely courteous

- Encouraging staff to be fair, understanding and flexible in their response
- Handling complaints in a constructive way
- Investigating mistakes and learning from them.

1	Smile; be polite, helpful and friendly.
2	Listen and show interest.
4	Do not guess, find out.
3	Satisfy queries positively.
5	Work tidily and satisfy.

Figure 10.3 An extract from Asda's customer care policy

Customer service skills

In many customer service situations, there are four ways that customers can be made happy and problems resolved:

- If customers are shown respect and understanding of things from their perspective
- If customers are listened to
- If staff ask what a customer actually wants
- If staff are proactive and offer suggestions or ways to resolve a situation.

This topic is developed further in Unit 5.

Improving customer interaction

Good customer communications are a vital part of customer care. The communication may be face to face with a customer, in writing or on the telephone – whatever the method, it is essential that the communication is clear, concise, courteous, creates the right impression and conveys the correct message.

Federal Express: A model of efficiency and customer service

Federal Express has for long been an enthusiastic innovator across a range of technologies relevant to its worldwide delivery operations. An early user of toll-free telephone hot-lines and fax facilities for customer service, it has established itself as a pioneer in electronic commerce and customer service back-up systems.

With a worldwide delivery throughout of over 2.5 million packages per day, across over 200 countries, the company has an obvious interest in staying at the cutting edge of any technology that supports its customer service vision.

While the company still offers customers the ability to track delivery progress by phone or fax, it is finding that more and more tracking requests (over 900, 000 per month), are coming on-line via 5000 websites linked to its customised tracking network Fedex InterNetShip. Of course, with a 99 per cent on-time delivery record, the majority of its customers have no pressing need to reassure themselves about timing and delivery!

www.fedex.com

Source: Adcock et al. *Marketing Principles and Practice*, 4th Edition, 2001.

Creating a good image

You can create a good first impression with customers through positive action, such as:

o   Good personal grooming
o   Smart clothes or uniform
o   Punctuality
o   A tidy and well-organized work environment
o   Smart reception areas
o   Establishing a consistent method for greeting people when they enter the organization
o   An overall positive image in all documentation such as invoices, application forms, instruction manuals, leaflets, posters, signs, company vans and shop windows.

Improving internal communication

Some organizations have had to spend time and resources in changing the way they do business to improve internal communication and so ultimately improve external customer service. One insurance company has changed its job roles so that clerks no longer deal with one aspect of a claim or a customer file but instead become 'case managers' who have full responsibility for seeing a process through and dealing with a customer at all stages of a claim. This approach has led to a 'seamless' process and directly contributed to a reduction in complaints and delays.

Other organizations have used technology to improve teamworking and internal communication. A new generation of desktop systems now makes small-scale videoconferencing affordable and easy to use. A single card, installed in a personal computer, can enable people to hear and see colleagues face-to-face wherever they are in the world and exchange and amend documents on screen.

In addition, more organizations are investing in 'knowledge networks' or 'knowledge management' to make the most of skills and experience that exist in an organization. This usually means establishing a database to store company procedures, templates of forms, file notes and projects so that staff anywhere in the firm can access current information and examples of past project work to improve the way they do their jobs.

Communication tools such as mobile telephones, pagers, voice mail and call routing are used so that personnel can be reached wherever they are working. Similarly more staff are allowed to work at home or on the move by using remote data access through lap tops or computers at home.

Staff at a large consumer electronics company, with 64 bases in 30 countries, found that the internal communication between international sites and the head office in Japan was difficult. There had been little face-to-face or even telephone communication in the past, which had led to poor working relationships and delays which in turn affected production and distribution. To overcome language and time differences, fax communication and personal videoconferencing meetings have been used with great success.

Activity 10.5

Find out what the following 'flexible office solutions' are and how they can help improve customer service:

o   Intelligent telephony services
o   Message and voice processing
o   Personal video conferencing.

213

According to Smith (*Meeting Customer Needs,* Butterworth-Heinemann, 1997) 'Good customer service often goes beyond your own organization. The relationship your organization has with suppliers, retailers, distributors and other members of the "demand chain" have an important effect on the service your customers enjoy.'

Smith advocates that everyone in the demand chain should be capable of delivering a quality service and that this can be achieved through training, good communication, support and a shared commitment to the customer.

Activity 10.6

You work in the export department at a bottling plant for a famous label drink and are having problems contacting distributors and retailers in one of the overseas sales regions by telephone. You are concerned that they are not receiving the latest product and sales promotion information because of different office opening times and time differences between the two countries. How can you ensure that they are kept fully informed?

Making it easy to do business

By making it easy for customers to do business, you can improve customer service and the way your organization is perceived by its customers. If the business receives a high volume of incoming calls, one way to achieve this could be by using telecommunications technology to improve customer telephone response. You could enhance call response by:

o   Using 0800 numbers that allow customers to call for free, thus improving convenience and demonstrating customer care
o   Having customer care lines to assist after-sales service
o   Ensuring that incoming calls are queued and answered in order
o   Giving information to those waiting to reduce the risk of callers hanging up
o   Allowing callers to leave messages using voice mail
o   Using integrated voice response order-processing systems to answer calls automatically and take details, e.g. some gas and electricty companies use systems that mean customers can access information or leave meter readings by keying certain digits.

Ultimately all systems and procedures impact on the external customer. For most organizations there are five key processes that need to be considered from a customer's viewpoint:

1.   Sales and ordering
2.   Accounts and invoicing
3.   Delivery
4.   After-sales
5.   Customer complaints.

If you are trying to improve any of these areas you could ask yourself the following questions to help you identify how you could improve customer service.

Sales and order systems

○ How easy is it for a customer to make a purchase or place an order?
○ Do customers receive confirmation or information about their order, for example, if there are delays?
○ How quickly are orders processed?
○ Can you deal with non-standard requests?

Accounts and invoicing systems

○ How accurate are invoices?
○ How are queries dealt with?
○ Can customers use a variety of ways to pay, e.g. in cash, by cheque, by direct debit
○ What credit arrangements are available and is the information easily available to customers?

Delivery systems

○ Do you deliver when and where people want?
○ How do you inform customers about deliveries?
○ Are deliveries reliable in terms of time expected and condition of goods?
○ What sort of quality checks are made before/after delivery?

After-sales

○ Do you make it easy for customers to contact you?
○ How well do you follow up requests, e.g. for repairs, for further information, for a follow-up visit?

Complaints

○ Do you get any? What do you do with them (do you have a recording mechanism)?
○ How easy is it for customers to complain?
○ How do you resolve complaints, what system is in place and what really happens when someone complains?

Life at the sharp end – fulfilling an order is not easy

As Laura Mazur (2000) notes, getting the idea up and running, and the website designed is just the start of the battle. There are increasing signs that Web-based businesses are, not surprisingly, finding delivery on customer service promises just as difficult if not more so than their traditional counterparts.

Mazur examined a report from Ernst and Young, based on over 125 companies. Firstly, companies found it very difficult to maintain consistency of service across different channels; for example, customers were accessing information on the website and then receiving a letter telling them something quite different.

More fundamental, however, were the examples of poor *fulfilment* found by Ernst and Young. Reports of the growth in online shopping were offset by others on just how unprepared many companies were for the rise in visitors to their sites. One researcher found that almost half the sites surveyed took more than five days to answer e-mail requests. Almost a fifth of the suppliers failed to respond to e-mails at all, while nearly one in three charged more than the RRP for a sample product.

One of the problems is the technology itself. The speed and convenience alluded to many times tends to raise expectations for subsequent service. But, as Mazur noted, it is not the technology that makes the relationship work, but the people in the company wanting to respond to customers' needs. Given the isolation between company and customer in a virtual market place, it is perhaps not surprising that home shopping is laden with tales of deliveries of the wrong products and late deliveries. Anecdotally, there are stories of supermarkets offering slots of delivery that are over a week later than the shopper requests.

As all traditional direct marketers know, in a 'direct company', it is the back end of operations, fulfilment, that is the hardest part of customer service to get right; it is also the most important.

Source: A. Tapp, *Principles of Direct and Database Marketing*, 2nd Edition, 2000.

 ## Activity 10.7

Think of four different ways that different types of businesses have enhanced customer service with technology.

Case history

Changing behind the scene processes to improve customer service and communication

One financial services organization wanted to increase personal loan sales by improving customer services. Personal loan applications had originally been handled by post, using a time-consuming process that occupied a large team working with separate IT systems. By establishing a 'direct' telephone operation and a computerized credit scoring system, the loan application and approval decision process was reduced from 7 days to one 12-minute telephone call, thus improving customer satisfaction levels.

Telephone operators can now deal with customers personally, instead of taking details of an application and passing it to a different work area. This gives staff greater satisfaction and the customer an immediate response. In turn, staff have the opportunity to build a relationship and rapport with the customer and as a result sales of additional products, such as loan insurance, have increased.

New integrated customer service systems using the organization's database, mean that accounts can be set up and tracked for the period of the loan. This streamlined process means that staff can deal with enquiries more efficiently.

In addition, new electronic filing systems mean that traditional paper-based filing systems are becoming a thing of the past. These new systems save space and money by converting bulky files to compact desktop systems. They improve customer service because the risk of losing documents is reduced; the time it takes for staff to find documents and respond to enquiries is also decreased.

Furthermore, new document management systems ensure that information and documents are available when and where they are needed, wherever they are located. It means that application forms and associated documents, such as proof of residence or past bank statements can be scanned and converted into electronic form. Staff can annotate documents and pass them to colleagues as and when needed, without ever having to get up from a chair and physically sort through file notes and documents.

Activity 10.8

1. You are the manager of an estate agents responsible for a team of six negotiators who regularly deal with customers buying and selling houses. The team deals with customers on the telephone and those who visit the estate agency office.

    To improve standards of customer care you decide to involve staff in determining the best practice for dealing with customers.

    To assist staff in formulating a protocol for best practice, draft five minimum standards you would expect to achieve when dealing with telephone calls from customers.

2. You overhear a customer complaining to one of the negotiators that the property details sheet for his house contains incorrect room measurements, incorrect room descriptions and a number of spelling mistakes.

    The member of staff's response to the customer is that he is not responsible for preparing the property information sheet and that prospective buyers will find out what the house is really like when they view it.

    In advising the member of staff how to provide good customer service, outline five main points that you would make to him about the above situation.

Establishing a customer care programme

Like many procedures, it is normally helpful for everyone who's going to be involved in the actual implementation of a system to have a list of the practical steps involved in establishing a customer care programme. That way, everyone knows what they should be doing.

The following are some of the most practical steps in establishing a customer care programme, according to Lancaster et al. (*Marketing Fundamentals*, pp. 212–213, Butterworth-Heinemann, 2001).

Identify customer needs and perceptions

This first step in establishing a customer-care programme illustrates that the start point is customer needs. We must clearly establish what these are and how our customer-care programme needs to be designed to meet them. We must also evaluate the perceptions that current and potential customers have with regard to our company and its standards of customer care.

Establish a mission statement

The approach to customer care and its importance in the company must be a key part of the mission statement. We also need a widely accepted mission statement for the approach to customer care itself.

Set service level standards and specifications

Clear standards must be set for levels of customer care and the key elements to be included. Examples include standards for courtesy, credibility, communication, responsiveness, empathy with customer and confidentiality.

Establish management processes and communicate this to all staff

There should be clear specifications of how jobs should be done with regard to achieving customer-care objectives. This should include for example:

o Who does what, and when – formal allocations of tasks and progress reviews
o Information flows and systems required to implement customer-care programmes
o The motivation, monitoring and control of people in the customer-care programme
o Obviously, responsibilities, and information on processes and procedures to be followed must be communicated to all staff.

Define tasks according to time factors

These factors include timing of recurrent work, seasonal factors, etc. This process should be accurately and comprehensively catalogued, and the programme of customer care must create systems by which the work can be handled according to the objectives of satisfying customer needs, using resources efficiently and cost effectively.

Establish a basic minimum level

Although customer-care programmes should be built around customer needs, wherever possible levels of customer care should meet the highest standards. However, it is also important to establish a baseline for standards of customer care, below which levels customer care should not drop.

Ensure systems for effective response to complaints

Although the idea of a customer-care programme is to reduce complaints, and indeed to remove the need for them altogether, it is unlikely that all complaints can be removed in this way. The customer-care programme therefore must have clear systems and procedures for ensuring effective responses to customer complaints.

Secure management commitment

It is important to ensure commitment to customer-care programmes. It is especially important that this commitment is established, throughout all levels of management, but especially at the head of the organization.

Implement effective and continuous measurement and control systems

The customer-care programme must be measured and controlled. It is pointless paying lip service to customer care, it must be supported by objectives and rigorously enforced measurement and control systems.

Case history

Customer care in Building Societies

The UK's Nationwide Building Society has a commitment to customer care. It has declared that it will not follow the lead of other building societies and become a bank, since this would mean paying dividends to shareholders rather than offering benefits to customers. The intention is to retain the existing customers as customers rather than encouraging them to become shareholders in a new institution.

Source: J. Blythe, *Essentials of Marketing*, 2nd Edition, Pearson Education Ltd

Case history

Customer care at Amazon.com

The philosophy of Amazon.com is that the customer is king. Jeff Bezos, the founder of the company, had several areas of the business which were seen as vital to success. One of these was how to attract and keep customers. Customer care was seen as being a vital element and a key growth driver of the company. It will be interesting to chart the future performance of the company and observe whether speedy deliveries, a discount on price, good selection of books and customized service will continue to attract customers in the years to come.

Source: D. Adcock, A. Halbourg, C. Ross, *Marketing Principles and Practice*, 4th Edition, Pearson Education Ltd

Why do customer care systems sometimes fail?

There is no doubt that thousands of organizations providing products and services implement customer care programmes and yet still have customers who receive poor service and complain about it.

The problem often lies in allocating a specific department for customer care instead of training and empowering all staff to deal with customer care issues.

A common problem is that companies impose customer care programmes on staff without explaining the reasons behind them, or do not allow staff who deal with customers every day to influence how customer care is implemented.

Other problems occur where firms have organized supposedly customer-centred systems and processes designed to enable staff to help customers but prospective customers are asked so many personal questions with no relevance to the actual query that they are put off from doing business with the organization.

In other cases organizations move from a localized branch network where staff may know customers quite well, to a round-the-clock service provision supported by centralized telephone services in a bid to give customers improved access to services. Unfortunately, customers may then find that they spend a long time explaining a particular problem or enquiry to an anonymous person and if they have to call again they are faced with another anonymous voice to whom they have to explain the whole thing all over again.

Customer service can also fail if it is commoditized through call centres with staff on short-term contracts. Often these staff fail to see the company's goals as they are often more concerned about their job security. It is also difficult to see how staff could be encouraged to take customer care seriously if senior managers do not treat their internal customers/staff appropriately.

Many staff feel that customer care is something that senior managers pay lip service to because they do not allocate adequate resources to it or establish any reward or recognition system aimed at customer care standards. Some companies persist in thinking that technology is the answer to tackling customer care issues. There needs to be a balance between using telephone technology to speed up response and put customers through to the right department without trapping them in voice mail jail. Technology on its own does not improve customer service if there are no humans available to help solve customers' problems.

In the final analysis, if the product breaks or does not work or the service does not arrive or does not do the job it was asked to do, no amount of apologies, discounts or gestures will change the situation, so quality still remains a key aspect of any customer care programme.

Complaints

Benefits of complaints

Most organizations that supply products and services find that there are occasions when customers are not satisfied and have need to complain. As part of their approach to customer care issues, some organizations have established customer service departments or introduced policies to handle complaints so that complaints are dealt with in a consistent and appropriate way.

The advantage of recognizing that things do go wrong and that customers do complain is that instead of seeing complaints as an unfortunate occurrence, they can be examined to help identify ways of improving products and services.

Resolving complaints satisfactorily usually means that the customer becomes more loyal in the long term because they appreciate that they have been listened to.

Organizations that recognize that it is useful to encourage customers to complain, because it provides valuable feedback, usually take active steps to obtain this feedback.

Figure 10.4 A complaints procedure

Handling complaints

There is obviously no one way to deal with complaints as the approach must be tailored to the circumstances. However, there are a number of general approaches that can be adapted to help deal with difficult situations where customers are dissatisfied and a complaint needs to be handled in a sensitive way. Here is a list of helpful approaches:

- Listen and say nothing until the customer has stated his grievance
- Give the customer your name so they are assured that you are committed to resolving the problem
- Use appropriate body language to show empathy with the customer
- Use an empathic tone of voice
- Use diplomatic phrases to calm angry customers, for example, 'This is obviously an unsatisfactory situation' or 'I'm sorry you're upset about this situation'
- Apologize for the fact that there has been a problem – this does not mean you are accepting full blame
- Do not interrupt the customer and use effective listening skills to get an overview of the problem and show that you are taking the customer seriously
- Clarify the problem by checking details and making notes so that you can fully investigate the complaint
- Be positive, not defensive. So, for instance, you could thank the customer for telling you about the situation because you need to know about the problem if it is to be rectified
- Tell the customer what steps you are going to take so that they know they have not just sounded off and wasted their time
- In cases of serious allegations you may need to explain that you cannot take the matter at face value and that you must investigate to verify the allegations
- Call for management help with customers who remain angry or dissatisfied.

 ## Activity 10.9

Read the scenario below, identify the areas where Orange could improve their customer service and explain how they might improve their customer communications.

A customer purchases an Orange mobile telephone and is promised connection to the service later that day. Unfortunately, the customer is unable to follow the complicated instructions in the user manual and rings the helpline telephone number. The customer tries to get through to the helpline number for three consecutive days but finds that it is constantly engaged. She eventually contacts the head office but there are no staff available to help because it is a weekend. However, the switchboard operator transfers her to the customer helpline. A call centre operator answers her call but he is unable to help because the customer was not allocated a security code number when she bought the telephone. However, the call centre operator promises to pass on the matter to head office to be dealt with after the weekend.

After the weekend the customer has not been contacted by anyone from the head office so she decides to contact them again. She complains bitterly to a person in the customer service department about the overcomplicated manual and the service she has received. The member of staff provides a lengthy explanation about how a shortage of staff means the helpline is constantly engaged. The customer becomes irate and says that she is not interested in Orange's staffing problems. She demands help with using her telephone, an apology for the way she has been treated and a discount on her bill to make up for the number of telephone calls she has made. The member of staff refuses to apologize, stating that it is not his fault that there have been problems. He explains that he has no authority to agree a discount on her bill and that it is not the company's policy to give discounts. However, he is able to give her the security code to enable her to use the telephone and clarifies the misleading instructions in the user manual. At the end of the call the customer can use her mobile telephone but she is still angry about the way she has been treated.

How to encourage customers to complain

Make it easy for people to complain by publicizing your complaints procedure. Stay close to your customers – regularly find out what customers think by asking them.

Put yourself in your customers' shoes by mystery shopping to find out what customers think.

Don't deflect complaints, find out what the customer expects and what can be done to put something right.

Using Information and Communication Technologies in customer service

Unit 5 goes into a lot more detail about Information and Communication Technologies (ICT), looking at areas such as the Internet and e-mails. Here, however, the role of ICT with regards to customer service and customer relationship marketing will be looked at briefly.

According to Kotler et al. (*Principles of Marketing*, p. 409, Pearson Education Ltd, 2001), 'Customer Relationship Management (CRM) systems are IT-based applications that integrate a company's information about customers with the knowledge of how to use that information. Their occurrence marks the meeting of the technology that has enabled the Internet with the humanity of relationship marketing. CRM systems are based on the basic marketing belief that an organization that knows its customers and how to treat them has an advantage.'

ICT can therefore be used to improve our relationships with our customers. For example, database systems can be used to compile information on our customers – the products they buy, their lifestyle and so on. This information can then be kept up-to-date and used in marketing communications.

For example, if Ford Motor Company built up a comprehensive database which contained information on which customer bought which car within the past twelve months, say a Ford Focus, then Ford would be able to target specific mailshots to these Ford Focus owners.

Many organizations around the world have large call centres which handle customer enquiries and complaints. Computer software allows call handlers to quickly call-up customer details on-screen, once they know the customer's details, e.g. postcode or account numbers. This software generally makes the procedure more efficient and effective and should hopefully provide the customer with a friendly voice to deal with their query.

Best use of communications technology to provide customer care

The Pokemon game support service, run by Telelab, was established by Wizards of the Coast to answer a marketing dilemma. Pokemon cards are the UK's best selling toys, but the craze for collecting and trading them has meant that the positive features of using them in a game of skill were being largely ignored.

In ten months, the service has received over 30,000 calls and 3,000 e-mails and letters. The balance of the questions is swinging increasingly toward how the game is played, away from trading aspects.

It has also been heavily involved in establishing a league, providing a safe environment where children can play the game and swap cards. To date, more than 10,000 children have enrolled.

A key indication of the service's success is that two million starter packs, essential for playing the game, have now been sold.

In another example, the five pilots who launched avbrief.com were convinced they had a winning formula if they could combine the right product with the superlative customer service.

They set up a flight information service, focusing on weather data, for weather pilots, who lacked access to the sophisticated resources of major commercial firms. The service includes airfield and navigation data from Racal Avionics, UK Met Office forecasts and weather reports.

Word-of-mouth recommendation has meant that as well as gaining twice as many subscribers in its first year, it has received subscription applications from commercial airlines, the armed forces and the UN in Bosnia.

Feedback is encouraged and acted upon. Most communication is by e-mail but telephone support is also available. Hosting and customer communications is provided by Telecom Potential.

The directors say that a policy of total honesty has helped create loyalty.

Source: Marketing, Nov 23, 2000, p. 9.

At the end of the day, the end result of this application of IT should hopefully mean better customer care for customers around the world. However, is this always the case?

IT Investment is not the same as customer care

Too many marketers work from the inside out, rather than the outside in.

Toward the end of 2000, one-to-one guru Don Peppers asked readers of his weekly newsletter to nominate their top ten CRM issues and trends for 2000.

Well, the results are in. And they are hardly inspiring. They are a reminder that there is still a lot of what you could call navel-gazing marketing. To put it another way, too many marketers work from the inside out, rather then the outside in.

Consider the two top picks: privacy protection and violations, and database management and integration.

Now privacy is indeed a prominent issue for business as more people get more unhappy about the use companies might make of the information they collect. Just look at the fury that greeted the once high-flying web agency DoubleClick when it announced it was meshing online and offline databases when it merged with a direct marketing company. It is yet to recover.

But should privacy management and database development be the key concerns when it comes to CRM? Of course not. What should be concentrating marketing minds are issues such as the realisation that it is not just about software, but about real people serving customers in real time and creating a rounded picture of the customer. Both of these, however, are well down the list.

What's even more worrying is that these upside-down priorities are being backed by such huge amounts of company investment. IT analysis company, Meta Group, for example, predicts that the global market for this technology could reach as much as $67 billion (£45 billion) by 2004. The cynics among us could be forgiven for being sceptical that this mania for CRM will actually result in a bright new dawn for customer relationships.

This inability to look beyond the end of the corporate nose is what Forrester Research calls self-centred marketing. In a new report, it castigates companies for failing to make enough of an effort to satisfy customers consistently across channels, including websites, mobile phones and call centres. According to Forrester, the average company can't even recognize its own customers when they move from one channel to another.

Even worse, they don't spend enough time trying to understand customers. So they get caught up in self-serving efforts that waste their customers' time, sending a message that the company cares more about itself than customers or prospects. It points to the example of a car company that fills its website with pointless animations that block visitors from getting quickly to information about the cars. Or there is the bank which clutters its 24-hour voice response service with unsolicited marketing messages that slow down customers.

What's dangerous about being self-centred is that by the time the damage is done, it's often too late. Marks & Spencer is an obvious example. Then there's Microsoft, which on the surface looks like the least likely contender for paying the price of self-obsession.

A new book, *World War 3.0: Microsoft and its Enemies,* claim that Bill Gates has created a culture that believes it always knows what's best for customers – whatever they really think. One ex-senior executive calls his former employer, the IBM of today. IBM didn't listen to customers and barely survived. It should be a salutary reminder to Microsoft of what happens when companies lose sight of who pays the bills.

Source: Laura Mazur, *Marketing,* Jan 18, 2001, pp. 22.

Summary

In this unit you have studied:

o   How customer expectations have increased

o   The importance of having a customer focus

o   How consumerism and ethical marketing have changed the way organizations do business

o   What is meant by 'customer care' and 'customer delight'

o   How relationship marketing improves communications with customers

o   How customer interaction can be improved

o   How to handle complaints.

Further study and examination preparation

Attempt Question 2(b) from the June 2000 examination paper and Question 2(c) from the December 2000 paper. Go to www.cimeduhub.com to access Specimen Answers and Senior Examiner's advice for these exam questions.

Exam hint

Be prepared to describe how and why customer expectations have changed and think of examples from your own industry sector.

Consider how an organization's image might be affected by poor first impressions. Think of some practical examples of this.

Use the examples and the activities in the unit to help you consider how you can apply your knowledge of customer care issues to a variety of contexts and situations.

appendix 1
guidance on examination preparation

Preparing for your examination

You are now nearing the final phase of your studies and it is time to start the hard work of exam preparation.

During your period of study you will have become used to absorbing large amounts of information. You will have tried to understand and apply aspects of knowledge that may have been very new to you, while some of the information provided may have been more familiar. You may even have undertaken many of the activities that are positioned frequently throughout your Coursebook, which will have enabled you to apply your learning in practical situations. But whatever the state of your knowledge and understanding, do not allow yourself to fall into the trap of thinking that you know enough, you understand enough, or even worse, that you can just take it as it comes on the day.

Never underestimate the pressure of the CIM examination.

The whole point of preparing this text for you is to ensure that you never take the examination for granted, and that you do not go into the exam unprepared for what might come your way for three hours at a time.

One thing's for sure: there is no quick fix, no easy route, no waving a magic wand and finding you know it all.

Whether you have studied alone, in a CIM study centre, or through distance learning, you now need to ensure that this final phase of your learning process is tightly managed, highly structured and objective.

As a candidate in the examination, your role will be to convince the Senior Examiner for this subject that you have credibility. You need to demonstrate to the examiner that you can be trusted to undertake a range of challenges in the context of marketing, that you are able to capitalize on opportunities and manage your way through threats.

You should prove to the Senior Examiner that you are able to apply knowledge, make decisions, respond to situations and solve problems.

Very shortly we are going to look at a range of revision and exam preparation techniques, and at time management issues, and encourage you towards developing and implementing your own revision plan, but before that, let's look at the role of the Senior Examiner.

A bit about the Senior Examiners!

You might be quite shocked to read this, but while it might appear that the examiners are 'relentless question masters' they actually want you to be able to answer the questions and pass the exams! In fact, they would derive no satisfaction or benefits from failing candidates; quite the contrary, they develop the syllabus and exam papers in order that you can learn and then apply that learning effectively so as to pass your examinations. Many of the examiners have said in the past that it is indeed psychologically more difficult to fail students than pass them.

Many of the hints and tips you find within this Appendix have been suggested by the Senior Examiners and authors of the Coursebook series. Therefore you should consider them carefully and resolve to undertake as many of the elements suggested as possible.

The Chartered Institute of Marketing has a range of processes and systems in place within the Examinations Division to ensure that fairness and consistency prevail across the team of examiners, and that the academic and vocational standards that are set and defined are indeed maintained. In doing this, CIM ensures that those who gain the CIM Certificate, Advanced Certificate and Postgraduate Diploma, are worthy of the qualification and perceived as such in the view of employers, actual and potential.

Part of what you will need to do within the examination is be 'examiner friendly' – that means you have to make sure they get what they ask for. This will make life easier for you and for them.

Hints and tips for 'examiner friendly' actions are as follows:

○ Show them that you understand the basis of the question, by answering *precisely* the question asked, and not including just about everything you can remember about the subject area
○ Read their needs – how many points is the question asking you to address?
○ Respond to the question appropriately. Is the question asking you to take on a role? If so, take on the role and answer the question in respect of the role.

For example, you could be positioned as follows:

'You are working as a Marketing Assistant at Nike UK' or 'You are a Marketing Manager for an Engineering Company' or 'As Marketing Manager write a report to the Managing Partner'.

These examples of role-playing requirements are taken from questions in past papers.

○ Deliver the answer in the format requested. If the examiner asks for a memo, then provide a memo; likewise, if the examiner asks for a report, then write a report. If you do not do this, in some instances you will fail to gain the necessary marks required to pass.

○ Take a business-like approach to your answers. This enhances your credibility. Badly ordered work, untidy work, lack of structure, headings and sub-headings can be off-putting. This would be unacceptable in the work situation, likewise it will be unacceptable in the eyes of the Senior Examiners and their marking teams.

○ Ensure the examiner has something to mark: give them substance, relevance, definitions, illustration and demonstration of your knowledge and understanding of the subject area.

○ See the examiner as your potential employer, or ultimate consumer/customer. The whole purpose and culture of marketing is about meeting customers' needs. Try this approach – it works wonders.

○ Provide a strong sense of enthusiasm and professionalism in your answers; support it with relevant up-to-date examples and apply them where appropriate.

○ Try to do something that will make your exam paper a little bit different – make it stand out in the crowd.

All of these points might seem quite logical to you, but often in the panic of the examination they 'go out of the window'. Therefore it is beneficial to remind ourselves of the importance of the examiner. He/she is the 'ultimate customer' – and we all know customers hate to be disappointed.

As we move on, some of these points will be revisited and developed further.

About the examination

In all examinations, with the exception of Marketing in Practice at Certificate level and Analysis and Decision at Diploma level, the paper is divided into two parts.

○ Part A – Mini-case study = 40 per cent of the marks
○ Part B – Option choice questions (choice of three questions from seven) = 60 per cent of the marks

Let's look at the basis of each element.

The mini-case study

This is based on a mini-case or scenario with one question, possibly subdivided into between two and four points, but totalling 40 per cent of the overall marks.

In essence, you, the candidate, are placed in a problem-solving role through the medium of a short scenario. On occasions, the scenario may consist of an article from a journal in relation to a well-known organization: for example, in the past, Interflora, easyJet and Philips, among others, have been used as the basis of the mini-case.

Alternatively, it will be based upon a fictional company, and the examiner will have prepared it in order that the right balance of knowledge, understanding, application and skills is used.

Approaches to the mini-case study

When undertaking the mini-case study there are a number of key areas you should consider.

Structure/content

The mini-case that you will be presented with will vary slightly from paper to paper, and of course from one examination to the next. Normally the scenario presented will be 400–500 words long and will centre on a particular organization and its problems or may even relate to a specific industry.

The length of the mini-case study means that usually only a brief outline is provided of the situation, the organization and its marketing problems, and you must therefore learn to cope with analysing information and preparing your answer on the basis of a very limited amount of detail.

Time management

There are many differing views on time management and the approaches you can take to managing your time within the examination. You must find an approach to suit your way of working, but always remember, whatever you do, you must ensure that you allow enough time to complete the examination. Unfinished exams mean lost marks.

A typical example of managing time is as follows:

Your paper is designed to assess you over a three-hour period. With 40 per cent of the marks being allocated to the mini-case, it means that you should dedicate somewhere around 75 minutes of your time to both read and write up the answer on this mini-case. Some students, however, will prefer to allocate nearer half of their time (90 minutes) on the mini-case, so that they can read and fully absorb the case and answer the questions in the context of it. This is also acceptable as long as you ensure that you work extremely 'SMART' for the remaining time in order to finish the examination.

Do not forget that while there is only one question within the mini-case, it can have a number of components. You must answer all the components in that question, which is where the balance of time comes into play.

Knowledge/skills tested

Throughout all the CIM papers, your knowledge, skills and ability to apply those skills will be tested. However, the mini-cases are used particularly to test application, i.e. your ability to take your knowledge and apply it in a structured way to a given scenario. The examiners will be looking at your decision-making ability, your analytical and communication skills and depending on the level, your ability as a manager to solve particular marketing problems.

When the examiner is marking your paper, he/she will be looking to see how you differentiate yourself, looking at your own individual 'unique selling points'. The examiner will also want to see if you can personally apply the knowledge or whether you are only able to repeat the textbook materials.

Format of answers

On many occasions, and within all examinations, you will most likely be given a particular communication method to use. If this is the case, you must ensure that you adhere to the requirements of the examiner. This is all part of meeting customer needs.

The likely communication tools you will be expected to use are as follows:

- o Memorandum
- o Memorandum/report
- o Report
- o Briefing notes
- o Presentation
- o Press release
- o Advertisement
- o Plan.

Make sure that you familiarize yourself with these particular communication tools and practise using them to ensure that, on the day, you will be able to respond confidently to the communication requests of the examiner. Look back at the Customer Communications text at Certificate level to familiarize yourself with the potential requirements of these methods.

By the same token, while communication methods are important, so is meeting the specific requirements of the question. This means you must understand what is meant by the precise instruction given. **Note the following terms carefully:**

- o **Identify** Select key issues, point out key learning points, establish clearly what the examiner expects you to identify
- o **Illustrate** The examiner expects you to provide examples, scenarios and key concepts that illustrate your learning
- o **Compare and contrast** Look at the range of similarities between the two situations, contexts or even organizations. Then compare them, i.e. ascertain and list how activities, features, etc. agree or disagree. Contrasting means highlighting the differences between the two
- o **Discuss** Questions that have 'discuss' in them offer a tremendous opportunity for you to debate, argue, justify your approach or understanding of the subject area – *caution* it is not an opportunity to waffle
- o **Briefly explain** This means being succinct, structured and concise in your explanation, within the answer. Make your points clear, transparent and relevant
- o **State** Present in a clear, brief format
- o **Interpret** Expound the meaning of, make clear and explicit what it is you see and understand within the data provided
- o **Outline** Provide the examiner with the main concepts and features being asked for and avoid minor technical details. Structure will be critical here, or else you could find it difficult to contain your answer
- o **Relate** Show how different aspects of the syllabus connect together
- o **Evaluate** Review and reflect upon an area of the syllabus, a particular practice, an article, etc., and consider its overall worth in respect of its use as a tool or a model and its overall effectiveness in the role it plays.

Source: Worsam, Mike, *How to Pass Marketing*, Croner, 1989.

Your approach to mini-cases

There is no one right way to approach and tackle a mini-case study, indeed it will be down to each individual to use their own creativity in tackling the tasks presented. You will have to use your initiative and discretion about how best to approach the mini-case. Having said this, however, there are some basic steps you can take.

o Ensure that you read through the case study at least twice before making any judgements, starting to analyse the information provided, or indeed writing the answers.

o On the third occasion, read through the mini-case and, using a highlighter, start marking the essential and relevant information critical to the content and context. Then turn your attention to the question again, this time reading slowly and carefully to assess what it is you are expected to do. Note any instructions that the examiner gives you, and then start to plan how you might answer the question. Whatever the question, ensure the answer has a structure: a beginning, a structured central part of the answer and, finally, always a conclusion.

o Keep the context of the question continually in mind: that is, the specifics of the case and the role which you might be performing.

o Because there is limited material available, you will sometimes need to make assumptions. Don't be afraid to do this, it will show initiative on your part. Assumptions are an important part of dealing with case studies and can help you to be quite creative with your answer. However, do explain the basis of your assumptions within your answer so that the examiner understands the nature of them, and why you have arrived at your particular outcome. **Always ensure that your assumptions are realistic.**

o Only now are you approaching the stage where it is time to start writing your answer to the question, tackling the problems, making decisions and recommendations on the case scenario set before you. As mentioned previously, your points will often be best set out in a report or memo type format, particularly if the examiner does not specify a communication method.

o Ensure that your writing is succinct, avoids waffle and responds directly to the questions asked.

Part B

Again, with the exception of the Analysis and Decision case study, each Part B is comprised of six or seven more traditional questions, each worth 20 per cent. You will be expected to choose three of those questions, to make up the remaining 60 per cent of available marks.

Realistically, the same principles apply for these questions as in the case study. Communication formats, reading through the questions, structure, role-play, context, etc. – everything is the same.

Part B will cover a number of broader issues from within the syllabus and will be taken from any element of it. The examiner makes the choice, and no prior direction is given to students or tutors on what that might be.

As regards time management in this area, if you used about 75 minutes for the mini-case you should have around 105 minutes left. This provides you with around 30 minutes to plan and write a question and 5 minutes per question to review and revise your answers. Keep practising – use a cooker timer, alarm clock or mobile phone alarm as your timer and work hard at answering questions within the time frame given.

Specimen examination papers and answers

To help you prepare and understand the nature of the paper, go to www.cimeduhub.com to access Specimen Answers and Senior Examiner's advice for these exam questions. During your study, the author of your Coursebook may have, on occasions, asked you to refer to these papers and answer the questions. You should undertake these exercises and utilize every opportunity to practise meeting examination requirements.

The specimen answers are vital learning tools. They are not always perfect, as they are answers written by students and annotated by the Senior Examiners, but they will give you a good indication of the approaches you could take, and the examiners' annotations suggest how these answers might be improved. Please use them.

Other sources of information to support your learning through the Virtual Institute are 'Hot Topics'. These give you scope to undertake a range of associated activities related to the syllabus and study areas, and will also be very useful to you when you are revising.

Key elements of preparation

One Senior Examiner suggests the three elements involved in preparing for your examination can be summarized thus:

- o Learning
- o Memory
- o Revision.

Let's look at each point in turn.

Learning

Quite often students find it difficult to learn properly. You can passively read books, look at some of the materials, perhaps revise a little, and regurgitate it all in the examination. In the main, however, this is rather an unsatisfactory method of learning. It is meaningless, shallow and ultimately of little use in practice.

For learning to be truly effective it must be active and applied. You must involve yourself in the learning process by thinking about what you have read, testing it against your experience by reflecting on how you use particular aspects of marketing, and how you could perhaps improve your own performance by implementing particular aspects of your learning into your everyday life. You should adopt the old adage of 'learning by doing'. If you do, you will find that passive learning has no place in your study life.

Below are some suggestions that have been prepared to assist you with the learning pathway throughout your revision.

- o Always make your own notes, in words you understand, and ensure that you combine all the sources of information and activities within them
- o Always try to relate your learning back to your own organization

- o Make sure you define key terms concisely, wherever possible
- o Do not try to memorize your ideas, but work on the basis of understanding and, most important, applying them
- o Think about the relevant and topical questions that might be set – use the questions and answers in your Coursebooks to identify typical questions that might be asked in the future
- o Attempt all of the questions within each of your Coursebooks since these are vital tests of your active learning and understanding.

Memory

If you are prepared to undertake an active learning programme then your knowledge will be considerably enhanced, as understanding and application of knowledge does tend to stay in your 'long-term' memory. It is likely that passive learning will only stay in your 'short-term' memory.

Do not try to memorize parrot fashion; it is not helpful and, even more important, examiners are experienced in identifying various memorizing techniques and therefore will spot them as such.

Having said this, it is quite useful to memorize various acronyms such as SWOT, PEST, PESTLE, STEEPLE, or indeed various models such as Ansoff, GE Matrix, Shell Directional, etc., as in some of the questions you may be required to use illustrations of these to assist your answer.

Revision

The third and final stage to consider is 'revision', which is what we will concentrate on in detail below. Here just a few key tips are offered.

Revision should be an ongoing process rather than a panic measure that you decide to undertake just before the examination. You should be preparing notes *throughout* your course, with the view of using them as part of your revision process. Therefore ensure that your notes are sufficiently comprehensive that you can reuse them successfully.

For each concept you learn about, you should identify, through your reading and your own personal experience, at least two or three examples that you could use; this then gives you some scope to broaden your perspective during the examination. It will, of course, help you gain some points for initiative with the examiners.

Knowledge is not something you will gain overnight – as we saw earlier, it is not a quick fix; it involves a process of learning that enables you to lay solid foundations upon which to build your long-term understanding and application. This will benefit you significantly in the future, not just in the examination.

In essence, you should ensure that you do the following in the period before the real intensive revision process begins.

- o Keep your study file well organized, updated and full of newspaper and journal cuttings that may help you formulate examples in your mind for use during the examination
- o Practise defining key terms and acronyms from memory

   o Prepare topic outlines and essay answer plans

   o When you start your intensive revision, ensure it is planned and structured in the way described below. And then finally, read your concentrated notes the night before the examination.

Revision planning

You are now on a critical path – although hopefully not too critical at this time – with somewhere in the region of between four and six weeks to go to the examination. The following hints and tips will help you plan out your revision study.

   o You will, as already explained, need to be very organized. Therefore, before doing anything else, put your files, examples, reading material, etc. in good order, so that you are able to work with them in the future and, of course, make sense of them.

   o Ensure that you have a quiet area to work. It is very easy to get distracted when preparing for an examination.

   o Take out your file along with your syllabus and make a list of key topic areas that you have studied and which you now need to revise. You could use the basis of this book to do that, by taking each unit a step at a time.

   o Plan the use of your time carefully. Ideally you should start your revision at least six weeks prior to the exam, so therefore work out how many spare hours you could give to the revision process and then start to allocate time in your diary, and do not double-book with anything else.

   o Give up your social life for a short period of time. As the saying goes 'no pain – no gain'.

   o Looking at each of the subject areas in turn, identify which are your strengths and which are your weaknesses. Which areas have you grasped and understood, and which are the areas that you have really struggled with? Split your page in two and make a list on each side. For example:

Planning and control	
Strengths	Weaknesses
Audit – PEST, SWOT, Models	Ratio analysis
Portfolio analysis	Market sensing
	Productivity analysis
	Trend extrapolation
	Forecasting

   o Break down your list again and divide the points of weakness, giving priority in the first instance to your weakest areas and even prioritizing them by giving them a number. This will enable you to master the more difficult areas. Up to 60 per cent of your remaining revision time should be given over to that, as you may find you have to undertake a range of additional reading and also perhaps seeking tutor support, if you are studying at a CIM Accredited Study Centre.

   ○ The rest of the time should be spent reinforcing your knowledge and understanding of the stronger areas, spending time testing yourself on how much you really know.

   ○ Should you be taking two examinations or more at any one time, then the breakdown and managing of your time will be critical.

   ○ Taking a subject at a time, work through your notes and start breaking them down into subsections of learning, and ultimately into key learning points, items that you can refer to time and time again, that are meaningful and that your mind will absorb. You yourself will know how you best remember key points. Some people try to develop acronyms, or flowcharts or matrices, mind maps, fishbone diagrams, etc., or various connection diagrams that help them recall certain aspects of models. You could also develop processes that enable you to remember approaches to various options. (But do remember what we said earlier about regurgitating stuff, parrot fashion.)

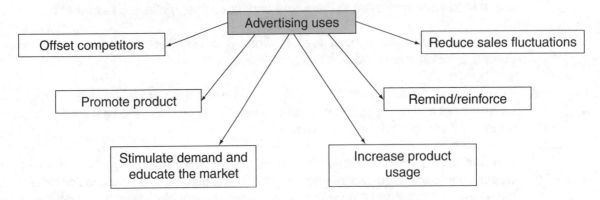

Figure A1.1 Use of a diagram to summarize key components of a concept
Source: Adapted from Dibb, Simkin, Pride & Ferrell, *Marketing Concepts and Strategies*, 4th edition, Houghton Mifflin, 2001

Figure A1.1 is just a brief example of how you could use a 'bomb-burst' diagram (which, in this case, highlights the uses of advertising) as a very helpful approach to memorizing key elements of learning.

   ○ Eventually you should reduce your key learning to bullet points. For example: imagine you were looking at the concept of Time Management – you could eventually reduce your key learning to a bullet list containing the following points in relation to 'Effective Prioritization':

       ○ Organize
       ○ Take time
       ○ Delegate
       ○ Review.

Each of these headings would then remind you of the elements you need to discuss associated with the subject area.

   ○ Avoid getting involved in reading too many textbooks at this stage, as you may start to find that you are getting confused overall.

   ○ Look at examination questions on previous papers, and start to observe closely the various roles and tasks they expect you to undertake, and importantly, the context in which they are set.

- **Use the specimen exam papers and specimen answers** to support your learning and see how you could actually improve upon them.

- Without exception, find an associated examination question for the areas that you have studied and revised, and undertake it (more than once if necessary).

- Without referring to notes or books, try to draft an answer plan with the key concepts, knowledge, models and information that are needed to successfully complete the answer. Then refer to the specimen answer to see how close you are to the actual outline presented. Planning your answer, and ensuring that key components are included, and that the question has a meaningful structure, is one of the most beneficial activities that you can undertake.

- Now write out the answer in full, time-constrained and written by hand, not with the use of IT. (At this stage, you are still expected to be the scribe for the examination and present handwritten work. Many of us find this increasingly difficult as we spend more and more time using our computers to present information. Do your best to be neat. Spidery handwriting is often off-putting to the examiner.)

- When writing answers as part of your revision process, also be sure to practise the following essential examinations techniques:

  - **Identify and use the communication method** requested by the examiner
  - **Always have three key parts to the answer** – an introduction, a middle section that develops your answer in full and a conclusion. Where appropriate, ensure that you have an introduction, main section, summary/conclusion and, if requested or helpful, recommendations
  - **Always answer the question in the context or role set**
  - **Always comply with the nature and terms of the question**
  - **Leave white space**. Do not overcrowd your page; Leave space between paragraphs, and make sure your sentences do not merge into one blur (Don't worry – there is always plenty of paper available to use in the examination)
  - **Count** how many actions the question asks you to undertake and double-check at the end that you have met the full range of demands of the question
  - **Use examples** – to demonstrate your knowledge and understanding of the particular syllabus area. These can be from journals, the Internet, the press, or your own experience
  - **Display your vigour and enthusiasm for marketing**. Remember to think of the Senior Examiner as your Customer, or future employer, and do your best to deliver what is wanted to satisfy their needs. Impress them and show them how you are a 'cut above the rest'

- Review all your practice answers critically, with the above points in mind.

Practical actions

The critical path is becoming even more critical now as the examination looms. The following are vital points:

- Have you registered with CIM?
- Do you know where you are taking your examination? CIM should let you know approximately one month in advance.

o   Do you know where your examination centre is? If not find out, take a drive, time it – whatever you do, don't be late!

o   Make sure you have all the tools of the examination ready. A dictionary, calculator, pens, pencils, ruler, etc. Try not to use multiple shades of pens, but at the same time make your work look professional. *Avoid using red and green as these are the colours that will be used for marking.*

Summary

Above all, you must remember that you personally have invested a tremendous amount of time, effort and money in studying for this programme and it is therefore imperative that you consider the suggestions given here as they will help to maximize your return on your investment.

Many of the hints and tips offered here are generic and will work across most of the CIM courses. We have tried to select those that will help you most in taking a sensible, planned approach to your study and revision.

The key to your success is being prepared to put in the time and effort required, planning your revision, and equally important is planning and answering your questions in a way that will ensure that you pass your examination on the day.

The advice offered here aims to guide you from a practical perspective. Guidance on syllabus content and developments associated with your learning will become clear to you as you work through this Coursebook. The authors of each Coursebook have given subject-specific guidance on the approach to the examination and on how to ensure that you meet the content requirements of the kind of question you will face. These considerations are in addition to the structuring issues we have been discussing throughout this Appendix.

Each of the authors and Senior Examiners will guide you on their preferred approach to questions and answers as they go. Therefore, where you are presented with an opportunity to be involved in some activity or undertake an examination question either during or at the end of your study units, do take it. It not only prepares you for the examination, but helps you learn in the applied way we discussed above.

Here, then, is a last reminder:

o   Ensure you make the most of your learning process throughout

o   Keep structured and orderly notes from which to revise

o   Plan your revision – don't let it just happen

o   Provide examples to enhance your answers

o   Practise your writing skills in order that you present your work well and your writing is readable

o   Take as many opportunities to test your knowledge and measure your progress as possible

- ○ Plan and structure your answers

- ○ Always do as the question asks you, especially with regard to context and communication method

- ○ **Do not leave it until the last minute!**

The writers would like to take this opportunity to wish you every success in your endeavours to study, to revise and to pass your examinations.

Karen Beamish
Academic Development Advisor

appendix 2
undertaking CIM assignments and the integrative project

Introduction – the basis to the assignments and the integrative project

Within the CIM qualifications at both Stage One and Stage Two, there are several assessment options available. These are detailed in the outline of modules below. The purpose of an assignment is to provide another format to complete each module for students who want to apply the syllabus concepts from a module to their own or a selected organization. For either qualification there are three modules providing assessment via an assignment and one module assessed via an integrative work-based project. The module assessed via the integrative project is the summative module for each qualification.

	Entry modules	Research & analysis	Planning	Implementation	Management of Marketing
STAGE 3	Entry module – Stage 3	New syllabus to launch September 2004			
		Currently all modules assessed via examination route only			
STAGE 2	Entry module – Stage 2	Marketing Research & Information	Marketing Planning	Marketing Communications	Marketing Management in Practice
		All assessed via examination or assignment			*Exam/Integrative Project*
STAGE 1		Marketing Environment	Marketing Fundamentals	Customer Communications	Marketing in Practice
		All assessed via examination or assignment			*Exam/Integrative Project*
Introductory Certificate		Supporting marketing processes (research & analysis, planning & implementation)			

Adapted from the outline of CIM 'standard' syllabus, October 2002

The use of assignments does not mean that this route is easier than an examination. Both formats are carefully evaluated to ensure that a grade B in the assessment/integrative project route is the same as a grade B in an examination. However, the use of assignments does allow a student to complete the assessment for a module over a longer period of time than a three-hour examination. This will inevitably mean work being undertaken over the time-span of a module. For those used to cramming for exams, writing an assignment over several weeks which comprises a total of four separate questions will be a very different approach.

Each module within the qualification contains a different assignment written specifically for the module. These are designed to test understanding and provide the opportunity for you to demonstrate your abilities through the application of theory to practice. The format and structure of each module's assignment is identical, although the questions asked will differ and the exact type of assignment varies. The questions within an assignment will relate directly to the syllabus for that particular module, thereby giving the opportunity to demonstrate understanding and application.

The assignment structure

The assignment for each module is broken down into a range of questions. These consist of a core question, a selection of optional questions plus a reflective statement. The core question will always relate to the main aspects of each module's syllabus. Coupled with this are a range of four optional questions which will each draw from a different part of the syllabus. Students are requested to select two optional questions from the four available. In addition, a reflective statement requires the students to evaluate their learning from the module. When put together, these form the assessment for the entire module. The overall pass mark for the module is the same as through an examination route, which is set at 50 per cent. In addition, the grade band structure is also identical to that of an examination.

Core question

This is the longest and therefore most important section of your assignment. Covering the major components of the syllabus, the core question is designed to provide a challenging assignment which both tests the theoretical element and also permits application to a selected organization or situation. The question itself will require a written answer of approximately 2,500 words (Stage One) or 3,000 words (Stage Two) in addition to any further information you may wish to provide. This additional information should be in the form of appendices. However, the appendices should be kept to a minimum. Advice here is that they should be no longer than five pages of additional pertinent information.

Optional questions

There are a total of four questions provided for Stage One and Stage Two of the syllabus from which a student is asked to select two. Each answer is expected to provide a challenge although the actual task required varies. The word counts are also lower than the core question at 1,000 words (Stage One) and 1,500 words (Stage Two) respectively.

These are designed to test areas of the syllabus not covered by the core question. As such, it is possible to base all of your questions on the same organization although there is significant benefit in using more than one organization as a basis for your assignment. Some of the questions specifically require a different organization to be selected from the one used for the core question. This only occurs where the questions are requiring similar areas to be investigated and will be specified clearly on the question itself.

Within the assignment there are several types of questions that may be asked, including:

- o **A report** The question requires a formal report to be completed, detailing an answer to the specific question set. This will often be reporting on a specific issue to an individual.
- o **A briefing paper or notes** Preparing a briefing paper or a series of notes which may be used for a presentation.
- o **A presentation** You may be required to either prepare the presentation only or to deliver the presentation in addition to its preparation. The audience for the presentation should be considered carefully and ICT used where possible.
- o **A discussion paper** The question requires an academic discussion paper to be prepared. You should show a range of sources and concepts within the paper. You may also be required to present the discussion paper as part of a question.
- o **A project plan or action plan** Some questions ask for planning techniques to be demonstrated. As such, the plan must be for the timescale given and costs shown where applicable. The use of ICT is recommended here in order to create the plan diagrammatically.
- o **Planning a research project** Whilst market research may be required, questions have often asked for simply a research plan in a given situation. This would normally include timescales, the type(s) of research to be gathered, sampling, planned data collection and analysis.
- o **Conducting research** Following on from a research plan, a question can require student(s) to undertake a research gathering exercise. A research question can be either an individual or a group activity depending upon the question. This will usually result in a report of the findings of the exercise plus any recommendations arising from your findings.
- o **Gathering of information and reporting** Within many questions, information will need gathering. The request for information can form part or all of a question. This may be a background to the organization, the activities contained in the question or external market and environmental information. It is advisable to detail the types of information utilized, their sources and report on any findings. Such a question will often ask for recommendations for the organization – these should be drawn from the data and not simply personal opinion.
- o **An advisory document** A question here will require students to evaluate a situation and present advice and recommendations drawn from findings and theory. Again, any advice should be backed up with evidence and not a personal perspective only.
- o **An exercise, either planning and/or delivering the exercise** At both Stage One and Stage Two, exercises are offered as optional questions. These provide students with the opportunity to devise an exercise and may also require the delivery of this exercise. Such an activity should be evidenced where possible.
- o **A role-play with associated documentation** Several questions have asked students to undertake role plays in exercises such as team-building. These are usually videoed and documentation demonstrating the objectives of the exercise provided.

Each of these questions related directly towards specific issues to be investigated, evaluated and answered. In addition, some of the questions asked present situations to be considered. These provide opportunities for specific answers relating directly to the question to be asked.

In order to aid students completing the assignment, each question is provided with an outline of marking guidance. This relates to the different categories by which each question is marked. The marker of your assignment will be provided with a detailed marking scheme constructed around the same marking guidance provided to students.

For both the core and the optional questions, it is important to use referencing where sources have been utilized. This has been a weakness in the past and continues to be an issue. There have been cases of plagiarism identified during marking and moderation, together with a distinct lack of references and bibliography. This becomes more important at Stage Two where the nature of the syllabus lends itself to a more academic approach. It is highly recommended that a bibliography be included with each question and sources are cited within the text itself. The type of referencing method used is not important, only that sources are referred to.

The reflective statement

This is the final aspect to each module assignment. The purpose of the reflective statement is for each student to consider how the module has influenced him or her as individuals and reflected upon their practice. A shorter piece of work than for other aspects at 500 words (Stage One) or 750 words (Stage Two), it is also more personal in that your answer will often depend upon how you as an individual have applied the learning from the module to your work and other aspects.

A good reflective statement will comprise a number of aspects, including:

o Details of the theoretical aspects that you found beneficial within the module, and their reasons. If you have found particular resources beneficial, state this and the reason why.
o How these concepts have affected you as a practitioner with examples of application of concepts from the module to your work and/or other activities.
o How you intend to progress your learning further after completing the module assessment.

When looking at the reflective statement, your tutor or an assessor will try to award marks for your demonstration of understanding through the module together with how you have applied the theoretical concepts to practice. They are looking for evidence of learning and application over time, rather than a student simply completing the question because they have a deadline looming. The result of this marking tends to be that students who begin to apply the module concepts early often achieve higher marks overall.

Integrative project structure

The integrative project is designed to provide an in-company approach to assessment rather than having specified assignments. Utilized within the summative module element of each level's syllabus, this offers a student the chance to produce a piece of work which tackles a specific issue. The integrative project can only be completed after undertaking other modules as it will rely on information in each of these as guidance. The integrative project is approximately 5,000 words in length and was introduced from September 2002 at the Stage One level. It will be introduced from September 2003 at Stage Two with the commencement of the new syllabus. The integrative project is marked by CIM assessors and not your own tutors.

Stage One assignments – Customer Communications

Divided into five different elements, the Customer Communications module covers a range of aspects. These present a number of potential questions which can be asked. For each of the five elements, a sample question is given together with an evaluation of the type of answer which would be expected at this level.

Element 1 – Customers and stakeholders

This element of the syllabus covers the role of stakeholders and the importance of internal and external customers. A typical question covering this aspect would be:

For your organization or an organization of your choice, prepare a report for the Marketing Manager which evaluates your organization's stakeholders. From this, select FOUR key stakeholder groups and evaluate the following:

- o *Their relationship with the organization*
- o *The best form of media to communicate with each stakeholder.*

In order to answer this question effectively, an answer would consider the following aspects:

- o A clear introduction to the organization selected as a basis for the question.
- o An analysis of the organization using a range of stakeholder mechanisms. This would include a map of stakeholders and a discussion of both internal and external stakeholders. This would include details of their interactions and level of influence on the organization.
- o Plotting of the stakeholders in a diagrammatic representation.
- o An evaluation of each of the stakeholders in order to identify the four key stakeholders. This would be presented best in a table format.
- o The rationale for identifying the key stakeholders.
- o For each of the four key stakeholders, cover in detail the relationship they have with the organization. Are they internal or external. In addition, how do they view the organization's products/services.
- o Drawing in part of element 3 (Implementing elements of the promotional mix), the range of potential media should be considered. From these the most appropriate for each of the four stakeholders identified should be considered. The rationale for each selection also needs to be given.
- o The assignment should be presented as a report, although not in a folder, as per the submission instructions for the module.

Element 2 – Buying behaviour

This element covers the role of the decision-making unit and buyer behaviour, both consumer and organizational. As such, a sample question from this element would be:

For your organization and another one of your choice, make a comparison of consumer and organizational buyer behaviour that will help a graduate trainee, with no marketing experience, understand the differences. Your analysis should address the Decision Making Process (DMP) and how the communications mix can be used by an organization to influence the DMP.

In order to create an effective answer, two organizations need to be selected to provide a comparison. One needs to provide a perspective of consumer buyer behaviour and the other organizational buyer behaviour. A suggestion for this would be to link up with another student whose organization has the alternative customer base. However, the assignments should be completed separately. An answer to the question would include the following:

- o A background to the organizations selected given, together with a picture of the types of customer(s) each organization has. This needs to provide a basis of comparison for the organizations.
- o A definition of consumer and organizational buyer behaviour, with the organizations placed into context. This should include the models of consumer and organizational buyer behaviour.

o   An explanation of the decision-making process for each organization – one covering the organization with consumers and the other with organizational buyers. This should highlight the differences between each organization's buyers. This could either be displayed diagrammatically or in a table to facilitate understanding and aid comparison.

o   The next stage would be to introduce the communications mix, which is drawn from element 3 (Implementing elements of the promotional mix). The differences and similarities between the buyers should be shown. Again, a table would be the best form of representation here.

o   Presentation as a report in this instance would be the most obvious choice.

Element 3 – Implementing elements of the promotional mix

There are a wide range of questions which could be asked from this element. The most obvious range around the use of communications mechanisms, as has been included in the previous questions. However, the element covers much more than simply communications, as the sample question below demonstrates:

Your manager has asked you to prepare a presentation to the Sales Team on the value and potential impact of 'below-the-line' methods of promotion to your organization or an organization of your choice. The presentation should take no longer than 40 minutes and include slides plus a handout to aid the sales team.

This question covers a number of aspects, together with drawing a presentation from element 4 (Face-to-face communication). The format of the question should not be ignored, nor the additional request. Therefore, an answer should cover the following:

o   A background to the organization selected as a basis for the question. This should show the relationship between the sales team and their customers. In addition, a picture of the current use of promotion methods would be helpful.

o   The presentation needs to include the different types of promotion, both above-the-line and below-the-line methods. The benefits and drawbacks of each should be highlighted, together with the use of examples.

o   From this, the below-the-line methods should be covered in more detail, providing a range of examples to illustrate points made.

o   A summary of the presentation is required. In addition, having a question-and-answer session at the end to reinforce learning would be beneficial. Suggestions for this would include a questionnaire or questions relating to each promotional method within the presentation slides themselves.

o   Each slide should be legible and understandable. A recommended number of words per slide is 20 +/−5 to aid understanding.

o   The format of the presentation covers the use of slides together with the handout. This additional information should include the slides together with documentation relating to above-the-line and below-the-line methods of promotion. It should also include sources of further information.

o   A copy of the presentation slides should be included with the answer to the question, together with the handout and a disk containing the presentation.

Element 4 – Face-to-face communication

This element provides some interesting opportunities for questions. They could relate to your own or a given organization. As such, questions drawn from this element may relate to external and internal customer communication, to the handling of meetings, to personal communication or to presentations. An example question would cover:

In recent months, the planning meetings at the local council offices have become heated affairs due to a long-running application to construct an accommodation centre for international refugees. Local and national media have also been covering the arguments that have reigned. In order to improve local relations, you have been asked to advise the council on how their meetings can be better operated.

An answer to this question would require consideration of the contentious nature of the subject. In addition, the question has been placed in a public-sector context and one where feelings are already likely to be running high. There has been global media coverage on the nature of refugees, both genuine and bogus. A significant number of refugees claiming asylum in many countries are genuine and therefore this should be the context in which the question is placed. An example answer would cover the following aspects:

- o The context of the question should be set, and its nature covered. The situation should be explained in detail in order that there is no confusion.
- o The question needs to cover both communication in meetings together with face-to-face communication.
- o An explanation of communications is required, together with coverage of the different types of communication. This should cover not just voice, but also body language, tone plus listening skills. Barriers to communication would need to be covered in detail within the question.
- o An answer would then move on to explaining the role of meetings. This should include guidance for holding meetings. It is also important here to place the answer in the context of the question.
- o The final element of the answer should cover advice on communication in general with stakeholders, together with recommendations for the next meeting to be held.
- o The most appropriate format for this question would be the use of a report highlighting the communication issues, together with advice on communication and meetings.

Element 5 – Customer service and customer care

Customer service is one of the smaller elements of the Customer Communications module. However, questions are likely to be asked on this element as customer service is a critical aspect of customer communications. A typical question covering this element would be:

More organizations are now using their websites to interact with their customers and to facilitate and fulfil on-line purchasing. You have decided to produce a report for the next marketing meeting to highlight the differences between your own website and those of your THREE main competitors, together with their ease of identification using search mechanisms.

An answer to this question would require the selection of a range of competitors in order to provide a comparison. The organization selected should have a website already although this is not essential. In addition, they would not need to undertake on-line purchasing.

o The answer should set the scene by identifying the organization selected together with their industry. The current use of a website within the organization needs discussing. This should cover the purpose of the website, together with the use of on-line purchasing if this occurs.

o The three competitor websites should be selected, with a clear rationale for their choice. They may include the key competitors within the market, the largest players are those with the most advanced on-line purchasing systems.

o The next stage would be to examine potential sources of information regarding the sites. This includes search engines (e.g. Google, Hotbot, Yahoo), directories (e.g. Yahoo and others), links (trade bodies). Issues within this which need considering are the use of domain names, on-line promotion and listings. Do competitors use paid-for listings and promote themselves or are they generally listed on a search engine.

o Each of the three competitors' websites should be examined. Areas to be considered are navigation, information searching, customer contact together with their on-line purchasing system. If possible, follow through an order as a customer. The best way to represent these would be in a table as a comparison. In addition, the organization selected as a basis for the assignment should be included.

o The final stage would be to make recommendations regarding the organization's own website. How does their website reflect in terms of the industry standard. Where can improvements be made to the website.

o This would be best presented as a report, detailing the three competitors' websites. In addition, examples taken from each website would be suitable as appendices.

Assignment regulations

There have been a number of changes to the assignment structure compared with previous years, timed with the introduction of the new syllabi. These have been designed to provide consistency in approach for a student whether they are completing the assessment for a module by examination, assignment or integrative project. The more significant changes include:

o For the current academic year tutors at CIM centres will mark assignments. These are then moderated by CIM assessors. An integrative project is marked by CIM assessors only.

o No resubmission of assignments, as per an examination. In previous years, a range of assignments were being submitted. Where a student does not achieve the 50 per cent pass mark, they are requested to retake the assessment for the module through examination or assignment/integrative project.

o Whichever assessment route selected is fixed rather than having the option to change at the last minute. Past history has shown that students sometimes begin on an assignment route, change to an examination at the last minute due to not meeting a deadline and then score badly in the examination. The paths to an assignment or examination are different and therefore it is unadvisable to switch, which is the reason for the change of rule.

o In the 2002–3 academic year, word limits for questions and assignments were introduced. This was introduced due to assignments being submitted which were of a wide variety of lengths. These ranged from under 2,000 words to over 25,000 words. Where a student is completing four modules by assignment this would equal over 100,000 words – the equivalent of a medium-sized textbook or novel. As such it became impossible for two assignments to be considered together. Therefore the word limit guidance was introduced in order to provide equality for all students undertaking assessment by assignment.

o Two sets of assignments per year as with the examination route. With this change students are required to complete the assignment aimed at the nearest examination session. Previously students had between 3 months and 9 months to complete an assignment depending upon whether it was given out in September for a June deadline or March for the June deadline. Therefore a decision was made to follow the examination route with the intention of giving all students equal time to complete an assignment.

These summarize the key changes which have occurred due to the introduction of new syllabi with the assignment/integrative project route in order that there is parity of assessment at all levels and using all formats. Some of these changes have been significant, others minor. However, all the changes have been considered thoughtfully and with the best intentions for the students in mind.

Use of case studies

For anyone who is not working or has difficulty in access to information on their or another organization, there are a number of case studies available which allow the completion of a module using a case-based approach rather than basing it upon an organization identified by the student. These case studies are provided on a request-only basis through your accredited CIM centre and should only be used as a last resort. Using a case study as the basis for your assignment will not mean an easier approach to the assignment. However, they do provide an opportunity to undertake assignments when no other alternative exists. Each case study comes with a certain amount of information which can be used specifically for the completion of a question. Additional information may need to be assumed or researched in order to create a comprehensive assignment.

Submission of assignments/integrative project

The following information will aid both yourself and your tutor who marks your work and also the CIM assessor who will be moderating your work and the integrative project. In addition, the flow diagram represents the process of an assignment/integrative project from start to final mark.

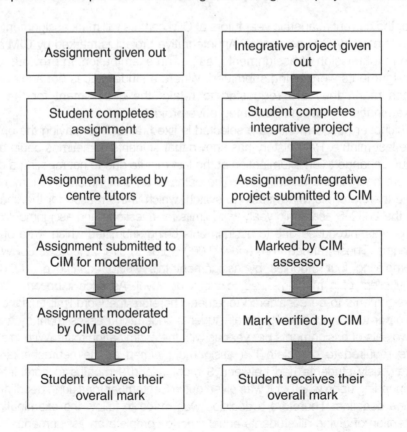

Assignment given out	Integrative project given out
Student completes assignment	Student completes integrative project
Assignment marked by centre tutors	Assignment/integrative project submitted to CIM
Assignment submitted to CIM for moderation	Marked by CIM assessor
Assignment moderated by CIM assessor	Mark verified by CIM
Student receives their overall mark	Student receives their overall mark

When completing and submitting assignments or the integrative project, refer to the following for guidance:

- Read through each question before starting out. Particularly with the core question there will be a considerable amount of work to undertake. Choose your optional questions wisely.
- Answer the question set and use the mark guidance given regarding the marking scheme.
- Refer to each question within the assignment and use a bibliography.
- Complete all documentation thoroughly. This is designed to aid both the CIM and yourself.
- Ensure that the assignment is bound as per instructions given. Currently assignments are requested not to be submitted in plastic wallets or folders as work can become detached or lost. Following the submission, instructions provided aids both the CIM administrators and the CIM assessor who will be marking (integrative project) or moderating (assignments) your work.
- Complete the candidate declaration sheet showing that you have undertaken this work yourself. **Please note that if you wish the information contained in your assignment to remain confidential you must state this on the front of the assignment.** Whilst CIM assessors will not use any information pertaining to your or another organization, CIM may wish to use the answer to a question as an example.

An assignment will be marked by a tutor at your CIM centre followed by moderation by a CIM assessor. The integrative project will be marked by a CIM assessor as per an examination with moderation by the CIM. To ensure objectivity by CIM assessors there exists a mark-in meeting prior to any marking in order that standardization can occur. The senior assessor for each subject also undertakes further verification of both examinations and assessments to ensure parity between each type of assessment.

David C. Lane
Senior Moderator (Advanced Certificate)
February 2003

appendix 3

answers and debriefings

The answers that follow are indicative and are not intended to be complete. Some of the answers to the activities are embedded in the course materials, the essential text, websites or simply in the mind of the reader.

Unit 1

Debriefing Activity 1.1

By doing this activity you should be able to see how important communication skills are to your job or daily life and be able to get a measure of areas for self-development where you may want to spend extra time. It may also steer you to take up opportunities for self-development in your workplace.

There is no one answer to the skills audit. You may have identified that, while you do not write business reports at the moment, you may be likely to do so when you take up another position within the firm where you work. Consequently this might be an area of special interest in your studies.

Alternatively you may have identified that you are highly skilled in writing press releases and therefore you may feel this is an area that you want to skim over. You could even go direct to the examination papers at the back of the book and spend some time answering any question relating to this area.

Debriefing Activity 1.2

Stakeholder	Message	Method	Why
Consumers – these would be broken down into various target groups in the consumer and business to business markets	Information about products, persuasive messages to brand the cars and persuade customers to buy.	All the promotional mix: advertising, branding, sponsorship, sales literature, direct marketing, public relations and a trained sales force.	To raise awareness. To increase sales.

Shareholders	Performance, dividend payout, future developments.	Annual general meeting. Annual report. PR to financial press.	Need shareholder support and need to promote correct image. Legal obligation to set out performance information.
Employees	Company performance. Future plans. Training information. Improvements in staff facilities. Staff news.	Internal newsletter. Memos, meetings, staff notice-board.	To maintain good industrial relations and staff motivation.
Potential employees	What the company does. What job opportunities are available.	Recruitment advertising. Corporate image.	To recruit from the biggest pool of available staff so will have better selection.
Suppliers	Company production plans and requirements.	Meetings. Tender documents. Contracts.	To help firms supply best components at the right time and to ensure that the organization and its suppliers work together in partnership.
Distributors	Product and technical information.	Point of sale material, sales literature and promotional items for branding purposes.	To assist dealerships in selling cars.
Local community – could be residents who live near factories, or local charities	That the firm cares for the local community.	PR activities. Sponsorship.	Good PR which could help, for example, if the firm applies for planning permission to extend factory premises.
The media	Product information and information about company performance.	Press releases. Events.	To raise the company's profile. To promote its image.
Government, local, national and international	They are an ethical firm and a good employer.	Via senior management on a personal level.	To establish good relations so can put pressure to bear regarding legislation that might affect the industry.
Pressure groups	They are an ethical firm that cares about the environment.	PR.	To negate effect of conflicting messages from environmental pressure groups.
Competitors	To develop strategic alliances.	Via senior management on a personal level.	To rationalize operations, cut costs and expand into other markets.

Debriefing Activity 1.3

Presentation notes internal marketing and internal communications

Introduction

I have been asked to deliver a short presentation on the importance of effective internal marketing and internal communications. I will explain what is meant by these terms and how they contribute to the success of a company and then will draw on my experience within other organizations to describe how they have improved their internal communication systems.

Key points
Internal marketing

Internal marketing means creating a culture where staff work together as a team, seeing each other as internal customers, who require good service. With internal marketing, the contribution of all staff is recognized and valued as helping to achieve the goals set by the organization.

For example, in my experience at a successful packaging firm where all the staff know what is expected of them and how their individual contribution affects whether a job is completed well and on time, they know this affects whether the client is retained. Contrast this example with that of a building firm where staff have to alter work that has been carried out badly by colleagues and time is wasted because builders are not given the correct information about the work that needs to be undertaken.

Benefits of internal marketing culture:

- o   Shared values
- o   Co-operation
- o   Efficiency
- o   Job satisfaction
- o   High-quality work
- o   Loyalty
- o   Effective communications.

Internal communications

The organization's internal communications system is vital in the creation and maintenance of an effective marketing culture among staff. This approach should transcend all petty differences and encompass both staff within a department and staff in different departments, on different sites and even in different countries.

Improving internal communications

Establish a two-way flow of information so that managers hear staff's views and opinions as well as staff hearing about management's objectives, views and plans by:

- o   Regular staff meetings and team briefings to discuss plans, work and how to get around difficulties
- o   Meetings with senior managers regarding current performance, future objectives, plans and how they affect staff
- o   Empower staff to become involved in improving quality, facilities, systems and procedures
- o   Performance reviews to tell staff how they are doing, what could be improved and to identify what training is needed to improve individual performance
- o   Feedback to managers on their performance
- o   Suggestion schemes
- o   Establish a culture where people are not afraid to air their views or grievances

- ○ Use the staff notice-board effectively to inform of events, training and even to quash rumours
- ○ Establish an internal newsletter
- ○ Train managers to run effective team briefings
- ○ Train staff to hold effective meetings
- ○ Establish a house style for letters, memos and reports
- ○ Encourage staff not to resort to sending an e-mail to everyone and anyone
- ○ Remind staff how to use the internal telephone system effectively
- ○ Establish effective recording systems, whether for taking messages, informing other staff of your whereabouts, recording sales visits or job instructions
- ○ Introduce staff manuals and policy documents so that staff are clear about systems and procedures in the firm.

Summary

A culture of internal marketing and an effective internal communications system is vital to the success of an organization. If staff are well informed, empowered and listened to, they are more likely to know and share the aims of the company and work together to play their part in achieving them.

Unit 2

Debriefing Activity 2.1

A consumer's internal stimuli are feelings that come from within them. In the case of a new car, a consumer may feel embarrassed by their old car if its not in very good condition. Alternatively, they may just feel the need to 'treat' themselves to something new like a car, which they can take pride in.

External stimuli can come from various sources, including the media, family and friends. For example, the consumer may see an advertisement on television for a nice, new car and this prompts the consumer to realize that a purchase is needed. Alternatively, if a bank is offering a very favourable interest rate on a loan, a consumer may feel that they can now afford to buy a car, whereas previously they couldn't.

Debriefing Activity 2.2

The buying process	AIDA model of communication	Promotional tool
Need recognition	Gain attention	PR
Information search	Stimulate interest	Advertising and point of sale material in car showroom
Evaluation of alternatives	Create desire	Test drives, sales brochure
Purchase decision	Generate action	Sales force
Post-purchase decision	Create satisfaction	Direct marketing material, follow-up calls to check customer satisfaction, warranty material

Debriefing Activity 2.3

PEST factors would be very influential to a buyer from John Deere tractors. For example, you would need to consider the general state of the economy before you bought in large amounts of new engines, bearing in mind these engines are probably very expensive to buy in bulk. If, say, the economy was in a down-turn and the farming community was severely affected by this, it is possible that the level of demand for tractors may decrease, therefore this would impact on the number of tractors you manufacture and ultimately your level of sales.

The level of technology required from the engines would be important, as it must tie-in with the level of technology of your tractors.

Other considerations would include your relationship with your supplier – is it an on-going one with a lot of trust and commitment, or are you looking for someone new.

What is your budget and what is your company's attitude to risk? How much influence does your DMU have in this purchasing decision.

These are just some of several external and internal factors to take into consideration.

Debriefing Activity 2.4

- o *Purchasing* This function may work closely with suppliers, either to develop a new relationship or to deepen an existing one. They may well act as the ultimate buyer within the DMU.
- o *Research and Development (R&D)* This function may work very closely with the marketing function in developing the specification for a new product. They may also liaise with the purchasing department when it comes to buying the materials for products. They may well act as influencers or gatekeepers within the DMU.
- o *Production* This function will be responsible for the actual manufacturing of the product(s). They will probably work closely with marketing when looking at production capacity for products, particularly when marketing or forecasting sales levels. They will act as influencers and users within the DMU.
- o *Finance* This function will have a very important role, and may well act as influencer, decider and possible buyer too in the DMU.
- o *Marketing* This function will probably work closely with all the major functions as they have to provide the initial information in terms of customer needs and wants. They will act as influencer in the DMU.

Debriefing Activity 2.5

1. For a General Practitioner, or GP, personal selling is quite probably the main method of communication, although this may well have been preceded by a very targeted mailshot to the GP, containing details of the drug (assuming there are no legal restrictions on mailing this type of information). As many GP surgeries are now made up of several practice managers who will make up the decision making unit, you may well need to do a brief presentation to all of them to try to convince them to try your new pharmaceutical product.
2. For a hospital, there will be several people or even departments who will make up the decision making unit, including nurses, doctors, surgeons and finance managers. Some of these individuals may attend exhibitions where you may well exhibit your pharmaceutical drug, or at least you will have literature which could provide written

details on the product. Members of your sales team should also be on hand to discuss key questions regarding the drug and its content, for example its potential uses or the amount of research that has been done on it and its success rate. Your company would possibly have a website too, which would offer restricted access to potential buyers from the medical profession.

Unit 3

Debriefing Activity 3.1

Barrier	Problems caused
Technical noise caused by crackly telephone line.	Mistake by the agency in arranging the duration of the placement.
Social noise caused by Sally's prejudice about Peter's age, gender and appearance. He lacked credibility in her eyes.	This not only irritated Peter but also stopped Sally working effectively with him.
Psychological noise caused by Peter's anger.	Peter misinterpreted what Sally said to him and this caused conflict.
Contradictory non-verbal communication caused by Peter smiling and saying one thing but really thinking something else.	Sally received the wrong message.

Debriefing Activity 3.2

Student's answer

1. Lack of credibility can be a barrier to communication if, for example, a young, inexperienced salesperson lacking product/market knowledge tries to sell a high-value, specialist, technical product. This barrier to communication could only be overcome if the salesperson had thorough training in both the sales technique and the product/market.

    The noise could be reduced if the salesperson had a professional appearance in terms of dress and used a professional demonstration kit to illustrate the product to potential customers. It would also be useful if the salesperson worked for a well-known company and had testimonials from previously satisfied clients. In this way customers would concentrate less on the weak traits of the salesperson, and be more aware of the credibility of the product and the manufacturer.

2. Perceptual bias refers to people hearing what they want to hear. By filling in the gaps and making assumptions, a significant barrier to the real message can be created. For example, if staff had heard rumours about potential job losses prior to a staff meeting they might 'tune out' from the information being delivered during the meeting and may only select the negative aspects of what was being said.

    The noise could be effectively reduced only if the manager addressed the rumours and allowed staff to ask questions so that he could allay fears and ensure that the staff heard the whole message.

3. Information overload is a barrier to communication because if a person is given too much information then the key message is not digested. For example, if a person delivered a talk to their local CIM branch on the effectiveness of an advertising campaign and the speaker provided too many facts and figures, the overall message might be lost in the detail.

   To avoid information overload, the speaker could reduce the amount of detail and emphasize the main points using visual aids, illustrations, demonstrations and anecdotal examples. In-depth background detail to the campaign could be provided in the form of notes or a handout for those who wanted to read this information in their own time.

4. Contradictory non-verbal signals might be conveyed by a person whose words say one thing whilst their body language says something else. For example, when a customer is complaining about the service in a bank, the cashier dealing with the complaint could be apologizing for the mistake made but at the same time avoiding eye contact and sounding disinterested and bored by speaking in a monotonous voice.

   To reduce the noise, the cashier would need to support the words being used by adopting a sympathetic tone, eye contact and positive body language such as nodding to show empathy with the customer's viewpoint.

Debriefing Activity 3.3

Here are some ways of rewriting the sentences:

1. We should attempt to plan ahead to meet future service requirements
2. The supplies manager has pointed out that the product is difficult to obtain
3. It is difficult to move as the price of land has gone up.

Debriefing Activity 3.4

1. You could use a poster campaign along the roads where the tolls will be introduced. As with all poster campaigns, you would need to keep the message simple because people need to be able to take in the message as they go past at speed.
2. You could do a demonstration and a short presentation. Your communication style should be persuasive in order to show the benefits of the new product. To communicate the financial data you might use visual communication, such as graphs and tables. Any slides or acetates that you produce may just feature key words that you will explain as part of your presentation.
3. You may write a lengthy, formal report to the Director that deals with the problems and suggests solutions. You may adopt an impersonal tone, using a 'third person' style. For example, 'It appears that the road works on the local motorway network have caused significant delays when our vans depart for the mid-morning delivery run.' As you are writing to your line manager you would not use an authoritative 'tell' style of communication. In your report you would not necessarily avoid longer, more complex sentences or technical terms.

Unit 4

Debriefing Activity 4.2

1. Calvin Klein fragrances are unisex and aimed at younger people. They are a highly branded product and are usually advertised using photogenic models in creative adverts on television. Consequently local press advertising does not seem to fit in with the image of the product.

2. A small hotel in Wales is unlikely to have the marketing budget to afford television advertising. Also, it would be rather wasteful as it is a mass-market medium. The hotel should specifically target holidaymakers who want to spend their holidays in Wales. They could consider the national press, perhaps a Sunday newspaper, that has a travel section and they should choose an edition when there is editorial coverage about holidays in Wales.

3. Harvey Goldsmith Entertainments are right to use radio as the 'product' fits the medium. They could advertise on national radio, specifically Classic FM, as that station appeals to opera fans. They may even use local radio to tie-in with the locations of the concerts.

4. ASH has chosen a good mix of media to target young women. The cinema will be a good choice if they make sure their adverts appear before films that specifically appeal to young women. The magazines aimed at young women also seem an ideal choice for such a campaign.

Debriefing Activity 4.3

The instructions to the printer might be as follows:

o   Midchester logo to be inserted where it says 'logo' (see attached compliment slip and pantone references)
o   120 gsm white card with gilt edging
o   Black print
o   Typeface Arial
o   Typesize 12 point
o   Type to be centred as indicated on attached rough layout
o   Print run 250.

Midchester Chamber of Commerce
LOGO
in association with National Westminster Bank

Invite

....

to the e-commerce gala dinner
on
Friday 11th June 20XX
at
The palace Hotel, Oxford Street, Midchester
7.00pm for 7.30pm pre-dinner drinks will
be served in the Hexagon bar.

RSVP by 30.5 XX to A.Candidate, Chamber of Commerce

Debriefing Activity 4.4

To those consumers that The Body Shop products appeal to, its environmentally friendly appeal evokes a feeling of comfort because these consumers see it as an extension of themselves because they either aspire to be or are environmentally friendly in their lifestyle or behaviour.

To those consumers that Benetton products appeal to, its global village branding evokes a feeling of warmth and belonging.

Debriefing Activity 4.5

The two main criticisms are that the content is dull and the language is indecipherable.

Somewhere in the text there is possibly a news story but the way it is written makes it difficult to find.

The readers of a local newspaper want to read interesting human-interest stories that relate to the area they live in.

XYZ Farming Ltd is probably a local firm in the area covered by the newspaper, and the writer should make reference to this in the release.

The news story the writer could have developed is that XYZ Farming Ltd has introduced a new product that helps local farmers produce milk that is more popular with consumers and dairies pay higher prices for it.

To add some human interest to the story, the writer could have found a local farmer who actually had sold more milk to the dairies because of this new product. The writer could then have provided him with a suitable quote in the release, stating his delight with the new product. The firm could then have organized a photograph of the farmer, holding a bag of the miracle new product, standing beside one of his cows.

The press release could also have been improved even further if the writer had avoided jargon and used short, punchy sentences. It would also have been a useful tactic to get the name of the product (Granary) into the first few paragraphs of the release, as presumably the objective was to publicize the Granary feed and the fact that XYZ produced it.

Debriefing Activity 4.6

1. **MIDCHESTER CHAMBER OF COMMERCE**
   PRESS RELEASE

   Date of release: 14 June 20XX

   A gala dinner to launch the first e-commerce conference ever held in Midchester took place last night.

   Celebrity guest speaker at the event, Bill Gates, said, 'It's great to see all the best minds involved in the Internet business gathered in one place'.

'This event certainly puts Midchester on the map as the place if you want to be involved in any aspect of e-commerce'.

Over 200 people attended the dinner and Andy Potts, the Chairman of the Chamber of Commerce, said, 'It's an unprecedented success and there's already talk about holding another dinner next year'.

'It's a great opportunity for business people at the forefront of technology to get together to network and enjoy themselves at the same time. It will probably result in the region attracting lots more inward investment from this area of business.'

The dinner launched a two-day e-commerce conference, which will be held this week at the town hall and will be attended by business people from all over the world. It will feature a series of lectures and a number of workshops, some of which will be held online with other Internet businesses in the United States and Japan.

Tickets are still available at £100 per person from the Midchester Chamber of Commerce.

For further information about the dinner or conference, please contact Sally Moss at Midchester Chamber of Commerce, Market Street, Midchester. 0161 234 7890. Fax 0161 245 8923. E-mail s.moss@madeupnamenet.co.uk

2. The objective in sending this press release was to promote the chamber of commerce and to publicize the conference. It could even be issued to attract inward investment from e-commerce businesses

3. The press release could be sent to the local newspaper and also to specialist Internet magazines.

Debriefing Activity 4.7

Specimen answer: The Society for the Prevention of Accidents
To: Ruth Arnold, Marketing Officer

From: Davina Darcy, Chief Executive

Date: 7 May 20XX

Subject: Brief for marketing campaign

Project details
Marketing campaign 8, summer 1999, highlighting health and safety issues in the workplace.

Background information
Government statistics show a rise of 25 per cent in the last two years in workplace accidents. A recent *Law Gazette* article has revealed a dramatic rise in employer negligence cases where damages have had to be awarded and in some cases the head of the company has been given a jail sentence.

The SPA has a large database of companies that have requested information on accident prevention, have attended one of our training courses or have been added to our list through our own research into accidents.

Objectives

○ To send out 3000 posters illustrating workplace health and safety hazards
○ To generate 1000 requests from personnel managers in industry for leaflets about accident prevention. This information to be added to our database
○ To generate 1000 requests from managers in the construction industry for leaflets about accident prevention. This information to be added to our database.

Target audience

○ Companies on SPA's database
○ Personnel managers in industry
○ Managers in the construction industry.

Message to be conveyed

○ Government statistics show a 25 per cent rise in workplace accidents over the last two years
○ Accidents can result in employers paying substantial damages and they can be held criminally negligent
○ More accidents than ever before are happening in the construction industry.

Media

○ Posters illustrating health and safety issues in the workplace to be sent to all the companies held on SPA's database. Each poster to be sent with a covering letter addressed to health and safety officers highlighting the penalties and pointing out methods of prevention. A copy of the letter should be provided so that the health and safety officer can give it to the company's Managing Director
○ Advertising and PR campaign in *People Management* with a direct response mechanism for personnel managers to request more information about accident prevention
○ Advertising and PR campaign in *Construction News* with a direct response mechanism for senior managers to request more information about accident prevention.

Timescale

Campaign should run from the beginning of September to the end of October 20XX.

Budget

A total budget of £8000 is available.

Unit 5

Debriefing Activity 5.1

You should have been able to:

○ Check the Frequently Asked Questions section
○ Get access to past papers and examiner reports
○ Update your details, register for exams
○ Voice your view in the voting area.

Debriefing Activity 5.2

The Internet is being used in the following ways:

- o To provide information to customers and prospects as another promotional activity
- o To provide information and other services to add value to the customer offering
- o To create a two-way communication flow
- o To capture customer information and for research purposes
- o To sell goods and services
- o To improve internal communication
- o To improve business relationships with suppliers and distributors, etc.

Debriefing Activity 5.3

ICT developments have changed the way people communicate as follows:

- o E-mail has become a major means of internal and external communication and large documents can be sent as attachments quickly, which reduces time and cost on paper distribution.
- o Fax machines are still used where recipients of messages do not use e-mail and are useful for sending visual information where offices do not have access to scanners.
- o Mobile telephone use means staff on the move can keep in touch with colleagues and customers.
- o Laptop technology means sales staff have remote access to information when out in the field with clients.
- o Laptop computers ensure sales staff can give quality presentations to clients.
- o Videoconferencing means excess travel to meetings is reduced but that staff working at different sites can communicate almost face-to-face without too much advance notice.
- o Databases are used to track customer purchases and to mailmerge documents when sending out mailshots to different groups of customers.
- o An EDI system means that when outlets in the network use up materials, re-stocking requests are automatically received which reduces paper and telephone calls.
- o An intranet can be set up for managers to access information on previous projects and client requirements easily and quickly.
- o Internet research means that information can be found out more quickly and easily.

The Law courts are a good example of an organization using ICT to improve the way it operates. Computer screens can be used to present evidence electronically. So photographs, maps, witness statements, video stills and Internet pages will all appear on screens in front of judges, prosecution lawyers and witnesses, jury members and defendants.

The technology will speed up the process of communicating information during court sessions. In addition, a digital audio system with microphones is being used to reduce the need for witnesses to speak loudly, recording equipment will speed up the production of court transcripts and e-mail requests will be used to speed up requests for plea and directions hearings.

Unit 6

Debriefing Activity 6.1

1. 'I'm not sure what we can do about that but if you give me your details I will make sure that someone gets back to you – when would it be convenient for them to contact you?'
2. 'I don't actually handle the payments but if you hold on . . .' either 'I will transfer you to x in y department who will help you' or 'I will ask x in y department to come down to speak to you if you could just wait for a few minutes'
3. 'I don't think we have that in stock but I'll just go and check for you'
4. 'X is not at their desk at the moment but if you give me your telephone number I will ask them to call you back.'

Debriefing Activity 6.2

MEMORANDUM

To: All Managers

From: Maggie Yorke, Communications Manager

Date: 30 July 20XX

Subject: Weekly team briefings

A number of managers have asked for some guidance on the best way to present themselves in the regular team briefings that have recently been introduced in all departments.

I have observed a number of the meetings and body language is one important area where some simple tips could improve the way messages are put across to teams.

It is important to communicate your verbal message and keep in the back of your mind how the following can either add to or detract from the message you are trying to put across.

Facial expressions

Staff will react more favourably to you if you have a warm, friendly smile instead of looking rather tense or aggressive, which is the message that can be communicated if you have a furrowed brow or pursed lips.

Posture

You may feel more comfortable sitting down with your team round a table rather than standing up in front of them, which creates a more formal atmosphere. If you do sit down, avoid folding your arms as that can appear as if you are creating a barrier. Make sure that you sit upright rather than slouched in the chair as that could communicate that you are too tired or bored to be bothered with the briefing.

Gesture

Many people like to use their hands to express themselves but too much hand waving can be distracting for those listening. Even if you are displeased with the team's performance or recent events, it is better to avoid emotional displays such as banging your fists on the table.

Eye contact

It is very easy to find yourself making eye contact with just one person in the team. However, this may make the person feel uncomfortable as they will feel they are being stared at. Another problem could be that you are tempted to read from your notes and may end up not making eye contact with your team. You should avoid this as it can result in the team not being involved in what you are saying.

I am sure that most of you are happy with your departmental team briefings. However, I do hope that you find these tips helpful so that we can continue to improve our internal communications which are so important in helping to motivate and inform the workforce.

Debriefing Activity 6.3

There are a number of ways in which you can ensure that you are listening effectively in interviews:

- º Be patient and let the person express themselves – do not interrupt or complete sentences for the interviewee
- º Use appropriate body language, such as eye contact and nodding, to show interest in what is being said – this will encourage the interviewee to answer your questions fully
- º Ask questions to clarify your understanding of what has been said
- º At intervals, sum up what the interviewee has said to show that you have listened and understood.

Debriefing Activity 6.4

BLUEBIRD HOTELS MEMORANDUM

To: All reception staff

From: George Stakis, Marketing Manager

Date: 9 August 20XX

Subject: Effective telephone use

A recent research survey into the service provided by Bluebird Hotels has revealed a number of areas where we can improve our service. One of these areas is the way customers' telephone calls are dealt with. The following recommendations need to be adopted by reception staff when dealing with calls.

Incoming calls

All calls should be answered by the fifth ring. Too many callers are left waiting for several minutes before their call is picked up.

When calls are answered, it is important that they are dealt with correctly. Staff should clearly state their name and that of the hotel, followed by the question, 'How can I help you?'

Transfer of calls

It is important that reception staff are familiar with the extension numbers for the hotel's various departments and the numbers in guests' rooms, so that calls can be transferred quickly and efficiently.

It is apparent that many calls are being cut off whilst they are being transferred. Therefore it is vital that reception staff ensure that they press the gate (#) button before dialling the extension number they require.

Many suppliers have complained that they are transferred to various departments in the hotel when they are in the middle of speaking to the person on reception. Before transferring calls, please briefly explain to the caller why you need to transfer them and ask for their permission to do so.

Message taking

If the extension number is engaged or not answered, then it is important that an accurate message is taken. Messages should be noted on hotel message pads only. They should state the date and time of the call, name of the caller (company name if it is appropriate) and the telephone number of the caller. Messages for staff should state the purpose of the call. All messages should be put in guest or staff pigeon-holes immediately after they have been taken.

Thank you for your co-operation in this matter.

Unit 7

Debriefing Activity 7.1

MEMORANDUM

To: Dennis Law

From: George Best

Date: 4 March 200X

Subject: Guidance on leading project management meetings

An important aspect of leading a meeting is to be well organized. This means making sure a room is booked for the meeting and that it is prepared in advance with enough seats, paperwork and refreshments if appropriate.

It also means having the correct paperwork and if there is an agenda, following it.

Being responsible for leading a meeting means opening the discussion, setting the objectives of the meeting and then moving on to the items you need to discuss.

Another aspect is to make sure that everyone participates, by ensuring that a few do not dominate and some are left feeling they cannot contribute.

To lead the meeting effectively, you need to judge when everyone has contributed, summarize the discussion so that everyone knows what has been decided. For example, who has to do what next as part of progressing the project effectively or that it has been agreed that deliveries of x materials must be increased before y production can go ahead.

One difficult thing to watch is that discussion does not run over and the meeting does not keep to time. Sometimes it is necessary to be quite firm that discussion needs to be hurried along and a decision or a point made.

Finally, you should ensure you clearly inform the people attending when the meeting is closing and after the meeting make sure that a record of the meeting, usually action minutes, is distributed to everyone who attended.

Debriefing Activity 7.2

The role of meetings

- o Decision-making/Problem-solving
- o Dissemination of information
- o Motivating staff
- o Two-way discussion
- o Building relationships.

Different types of meetings

- o Informal meetings – these occur daily in the work place. Employees getting together on ad hoc basis to discuss progress on work, share out work, agree plans, gather information or generate ideas.
- o Formal meetings – likely to feature a chairperson, formal agenda and minutes from the last meeting. These meetings may require a quorum and have a formal voting procedure. These meetings may be at board level where strategic decisions are discussed.

Leading meetings
It is the responsibility of the person leading the meeting to do the following:

- o Ensure there is an accurate record of the meeting
- o Effectively control and manage the meeting ensuring that participants listen and give each other a chance to contribute
- o Ensure there is adequate discussion of each item and that the meeting runs on time
- o Bring a conclusion to discussion, clarifying points made, taking a vote and summarising the decision
- o Delegate responsibility as actions arise.

Meetings documentation

- o Notice of meeting – gives notice of when and where a meeting will take place
- o Agenda – a list of what will be discussed, sometimes has formal proposals
- o Chairperson's agenda – the agenda plus background notes to help run the meeting
- o Minutes – a note of what was discussed and decisions taken
- o Discussion papers – papers put forward to participants for consultation and discussion.

Debriefing Activity 7.3

MEMORANDUM

To: All Managers

From: Ann Candidate

Date: 11 August 200X

Subject: Checklist outlining five stages of the interview process

- o *Preparation* This includes preparing the content of the interview in terms of the information that needs to be given to candidates and the questions that need to be added. In addition, some thought needs to be given to the logistics in terms of the desk and chair arrangements, paperwork that is needed and identifying the staff who will conduct the interviews.
- o *Opening* Interviewers must be prepared to set the tone and the atmosphere of the interview with a friendly greeting and an outline of the structure of the interview.
- o *Conducting* This refers to the main body of the interview when the interviewer will be asking questions, listening to answers and making any relevant notes.
- o *Closure* It is appropriate for interviewers to make it clear when the interview is about to end, perhaps by saying, for example, 'And now a final question' or perhaps asking the interviewee if they have any questions before the interview is completed.
- o *Follow-up* The interviewer needs to collate the information obtained during the interview and decide on the follow-up action. This could be an appointment letter or one informing the candidate that they were not successful on this occasion.

The benefits of using open questions are that they encourage two-way communication. An open question allows interviewees to express themselves. Open questions tend to begin with words like 'how', 'what', 'when' and 'why'. By using probing questions you can find out about the reasons why a person has said something or help them to justify their answer. For example, 'Why do you feel that you would be suitable for this job?' could be the open question you initially ask and then you could probe deeper into the answer by asking 'How have you recently demonstrated the research skills that you have just mentioned?'

Debriefing Activity 7.4

1. Negotiation is designed to achieve agreement that is mutually acceptable to both parties
2. To be an effective negotiator, I would need to carefully control my body language in order to appear and act confidently, take client feedback positively and not to create communication barriers. For instance, I would demonstrate confident body language by using eye contact and adopting an appropriate posture. I would be sitting upright but also slightly leaning forward to show that I was interested and paying attention to what the client was saying. I would not show impatience with any feedback on my firm's performance by tapping my fingers or frowning and would not shuffle nervously from side to side in my seat. I would not fold my arms and would sit with an open posture with my hands on my knees. I would use a calm, professional tone to offset whatever underlying feelings of nervousness or stress I might feel.

Unit 8

Debriefing Activity 8.1

Specimen answer
The first point to note is that 15 marks are allocated to this part of the question, and therefore we can safely conclude that 5 marks per drawing of a chart or graph will be awarded. The tables are all reproduced below (by kind permission of the CIM) and it is a question of personal

choice as to which are to be used in answer to the question. You must make sure that each graph or chart is clearly labelled, on each axis and also given a title.

I have presented below a different graph for each set of data corresponding to the first five tables.

Table 1 I have chosen a column/bar chart to represent the data in this table.

Figure 1 Shopping for groceries

Table 2 I have chosen a pie chart to represent this data.

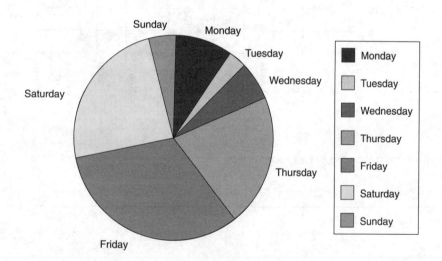

Figure 2 Shopping days

Table 3 I have chosen an area graph to represent this data.

Figure 3 Reasons for choice of day

Table 4 I have chosen a standard line graph for the data in this table.

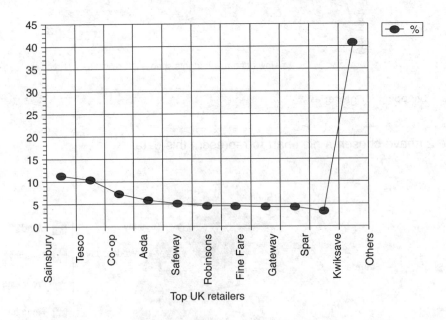

Figure 4 Store shopped at for groceries most often

Table 5 I have chosen a 3-dimensional column/bar chart for this data.

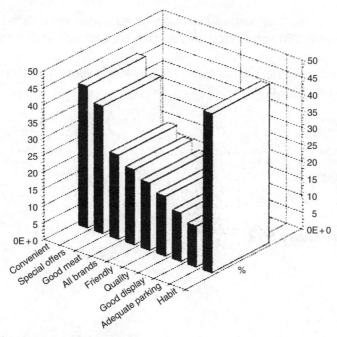

Figure 5 Reasons for shopping at a certain shop

Debriefing Activity 8.2

See Figure 2 in the debriefing for Activity 8.1

Unit 9

Debriefing Activity 9.1

Healthy Living
17 Haymill Road
Birmingham BH4 2UT

Dear Miss Murray

I notice from our records that your subscription is due for renewal. I thought you would like to know that all current and lapsed members who renew before 30 June qualify for a 25 per cent reduction on their subscription fee to Healthy Living.

This means a 12 month membership for £350!

The next 12 months are looking even better at Healthy Living as we have several new facilities on offer for all our members. We have added two new stretch-and-tone classes to our midweek schedule and have had a new running machine installed in the gym area. We have also extended our opening hours to 10.00 p.m.

Renewing your membership could not be easier – just return the tear-off slip below with any amended name and address details to our address with a cheque for £350 before 30 June.

By updating your contact details, you will also be automatically entered into a prize draw. The winner will receive a £50 sports clothes voucher, redeemable at our on-site sports shop.

If for any reason you are not able to rejoin right now, still send in your completed slip, which will be entered into the prize draw.

Yours sincerely

Michael Motivator

Health Studio Manager

Debriefing Activity 9.2

The Lime Tree
Lime Tree Lane
Hightown
Herts

14 June 200X

Mr Beckett
Longley Lane
Northenden
Hightown

Dear Mr Beckett

Thank you for your letter of 10 June with regard to the quality of service you received on 5 June.

I would like to take this opportunity to apologise on behalf of all the staff at the restaurant for the unacceptable behaviour by one member of my staff.

Although I am most concerned to hear about how you were treated, I am pleased that you took the trouble to inform me of what happened. I can assure you that the matter was thoroughly investigated and that the member of staff has been disciplined as part of company policy. It is company policy to monitor performance in a case such as this and the member of staff is fully aware of the consequences if there is any repeat of such an incident in future.

I would be very pleased if you would accept a refund of £50 as a small token for the trouble you have been caused. I am also enclosing vouchers to the value of £50 that can be used at any of our restaurants in the town.

Again I would like to express my apologies and hope to see you at the Lime Tree in the near future.

Yours sincerely

Michael

Manager

Debriefing Activity 9.3

MEMORANDUM

To: Sales Managers

From: Meredith Chapman

Date: 19 June 200X

Subject: Internal communication

With the new sales structure in place, it is vital to establish effective communications between the different regions. Although letters are traditionally used at S&G, we need to speed up internal communication because there are several disadvantages in relying on the postal system as the sole means of communication.

Problems with sending letters:

- o Letters can be delayed through postal difficulties in certain countries
- o Letters can be quite expensive
- o Letters do not allow for immediate feedback.

It is important for staff to remember that we can opt for a number of different ways to communicate with colleagues in other regions using our existing ICT facilities.

E-mail

Messages go direct to the recipient and can be copied to as many people as required. A hard copy of the message can be printed out if required. It is a quick method of communication and enables our company to protect the security and confidentiality of our internal communication. However, confidential documents should be password protected.

Fax

The fax machine allows immediate communication. Even where there is a time difference and the office you are communicating with is closed, the fax message will be there when staff are next in. It is possible to send hard copies of diagrams and drawings/plans of construction sites quickly and cheaply (for the cost of a telephone call).

Voicemail

This enables the sender's spoken message to be recorded in a digital form by a network computer so the recipient can access the message via a telephone handset at any convenient time. This means that, in spite of the time differences that are experienced in running an international sales operation, colleagues can communicate and express themselves in a way that is not possible with written information.

Unit 10

Debriefing Activity 10.1

For this answer, the assumption made is that the issue is genetically modified foods and the company is a manufacturer of baby food. The stakeholders might be customers who purchase the products and a pressure group such as the National Childbirth Trust (NCT). Customers might communicate their objection to the use of genetically modified components in baby food by telephoning and writing to the company, and boycotting its products. The NCT might undertake a media campaign using print and broadcast media.

The firm could deal with the objections by trying to assure consumers that the genetically modified products are safe via an extensive PR campaign. This would be unlikely to succeed against an intensive lobbying campaign. Ultimately, the manufacturer may have to give in to consumer demands to ban genetically modified foods from the production cycle.

If they did give in to public pressure, it would then be advisable to publicize the fact to maintain good relations with stakeholders. The changed stance could be publicized through a PR campaign, changing product labels to announce the change and via advertising. They would also need to set up a customer-care line and communicate the news to all concerned callers. They might also get involved in a joint campaign with the pressure group to promote the banning of genetically modified products in all other baby foods.

Debriefing Activity 10.2

Experiences where customers are delighted will be as varied as the people reading this workbook. You could have gone to the local supermarket, asked for help with packing your bags and been pleasantly surprised when you were also helped to your car with the bags. You may have wanted to buy certain items that were out of stock at the chemist's and were surprised that the manager not only arranged to order them but also arranged next-day delivery too. You may have asked for the balance of your bank account and been surprised that it was overdrawn. If the bank clerk cancelled the interest charges and arranged for you to have your bank statements sent out more frequently so that you could keep a better check on your account, you would have been delighted. Or you may have been travelling by plane on business and needed something to read but not had time to buy a newspaper. You may have been pleased to find that a free newspaper had been provided and delighted that a selection of all the daily newspapers was available.

In estimating the cost of improving a service, you could, for example, calculate the cost of sending out a bank statement every week to a customer in comparison to the cost of attracting a new customer. A weekly bank statement costing £15 over a year to produce and post, is probably much cheaper than the annual cost of marketing and advertising divided by the number of new customers gained each year.

Debriefing Activity 10.3

Tesco Baby Club Card
Pregnant women are encouraged to apply for a club card and the reward is money-off coupons for baby products. The mother-to-be completes an application form, providing information such as name, address, information about the family and the baby's expected birth date.

The money-off coupons encourage repeat purchase at Tesco's stores. The card means the company can record each customer transaction and establish a customer profile. The company can then target the customer with information about relevant products and services. The organization can also sell this information to other organizations wishing to communicate with customers of a certain age, living in a certain area, who have a particular purchase history.

The baby club card scheme also features a frequent customer contact programme. Mothers are sent magazines with hints and advice to coincide with the various developmental stages that babies go through. So, for example, when the baby is aged four months old, the mother is sent a magazine which gives advice on how to wean babies onto solid food and contains advertising and money-off coupons relating to first-stage baby food products.

In this way, both the organization and the customer receive benefits from the relationship that is established between the two parties.

Debriefing Activity 10.4

1. The minimum need is for the customer to be able to obtain the type of petrol wanted without having to wait too long. The additional customer service need that should be met is that the forecourt is clean and tidy with towels available to clean hands. In addition, the instructions for obtaining petrol should be clear, concise and friendly, helpful staff should deal with payment. If the service station does not have staff and has automatic credit card payment facilities, then instructions for use should be clear with graphical images to reinforce the message and avoid confusing the customer, who may not have used this method of payment before.
2. The minimum need is to travel from one place to another on time in a clean, comfortably lit and heated or ventilated train. In addition, customers should be communicated with if there are timetable problems, and all announcements should be spoken in a clear, well-articulated voice that is not distorted by the public address system. Similarly, timetable notices and platform signage should be visible.

Debriefing Activity 10.5

Intelligent telephony services are computer-based applications that fully integrate with a telephone system to provide routing of voice and fax calls to an individual or team regardless of location.

Messaging and voice processing are message management and call processing systems that help organizations deal with internal and external calls more effectively, with the potential to increase productivity and reduce call-handling costs.

Personal videoconferencing enables video and data conferencing from any location connected to the ISDN network by using a card that can be slotted into a personal computer.

These services mean that voice, fax and data communication is available to users wherever they are which makes people more accessible. Customers can be automatically routed to the correct department and should get a quicker response.

Debriefing Activity 10.6

You can ensure that personnel in the overseas sales region are kept fully informed by using fax and e-mail communication.

Debriefing Activity 10.7

o   Banks have used automatic teller machines (ATMs) or 'hole in the wall' machines where customers can withdraw or deposit money and get account balances, effectively providing 24-hour service.
o   Retailers have invested in electronic tills that allow staff to scan goods. This process allows for quicker service, fewer mistakes, itemized bills so that customers can check

> purchases, automatic re-ordering of stock and provides information for retailers to build customer profiles to help target future customer communication.
> - Utility organizations use automated telephone systems so that customers can get a quicker response or just leave information without having to speak to an operator.
> - Distribution companies use e-mail which enables immediate communication within and between organizations.

Debriefing Activity 10.8

Specimen answer 1(a)

- Minimum standards for dealing with customer telephone calls:
- Answer the telephone within six rings
- Introduce yourself by name and state the name of the firm
- Smile when you answer the telephone
- When taking messages for colleagues, always use company message pads and ensure that all details are taken down correctly
- When dealing with telephone messages, return all calls the same day.

Specimen answer (b)

Main points about how the member of staff's customer service could be improved:

- He should appreciate that all documentation and communications with customers should be right first time, as mistakes give the bad impression that the firm is careless in all its dealings with customers
- He should have apologized to the customer on behalf of the company about the mistakes, not tried to minimize the importance of the mistakes made
- He should not have been defensive with the customer about the mistakes made. It is not relevant to the customer whether he or someone else prepared the property details sheet and made the mistakes
- He should have arranged for the mistakes to be rectified and a new sheet sent out to the customer immediately
- He should have spoken to the person responsible for the mistakes and made sure that it did not happen again.

Debriefing Activity 10.9

To improve customer communications, Orange would have to improve their instruction manual so that customers find it easy to operate their telephones. They need to provide adequate staffing so that the system they have established to provide customer service actually works and customers can get through to the helpline. They need to rethink the process involving the allocation of security code numbers so that dealerships always allocate a security code and/or that call centre operators can still help customers who do not know their code.

Internal communications need to be improved to ensure that if staff in one department take a message it is always logged and passed on to the relevant staff in another department. Staff need to be trained to deal with customer complaints. The member of the customer service team should have apologized on behalf of Orange about the service the customer has received. He should have concentrated on helping her use the telephone, not wasted the customer's time explaining internal staffing problems.

The company should also empower its staff to use reasonable judgement in giving a discount on a bill where a customer has good reason to be unhappy about the product or service received.

appendix 4
curriculum information and reading list

Syllabus

Aim

The Customer Communications module provides the entry level skills and application in the development and use of communications for Stage 1. It aims to provide participants with a working knowledge of customers' buying behaviour and the promotional mix as well as communications techniques.

Participants will not be expected to have any prior qualifications or experience in a marketing role. They will be expected to be conversant with the content of the Marketing Fundamentals module before undertaking this module.

Related statements of practice

- ○ Cb.1 Develop direct or indirect communications.
- ○ Cb.2 Deliver direct or indirect communications.
- ○ Gb.1 Support the management of customer relationships.
- ○ Gb.2 Deliver effective customer service.

Learning outcomes

Participants will be able to:

- ○ Recognize organizations as open systems and explain the importance of relationships between the organization and its suppliers, intermediaries, customers and other key stakeholders in a changing environment
- ○ Explain why it is important for marketers to understand consumer and industrial buying behaviour for marketing decisions
- ○ Explain the elements of the promotional mix and its fit with the marketing planning process
- ○ Explain the advantages and disadvantages of the range of communications tools available to an organization

- o Develop internal and external communications using appropriate tools to suit a variety of target audiences and using an understanding of customer behaviour and customer information
- o Select appropriate verbal and non-verbal communications with people inside and outside the organization
- o Demonstrate the importance of customers and customer service and apply customer care principles to create positive relationships with customers in a variety of contexts.

Knowledge and skill requirements

Element 1: Customers and stakeholders (20%)

1.1 Explain what is meant by the terms 'customer', 'stakeholder' and 'user'

1.2 Demonstrate the fundamental importance of 'customers' to all forms of organizations, including services and the need to clearly identify them

1.3 Describe the link between the marketing concept, a customer focus and relationship marketing

1.4 Appreciate the need for effective internal and external customer communications and their link to and role in maintaining customer focus, developing and sustaining good customer relations and relationship marketing in creating loyalty and customer retention

1.5 List the factors that cause change in customers and the subsequent impact on marketing programmes.

Element 2: Buying behaviour (10%)

2.1 Explain the difference between consumer buyer behaviour and organizational buyer behaviour

2.2 Explain the importance of understanding buyer behaviour

2.3 Describe the decision-making unit (DMU) and the roles of its constituents

2.4 The decision-making process (DMP) for consumers and organizations

2.5 The impact and effect of the DMU and the DMP on the communications mix.

Element 3: Implementing elements of the promotional mix (50%)

3.1 Explain the concept of, and need for, an integrated marketing communications approach and the links between communications and marketing planning

3.2 Explain the role and importance of promotion in marketing

3.3 Explain the structure and function of the communication process

3.4 Describe the tools of promotion (the promotion mix)

3.5 Explain the planning process for developing and implementing promotional strategies and individual elements of the promotional mix

3.6 Explain how above-the-line and below-the-line activities are used

3.7 Explain the key stages and considerations when developing and designing advertisements

3.8 Describe the role and scope of PR and its contribution to the promotional mix

3.9 Explain the role of corporate identity, brand image and logos in corporate communication with customers

3.10 Distinguish between the different forms of integrated mail media, such as direct mail leaflets and mail order advertising.

3.11 Explain the role of point of sale (POS) material and how it is developing in response to changing customer needs

3.12 Explain the role of packaging in the promotions mix

3.13 Describe the role of exhibitions as a communications tool and their role in promotions

3.14 Explain the role of information and communications technology (ICT) in communications, including digital TV and interactive marketing

3.15 Describe current trends and developments in promotions and their impact on organizations.

Element 4: Face-to-face communication (10%)

4.1 Describe the communication process and explain the importance and the advantages and disadvantages of different types of communication in a variety of face-to-face situations

4.2 Identify barriers to communication and explain how they can be avoided and overcome

4.3 Explain the communications planning process to produce effective strategies for improving alternative communications formats

4.4 Explain the importance of effective body language, tone, verbal and listening skills in communication and strategies for developing and improving verbal, non-verbal and listening skills

4.5 Interpret, summarize and present oral, written and graphical information

4.6 Explain key communication factors to consider in meetings, including arranging and convening a meeting, documentation involved and strategies for conducting a meeting

4.7 Plan, prepare and deliver a presentation using appropriate and effective visual aids and media

4.8 Use a variety of formats to communicate with internal and external customers including telephone, letters, memoranda, notices, reports and e-mails.

Element 5: Customer service and customer care (10%)

5.1 Explain the concept of customer care and its importance in consumer, business-to-business, not-for-profit and public sector organizations

5.2 Explain the importance of quality and customer care and methods of achieving quality

5.3 Explain the relationship between customer care, customer focus and relationship marketing

5.4 Explain the importance of obtaining customer feedback and devising contingencies for dealing with customer complaints

5.5 Describe how to plan and establish a customer care programme

5.6 Demonstrate an understanding of how ICT is used in customer service, for example, through the use of databases.

Related key skills for marketers

o Using ICT and the Internet
o Using financial information and metrics
o Presenting information
o Improving own learning and performance
o Working with others
o Problem-solving
o Applying business law.

Assessment

CIM will offer two forms of assessment for this module from which centres or participants may choose: written examination and continuous assessment. CIM may also recognize, or make joint awards for, modules at an equivalent level undertaken with other professional marketing bodies and educational institutions.

Overview and rationale

Approach

The ultimate importance of Customer Communications is based on the importance of both customers and communications to the success of organizations. Without identifying who customers are and their buying habits, we cannot begin to understand them. Without this fundamental understanding, we cannot develop appropriate and effective communications.

Therefore, the rationale for the module is that it provides marketers with a comprehensive range of communication tools aimed at establishing and maintaining relationships with our customers, both internal and external. In addition, it emphasizes the role that we have to play in nurturing and developing our relationships.

The syllabus has now been greatly refined, ensuring both horizontal and vertical separation and integration.

o *Horizontally* the module includes customer behaviour and customer care moved from the Marketing Fundamentals module of the current Certificate syllabus. The use of marketing research, previously included in this module, has been moved to Marketing Environment to avoid overlap. The practical application of communications skills is reinforced in Marketing in Practice.

o *Vertically* this module provides a foundation for Marketing Relationships at Stage 2, which builds on this module by developing higher levels of knowledge and understanding for communicating.

Syllabus content

This module, like the other modules across all levels of the CIM Syllabus, has been modified and improved. These modifications have tried to take into account the changes to The Marketing Customer Interface, to be renamed Marketing Relationships, the Stage 2 module which is a logical follow-on and progression from Customer Communications.

With this in mind, the percentages for indicative weightings are:

- o Customers and stakeholders (20 per cent)
- o Buying behaviour (10 per cent)
- o Implementing elements of the promotional mix (50 per cent)
- o Face-to-face communication (10 per cent)
- o Customer service and customer care (10 per cent).

Those tutors already familiar with the previous Customer Communications syllabus will be able to identify key changes to the content, particularly the inclusion of, and greater emphasis on, buying behaviour and customer care, previously covered in Marketing Fundamentals although both areas were covered in the previous syllabus to an extent, and building relationships with stakeholders.

Element 1 – Customers and stakeholders

The key message that needs to be communicated to participants is the importance of customer centred organizations. Tutors need to differentiate between the different types of 'customers' that marketing participants will communicate with. The difference between internal and external customers should be reinforced and the differences between customers and consumers should be emphasized. The link and the importance between good communications and maintaining and nurturing good relationships with customers should be discussed along with the many factors which cause changes in customers and the subsequent impact on marketing programmes. Tutors should introduce the concept of relationship marketing and its importance, although this will be covered in greater depth in Element 5. The key message here is the role of communication in managing this relationship, to guiding and supporting customers through changing circumstances and situations, including for example, the need to develop new products in response to changing consumer attitudes.

Element 2 – Buying behaviour

The concepts of the decision-making units and the role of stakeholders should be introduced in relation to the communication process. At a basic level, participants should be able to understand and identify the needs of different target audiences in both not for profit organizations and a variety of business sectors. Participants need to have a good understanding of buying behaviour within decision making units and the impact of the DMU on both the decision making process and ultimately on the communications mix.

Element 3 – Implementing elements of the promotional mix

The key point here is that participants should be aware of basic theories about the communication process and customer behaviour so that participants can design effective customer communications at a basic level.

Consequently it would be appropriate to introduce the encoding/decoding process of communication. In addition, it would be appropriate to introduce participants to a simplified black box model of consumer behaviour and combine it with the various influences on consumer behaviour.

Participants should develop a comprehensive understanding of the range of promotion tools available to them and be able to develop and implement promotional activities and individual elements of the promotional mix. Therefore, practical exercises around developing advertisements, planning exhibitions, developing effective sales promotion and devising PR campaigns would all be useful practical measures to deepen understanding and assist in application.

The role of ICT should be discussed, including digital TV and interactive marketing. Participants are not expected to have technological expertise in this area. Tutors should impress upon candidates that they need to be aware of developments in this area and their dynamic nature and impact by reading appropriate marketing magazines and the quality press. Key points for discussion will include how digital technology will impact upon media decisions and how developments in digital technology (for example interactive catalogues, newsletters and video conferencing) will influence media decisions and improve communication.

A basic knowledge of consumer behaviour can be applied so that participants are capable of drafting a variety of communications, bearing in mind their target audience, and the use of appropriate tone and language.

The concept of, and need for, an integrated marketing communications approach should be introduced as a way of pulling together this element. It will introduce participants to the strategic role of communications however, more importantly, it will encourage participants to view and consider each element of the promotional mix as part of a cohesive whole, whose individual elements go towards creating an overall picture.

Finally, participants should look beyond current practice and give consideration to trends and developments in promotions and their impact on organizations.

Element 4 – Face-to-face communication
Tutors will again describe the communications process and explain the importance and the advantages and disadvantages of different types of communication in a variety of face-to-face situations. Tutors will explain the importance of effective body language, tone, verbal and listening skills in communication and strategies for developing and improving verbal, non-verbal and listening skills. Participants must also develop the skill of interpreting, summarizing and presenting oral, written and graphical information. Good practice for participants would be to write reports that interpret customer data, market trends and issues relating to electronic methods of communication.

Participants should be able to identify barriers to communication and be able to explain how they can be avoided and overcome.

Key communication factors to be considered in planning key communications events must be given due consideration, for example, the key communication factors involved in planning and conducting meetings or planning and preparing a presentation. This could involve approaches to pitching for work from clients or dealing with presentations from suppliers. Tutors should also encourage participants to look at the importance of effective listening.

Tutors should also highlight the variety of formats used to communicate with internal and external customers, including telephone, letters, memoranda, notices, reports and e-mails.

Element 5 – Customer service and customer care
Customer Relationship Marketing is important in marketing today. As such, it is critical that participants understand the concept of customer service and customer care and its importance in consumer, business-to-business, not-for-profit and public sector organizations.

Tutors should explain the importance of quality and customer care and methods of achieving quality of service. Tutors should also explain the relationship between customer care, customer focus and relationship marketing.

Participants should be able to devise contingency plans for dealing with customer complaints in the context of a well-planned customer care programme. As a result of this, participants will be better informed as to how to develop and establish a customer care programme.

Finally, participants should demonstrate an understanding of how ICT is used as part of the delivery of customer service, for example building customer databases and using Customer Relationship Management (CRM) software programmes as part of automated customer handling processes.

Delivery approach

Marketing Communications should ideally be taught either in conjunction with or following Marketing Fundamentals, as Fundamentals will provide the basic knowledge required regarding the marketplace and customers and their role. Furthermore, the teaching of the Marketing Environment will emphasize the role of different stakeholders within marketing and also the key external factors, which impact upon these very groups of people. This understanding will aid in appreciating the need for establishing appropriate forms of communication for different target audiences and for different communications circumstances.

As stated earlier, this module provides a good grounding for the Stage 2 module which logically follows on from this, i.e. Marketing Relationships. Therefore, it is fundamental that participants assume a good grasp of the knowledge and skills components covered within this module. Furthermore, it is recommended that tutors devise or utilize a variety of practical exercises to allow participants the opportunity to practise their new-found knowledge.

The form of assessment for this module will be by examination or continuous assessment. This should be taken into consideration when developing the teaching strategy for the module.

Reading list

Core texts

Forsyth, P. (1999) *Communicating with Customers*. London, Orion Business.

Syllabus guides

CIM (2003) *CIM Companion: Customer communications*. Cookham, Chartered Institute of Marketing.

BPP (2003) *CIM Study Text: Customer communications*. BPP Publishing.

Cheeseman, A. and Wood, G. (2003) *Customer Communications Coursebook*. Oxford, Butterworth-Heinemann.

Supplementary reading

Blundell, R. (1998) *Effective Business Communication: Principles and practice for the information age*. London, Prentice-Hall.

Daffy, C. (1999) *Once a Customer Always a Customer: How to deliver service that creates customers for life*. 2nd edition, Dublin, Oak Tree Press.

Fiske, J. (1990) *Introduction to Communication Studies: Studies in culture and communication.* London, Routledge.

Foster, J. (1998) *Effective Writing Skills for Public Relations.* London, Kogan Page.

Godin, S. (1999) *Permission Marketing: Strangers into friends and friends into customers.* Hemel Hempstead, Simon and Schuster.

Knight, A. (1999) *Effective Customer Care.* London, Directory of Social Change.

McMillan, S. (1997) *How to be a Better Communicator.* London, Industrial Society/Kogan Page.

McQuail, D. and Windahl, S. (1993) *Communication Models for the Study of Mass Communication.* Harlow, Longman.

McQuail, D. (2000) *McQuail's Mass Communication Theory.* London, Sage.

Postma, P. (1998) *New Marketing Era: Marketing to the imagination in a technology driven world.* London, McGraw-Hill.

Simons, C. and Naylor-Stables, B. (1997) *Effective Communication for Managers: Getting your message across.* London, Cassell.

Whelan, J. (2000) *e-mail@work: Getting moving with digital communication.* London, ft.com

BPP (2002) *Customer Communications: Practice and revision kit.* London, BPP Publishing.

Customer Communications: Success tape. Learning cassettes by BPP Publishing.

Index